"Most hearers of Sunday homilies stand with the seekers in John 12:21 who said, 'Sir, we wish to see Jesus.' *We Preach Christ Crucified* leads the homilist, as well as faithful Catholic 'hearers of the Word,' to prepare for Sunday. Besides providing a comprehensive and solid grounding in the theology of preaching, the chapters include 'how-to' aids to hasten a true revival of Catholic preaching that fosters a deep encounter with the Crucified and Risen Lord Jesus. This book is a perfect companion to the United States Bishops' document, *Preaching the Mystery of Faith: The Sunday Homily*."

> Most Reverend Joseph Kurtz
> Archbishop of Louisville

"In *We Preach Christ Crucified* contemporary preachers respond combining theological sophistication with pastoral practicality. This book can serve as a review for preachers years away from a homiletics class as well as a basis for a discussion of contemporary issues in preaching."

> Honora Werner, OP
> Aquinas Institute of Theology

"Nothing should be more exciting than proclaiming God's invitation to friendship. These essays offer a marvelous mosaic of the various elements of catholic preaching that make the Word of God so dynamic, relevant and timely in today's church. In keeping with the spirit of Pope Francis we preach Christ crucified fully alive and life-giving."

> Reverend Virgilio Elizondo
> Professor of Pastoral and Hispanic Theology
> University of Notre Dame

"This single volume brings together a variety of perspectives on what it means to preach the living Word of God in such a way that it fosters a true encounter of the worshipping community with God. In eloquence and wisdom, these chapters both individually and as a unit offer excellent contemporary scholarship and theological reflection on the kind of preaching that transforms individual lives, communities, and reaches out far beyond with a compelling message of hope. The diversity of contributors and foci make this a rich work that speaks to the reality of the Church in our times—in the never ending struggles and joys of faithfully interpreting, communicating and living out the Word in many contexts."

> Deb Organ, LICSW
> Pastoral Associate
> Holy Rosary Parish
> Minneapolis, Minnesota

D1260218

We Preach Christ Crucified

edited by Michael E. Connors, CSC

LITURGICAL PRESS
Collegeville, Minnesota

www.litpress.org

1   2   3   4   5   6   7   8   9

Library of Congress Cataloging-in-Publication Data

We preach Christ crucified / edited by Michael Connors, CSC.
    pages cm
    ISBN 978-0-8146-3823-1 — ISBN 978-0-8146-3848-4 (ebook)
    1. Catholic preaching—United States.   I. Connors, Michael E., editor of compilation.

BV4211.3.W4   2013
251—dc23   2013027453

Contents

Preface

"We're in trouble here."

The founding narrative of the John S. Marten Program in Homiletics and Liturgics includes John Marten's remark that, after years of sitting faithfully in the pews of his Catholic parish, listening to hundreds of homilies that neither informed nor delighted nor moved him, he knew the church needed help in this area. A related vignette tells of Mr. Marten displaying a picture he had discovered, a drawing of Jesus with head in hands, weeping and seated in a church pew with the pulpit inhabited by yet another incompetent preacher. Presumably the good Lord was not weeping the kind of tears that flow when the soul is stirred to the love of God. Whether the pain was John Marten's own, or that of Christ, or both, John and his wife, Virginia, decided to try and do something about it. When faithful Catholics such as the Martens know we are in trouble, and begin to insist on better preaching, we could be on the cusp of something.

The poor state of Catholic preaching has become the standard stuff of self-deprecating jokes and comic routines among Catholic clergy themselves. Everywhere one goes, one hears anecdotes recounted about preaching that routinely fails to connect with the lives of ordinary folk, fails to open the beauty and power of God's Word, and about homilies prepared in slapdash fashion and delivered with all the verve and passion of a reading from an auto repair manual.

Moreover, as the attention spans of a younger generation who cut their teeth on Twitter and YouTube get shorter, and this generation's expectations for engaging presentation get higher, our preaching problem seems to be worsening. "It's boring," say the young of what they witness on Sundays, turning back to a glittery, dynamic, promising virtual world that is just an iPad away. We no longer have a captive audience. We are in a life-and-death competition for hearts, minds, souls.

We often feel ourselves to be losing that competition. Yet, perhaps the situation is not as dire as we may think on those days when we stare at empty pews, scratch our heads over the young, or face yet another homily preparation. After all, the post–Vatican II Catholic Church has produced some stunning preachers. I think of the late Fr. Walter Burghardt, SJ, the incomparable dean of Catholic preaching for the post-conciliar generation. I think of a marvelous ordination homily by William McManus, bishop of Fort Wayne–South Bend, and the always evocative preaching of Fr. Bill Toohey, CSC, director of campus ministry here at the University of Notre Dame. I think of the weekly radio addresses by Archbishop Oscar Romero, bathing the tortured landscape of El Salvador in the bright light of truth and casting a lifeline of hope to the poor and suffering. I think of scores of parish priests forging connections between the scriptural texts and the daily lives of their parishioners, responding to *Fulfilled in Your Hearing*'s challenge to make the homily a "scriptural interpretation of life." And I think of the modest revival of lay preaching we've seen here and there—how enriched we are to hear the voices of lay witness. Perhaps we simply underestimated the time and effort required for the renewal of attention to the Word demanded by the Second Vatican Council. Perhaps we still have a bit of an inferiority complex in a religious context long dominated by the likes of Billy Graham, William Sloane Coffin, Joel Osteen. By any measure we Catholics are latecomers to the party, and unsure of our identity.

The chapters that follow were all given as addresses at "We Preach Christ Crucified: A Conference on Catholic Preaching" at Notre Dame in June 2012. When we set out to plan the conference, the first of its kind, our hopes were modest. I crossed my fingers and hoped for 150 participants, mentally telling myself to be satisfied with a hundred. To my utter amazement, 360 people showed up. The mere number suggests that American Catholics are hungry for the Word, hungry for help in both delivering and hearing that Word. The interactions among the attendees those three days were marked by an intensity of interest that underscores the conviction that we are in trouble here, we need and want help. The atmosphere became prayerful, almost retreatlike, hopeful and tinged with a bit of the joy of the banquet, too.

I want to salute and thank those eighteen-score people for making those days together truly remarkable. Let me offer special thanks from all of us to our contributors, who gave us much to ponder and strengthened our hope for the future. And, finally, I extend a hearty expression of gratitude for the foresight, generosity, and support of John and Virginia Marten and their family, to whom this volume is dedicated. May the paradox at the heart of our preaching continue to light the way forward.

Michael E. Connors, CSC
Notre Dame, Indiana
Easter 2013

Chapter 1

We Preach a Living Word

Archbishop Gustavo García-Siller, MSpS

Nothing is more basic and more important than our preaching. It was the preaching of the apostles that gave rise to the church, and it is our preaching that continues to illuminate the minds, motivate the hearts, and encourage the lives of Christians. Preaching invites people to conversion and nourishes the faithful. As St. Paul states: "But how can they call on him in whom they have not believed? And how can they believe in him of whom they have not heard? And how can they hear without someone to preach? And how can people preach unless they are sent?" (Rom 10:14-15, NABRE). Moreover, as St. Francis told us, we are sent to preach the good news of our salvation at all times, if necessary by using words. Our lives of Christian charity give credibility to our words. It is a labor of love. The integrity of the preacher is key.

Unfortunately, one of the frequent complaints we hear from Catholics is about the poor quality of our preaching. People tell us that sermons are boring, superficial, irrelevant, and useless. Our people are hungry for good preaching that illuminates, encourages, consoles, challenges, and motivates. Some prefer to go to evangelical churches where they encounter dynamic preaching. Many of those who have drifted away from the Catholic Church in the last twenty years have said that they did so because their spiritual needs were not being met.

The Word of God is life, and just as the rain that falls softly on the earth to produce delicious fruit, so our preaching ought to come to our people to produce in their hearts the new life of the love of God. After all, giving thanks to God, every one of us Christians can pray: "Your words are spirit and life! *¡Tu Palabra nos da Vida!*"

We have the truth, but we need to beg the Holy Spirit to fill us with the same Spirit that moved Peter on the first Pentecost to preach with such fervor, conviction, and enthusiasm that people thought he had had too much wine to drink so early in the morning. We too need to be greatly inspired and emboldened by the Holy Spirit so that our fearless conviction and exuberant joy will not only bring people to Christ but likewise set them on fire with the spirit of Christian love. We preach God's love, we preach Christ crucified, we preach the word of mercy and forgiveness. We don't preach ourselves. We preach the word of freedom and love; we preach the word of a new life, truly a life in its fullness. We do not dare to fail!

Our preaching is nothing less than a conversation of love that makes people feel so good about being loved by God that they cannot wait to become lovers like God. Moreover, as the Second Vatican Council pointed out, "prayer should accompany the reading of sacred Scripture, so that a dialogue takes place between God and man" (*Dei Verbum* 25). This dialogue implies thinking, but above all, loving. God is love, and only with the enthusiasm of a lover can we communicate the wonders of the love of God. It is to love, more than to think.

In his Apostolic Exhortation on the Word of God, Pope Benedict has pointed out that "the preacher 'should be the first to hear the word of God that he proclaims,' since, as St. Augustine says: 'He is undoubtedly barren who preaches outwardly the word of God without hearing it inwardly'" (*Verbum Domini* 59). The Holy Father adds that "the faithful should be able to perceive clearly that the preacher has a compelling desire to present Christ. . . . For this reason preachers need to be in close and constant contact with the sacred text; they should prepare for the homily by meditation and prayer, so as to preach with conviction and passion" (ibid.).

"Your words are spirit and life! *¡Tu Palabra nos da Vida!*"

In the first Pentecost each one of the listeners from throughout the world heard the message in his or her own tongue (Acts 2:6). This is a tremendous challenge for us today, considering the fact of the growing cultural and linguistic diversity in our country and in a growing number of our parishes. It is not just a matter of preaching in different languages but even more so of being aware of the cultural particularities of our parishioners. We need to become keenly aware of the cultural expressions of sin and grace that are present within the ethnic groups that we serve. Using examples from their everyday lives brings the Scriptures to life in ways that are captivating and easily understood. Furthermore, the lesson must remain clear in our hearts, that the Holy Spirit lives in the hearts of the members of our church. The gifts and fruits of the Holy Spirit are at work in the preacher, but the Holy Spirit is also at work in the listeners, in the people who hear the Word and listen to the preaching. We speak, we are articulate, we stimulate, and we persuade, but the Holy Spirit moves the will of the listener. Our preaching must honor and reverence the presence of the Holy Spirit within those to whom we preach.

Because of the teaching of our Lord and the promptings of the Spirit in our lives, we have to be genuinely interested in and concerned for our brothers and sisters who live in the culture of poverty and destitution, in homeless shelters, children and teenagers who have never had a home, those who live in the streets and under the bridges, the permanently underemployed, and the many other marginal people of our society. With great love and compassion we need to reach out to those who live in fear, for instance, our undocumented brothers and sisters, or those who have experienced violence in so many ways.

It is very true that we have only one Gospel to preach, but it will take on very different language and emphasis depending on who is listening. We preach differently to the faithful who live with financial security but who might be taken in by the allure of self-reliance, than we do to the very poor who know what it is to trust in God but often have a hard time seeing hope. We must "preach glad tidings to the poor" (Isa 61:1), while challenging the wealthy to obtain the true riches that come from self-donation, and trust in God's will, for "wealth will not endure" (Job 15:29, NRSV).

Each culture is a world, and just as the Word is made flesh and lives among us, so our preaching will have life and be effective insofar as it makes use of words, examples, images, and metaphors common to the people. We have to be especially conscious of those among us who are poor, of the undocumented, of those who live in fear and dread, and of victims of injustice.

The effective proclamation of the Word of God is also an essential dimension of the new evangelization called for by Blessed John Paul II and Pope Benedict XVI. The new evangelization was the focus of the World Synod of Bishops in October 2012. As the Holy Father has pointed out, "nations, once rich in faith and invocations, are losing their identity under the influence of a secularized culture" (VD 96). In the increasing secularism and consumerism of our society so many people are losing their way to true happiness, not recognizing that God alone can satisfy the deepest hungers of the human heart. God does not tire of raising humanity up. Our preaching should help the souls of our faithful understand the beautiful truth exclaimed by St. Augustine in the opening words of his *Confessions*: "You have made us for yourself, O Lord, and our hearts are restless until they rest in you." Thus, the need for effective preaching is vital for the present and the future of the community of faith.

"Your words are spirit and life! *¡Tu Palabra nos da Vida!*"

Preaching the Word of God is a sacred privilege and an awesome responsibility, which turns into a duty. When I look at my own unworthiness and my human frailty, I have to ask myself how God could have ever called me to be a mediator of his Word. I often feel like the prophet Jeremiah who felt overpowered by God's call (Jer 20:7), but consoled and encouraged by St. Paul's words that it has pleased God to choose the foolish, the lowly, and the nothing of this world (1 Cor 1:27) to proclaim the mystery of God (1 Cor 2:1). This mystery is made known to us through the mystery of the Word made flesh, "not of 'a written and mute word, but of the incarnate and living Word'" (VD 7).

Through the mystery of Christ, through every detail of his life from his conception to his ascension, we come to know not only the truth of God but equally the truth of our own humanity, as Blessed John Paul II said at Puebla in 1979. The Second Vatican Council taught that it is only in the mystery of the Incarnate Word that our own mystery, the mystery of what it truly means to be human, is revealed and made clear (*Gaudium et Spes* 22). Only in Christ do we find the deepest meaning of our life, our activity, and even our death, for it is only in and through Christ that the deepest desires of the human heart will be clarified, purified, fulfilled (GS 42).

The hearts of the faithful are filled with many difficult tensions: economic stress, professional difficulties, problems with children and teenagers, domestic tensions, work issues, questions of sexual identity, drug, alcohol, and pornographic addiction, and many others. The faithful come to church looking for guidance, consolation, and loving accompaniment.

We may not have all the answers, but we can certainly walk with them, offering them the light and the love of God that will lead them to a new understanding of the heart, mind, and soul. The Word of God that comes through our preaching offers consolation, direction, and hope. As Pope Benedict says, "By recalling in this way the mysteries of redemption, the Church opens up to the faithful the riches of the saving actions and the merits of her Lord, and makes them present to all times, allowing the faithful to enter into contact with them and to be filled with the grace of salvation" (VD 52). Only in Christ can we satisfy the deepest desires of our hearts and come to the fullness of our humanity. He is the way, the truth and the life. We cannot solve all the problems of people, but certainly we can accompany them in their search with words of direction and hope, giving the Word, giving God Himself. "Whoever preaches, let it be with the words of God" (1 Pet 4:11, NABRE).

Preaching is not so much a lesson in scriptural exegesis as it is an attempt to interpret our human situation through the Scriptures, to bring out the divine meaning of our human situation. As the U.S. bishops have written, the homily is "a scriptural interpretation of human existence which enables a community to recognize God's active presence (Community), to respond to that presence in faith through liturgical word and gesture, and beyond the liturgical assembly, through a life lived in conformity with the Gospel (unity, communion)" (*Fulfilled in Your Hearing*, 29, cf. 26). Or, as our Holy Father has written, "the word of God is living and addressed to each of us, and all of us, in the here and now of our lives" (VD 32). Our preaching is an interpretation of the true significance of our lives in the light of the Word of God. The Word of God is life and gives life not only to individuals but to the community. It allows us to recognize the presence of God among us and to respond to his invitation to be his intimate friends.

Good preaching easily draws people into the mysteries of God's love, making the salvific events of the past present and very much alive for us today. Meditating and contemplating upon the imagery of these mysteries invites us to enter personally and communally into the very life that is the basis of these mysteries. In this context we see and experience our own life within a larger and exciting mystery that we did not expect nor could we have imagined—the beautiful mystery of the absolute gratuity of God's love experienced in the ordinary events of everyday life. In the words of our Holy Father, "Being a Christian is not the result of an ethical choice or a lofty idea, but the encounter with an event, a person, which gives life a new horizon and a definitive direction" (*Deus Caritas Est* 11).

"Your words are spirit and life! *¡Tu Palabra nos da Vida!*"

Preaching is not primarily about abstract knowledge, dogmatic pronouncements, or moralistic imperatives. Authentic Christian preaching begins by reflecting on the various images presented in the Scriptures so as to invite the believer and unbeliever alike into the mystery of God's infinite, merciful, and tender love, revealed from the very beginning of creation but especially evident in the mystery of the cross (1 Cor 1:1-2). The Vatican II *Constitution on Divine Revelation* brings this out beautifully when it states that out of the abundance of God's love, God speaks to us as friends and invites us into the intimacy of his company (DV 2).

I pray to Our Lady of Guadalupe, "Patroness of all America and Star of the first and new evangelization" (*Ecclesia in America* 11), to guide us so that, filled with the Holy Spirit, we will be faithful and effective messengers of God's infinite love for one another—the one and only force that will convert enemies into friends, strangers into family, hunger into abundance, enslavement into freedom, war-torn cities into peaceful neighborhoods, misery into well-being, tears into laughter, and cries of pain into songs of joy. Christ is the firstborn of the new humanity, of the new heaven and the new earth, and through our preaching we are called to give birth to children of the new creation and nourish their lives until we reach the ultimate fulfillment in heaven. Full of the Holy Spirit, we go with delight, courage, and joy to proclaim the new life of the love of God.

Following in the footsteps of our Master, let us fear no one and be filled with the freedom of the Spirit. Be enthusiastic, be creative, be bold, be courageous! For, like the faithful at Pentecost, we are to be on fire with the Holy Spirit of God's love—the only force that can save the world from destruction, by transforming it into the new civilization of justice, love, and compassion!

"Your words are spirit and life! *¡Tu Palabra nos da Vida!*"

We preach the Word: "*Una palabra habló el Padre, que fue su Hijo, y ésta habla siempre en el eterno silencio, y en silencio ha de ser oído del alma.* The Father spoke one word, which was His Son, and this Word He always speaks in eternal silence and in silence it must be heard by the soul."[1]

Endnote

1. Saint John of the Cross, *Maxims on Love* 21, in *The Collected Works of St. John of the Cross*, trans. Kieran Kavanaugh and Otilio Rodriguez (Garden City, NY: Doubleday, 1964), 675.

Chapter 2

Feasting at the Table of the Word:
From *Dei Verbum* to *Verbum Domini*

Mary Catherine Hilkert, OP

> Wisdom has built herself a house;
> she has prepared her table,
> has brought forth her wine;
> and she calls to her children.
>
> Come and eat of my bread,
> and drink of my wine;
> Come to the feast
> I prepared for you.[1]

That hymn based on Proverbs 9 usually calls to mind both our eucharistic celebrations and that final banquet of which Eucharist is a pledge. But as the Second Vatican Council's *Dogmatic Constitution on Divine Revelation, Dei Verbum,* reminded us, this image of a banquet where all are invited to feast also applies to the word of God, which is the bread of life. Chapter 6 of that constitution proclaimed that "The church . . . never ceases, above all in the sacred liturgy, to partake of the bread of life and to offer it to the faithful from the *one table* of the word of God and the Body of Christ" (DV 21, emphasis added).

Underlining the insight that word and sacrament form "one table" and the essential role that preaching plays in the entire life of the church,

Yves Congar, the French Dominican ecclesiologist and ecumenist (and later cardinal) who had such a significant influence on the Second Vatican Council, made an amazing statement about preaching soon after the Council ended. In a volume on the renewal of Catholic preaching published in 1968 he wrote: "If in one country Mass were celebrated without preaching and in another there was preaching for thirty years without the Mass, the people would be more Christian in the country where there was preaching."[2]

My hope is to reflect on why that is the case and what it means for those of us who share a concern—and a responsibility—for the mission of the church to proclaim the reign of God as Jesus did. The most obvious reason for Congar's privileging of the preaching of the Gospel is that without an invitation that draws a response from those who are invited, there can be no banquet, no matter how lavish the food and drink. Preaching is an invitation to those who hunger and thirst, and who long for companionship, to share in the banquet. The invitation is to be twofold: first, nourished by the word of God, and through that rich fare, to be drawn into the full celebration of the eucharistic banquet and the sacramental life of the church.

That same dynamic is evident in the Emmaus narrative where two disheartened disciples pour out their lament and grief to an unrecognized stranger who accompanies them along the way as they journey away from Jerusalem in grief, even close to despair, according to Timothy Radcliffe.[3] As Luke tells the story, the unknown preacher, who has the wisdom and compassion to listen before he speaks, is able to open up the Scriptures for them in a way that reconfigures their lives and rekindles their hope. The words that caused their hearts to burn within them moved them to invite the stranger to share a table where they finally recognized him in the breaking of the bread.

The country in which there was preaching (by which Congar means preaching that nourishes the faith of the community) for thirty years, even without Eucharist, would be more Christian than the country that lacked effective preaching because the sacraments are sacraments of *faith.* They can't function as visible signs of invisible grace if we don't have eyes and ears of faith that allow us to see and hear the invisible reality of God's presence. Faith is, of course, always God's free gift, but a key conviction of Catholicism is that God's gifts are communicated and made known through created realities and human persons and communities. The invitation to the banquet, like the one who offers it, remains hidden within our ordinary life, unless someone accompanies our journeys and speaks the word of life, as the risen Jesus did for his companions on the way to Emmaus. In the words of St. Paul, "Faith comes from what is heard, and what is heard comes through the word of Christ" (Rom 10:17, NABRE). In other words, we need someone to "name the grace"[4] that we might otherwise miss in our lives and world.

As all of the church's documents on evangelization emphasize, the invitation to believe that God is at work in our lives, despite all of the evidence to the contrary, needs to be spoken explicitly. But after reflection on the Emmaus narrative, we might add, "even if not immediately." In any ministry of the Word, especially when we are dealing with human doubt and anguish, one of the challenges is learning to listen carefully before speaking. One might say that part of the art of any ministry of the Word is speaking the word "God" neither too soon nor too late.[5]

Further, as the documents under consideration here remind us, the invitation to faith is precisely that: an invitation. As preachers we need to let people know that they are welcome to the banquet, and as a community we have to do our part to make our human gatherings around the word of God—as well as our liturgical gatherings—inviting ones. But the reign of God is God's feast. We are, at best, only the *sous-chefs*, the waiters at the table, those who deliver the invitations to the meal, and the dinner companions. It is the work of the Spirit to move the hearts of those who receive the invitation, and as we know from the Scriptures, the Spirit's guest list often differs from our own.

God's grace can and does operate in spite of our preaching as well as outside of our sacraments. I am reminded of the French bishop who once observed: "Every Sunday there are thirty thousand sermons in France . . . and the people *still* believe!"[6] But our hope is that our sermons—and the many forms our preaching takes—will contribute to the building up of the faith and life of the church. Quite simply, we hope that our preaching will draw others to Wisdom's feast because we have been so richly nourished there. One of my favorite definitions of preaching is one that I heard years ago from members of a preaching team in West Virginia: "one beggar telling other beggars where he or she has found bread."[7]

With that in mind, let me turn to my subtitle: "From *Dei Verbum* to *Verbum Domini*." I will not offer here a thorough analysis of both of those documents, let alone of all of the important ecclesial documents that relate to preaching and evangelization in the intervening four and a half decades. Instead, I want to focus primarily on two aspects of *Dei Verbum*, the Second Vatican Council's *Constitution on Divine Revelation*, both of which are fundamental to all of the later documents. First, how are we to understand what constitutes "the word of God?" and how is that mystery of revelation handed on? And second, what is the significance of the call to restore Scripture to the center of the life and spirituality of the church?

After a close reading of key passages in *Dei Verbum* with some additional reflections for preachers, I will point to insights from the other documents of Vatican II that also have rich implications for the preaching ministries of the church but that we won't have time to consider here. Instead, I will turn more briefly to the two apostolic exhortations that have dealt most explicitly with preaching as evangelization since the time of the Council: Pope Paul VI's *Evangelii Nuntiandi*, written a decade after the Council, and Pope Benedict XVI's *Verbum Domini*, published in 2010. Both documents celebrate the contributions of *Dei Verbum* and take it as a touchstone for their later reflections. Unfortunately, there also won't be time to deal fully with an important fourth document, *Fulfilled in Your Hearing: The Homily in the Sunday Assembly*, published by the U.S. Bishops' Committee on Priestly Life and Ministry in 1982. But I will allude briefly to the connections between the theology of preaching underlying that document and the theology of revelation found in *Dei Verbum*.

Dei Verbum: A Renewed Theology of the Word of God

As Joseph Ratzinger (later Pope Benedict XVI), Avery Dulles, and many other theologians writing at the time of the Council noted, a significant achievement of *Dei Verbum* was to move beyond an implicit neoscholastic identification of revelation with church teaching, or with a combination of propositions derived from both Scripture and tradition. Instead, in its final draft, *Dei Verbum* offers a far richer notion of revelation as God's offer of friendship to God's people—an invitation to share the divine life.

The *ressourcement*, or return to the sources of Scripture, liturgy, and the ancient heritage of the early church that was the basis for all of the *aggiornamento* or updating that was the goal of the Council, resulted in a biblical, sacramental, and trinitarian theology of revelation. To the delight of the Protestant observers at the Council and around the world, *Dei Verbum* calls the church first to listen reverently to the word of God and then to proclaim confidently words taken from the First Letter of John:

What was from the beginning,
>   what we have heard,
>   what we have seen with our eyes,
>   what we looked upon
>   and touched with our hands
>   concerns the Word of life—
> for the life was made visible;
>   we have seen it and testify to it
>   and proclaim to you the eternal life
>   that was with the Father and was made visible to us—
> what we have seen and heard
>   we proclaim now to you,
>   so that you too may have fellowship with us;
>   for our fellowship is with the Father
>   and with his Son, Jesus Christ. (1 John 1:1-3)

The role of the Holy Spirit in preaching and the trinitarian dimension of the theology of revelation in this document become more explicit in the opening words of chapter 1:

"It pleased God, in his goodness and wisdom, to reveal himself and to make known the mystery of his will (see Eph 9), which was that people can draw near to the Father, through Christ, the Word made flesh, in the Holy Spirit, and thus become sharers in the divine nature (cf. Eph 2:18; 2 Pet 1:4). By this revelation, then, the invisible God (see Col 1:15; 1 Tim 1:17), from the fullness of his love, addresses men and women as his friends (see Exod 33:11; John 15:14-15) and lives among them (see Bar 3:38), in order to invite and receive them into his own company" (DV 2). As preachers, we might consider that theology of the Trinity and of God's trinitarian mode of communication as a call to attend carefully to where and how God speaks God's own invitation to shared life—where God speaks God's word. The constitution locates God's first word of love in creation itself—what Augustine and the medieval theologians called "the Book of Nature," an insight to which Benedict XVI returns in *Verbum Domini*. For preachers, this means that since we have "two books of revelation," the created universe becomes not only the world deserving of our ecological concern but an actual source for discovering the word of God as spoken in every species, creature, landscape, and ocean. As with all revelatory events, of course, the lens of faith is necessary to perceive that nature is in fact God's beloved creation and speaks a word of summons to us.

Next, *Dei Verbum* turns to God's desire to offer the gift of friendship or salvation to all human beings. That desire, according to *Dei Verbum*, was God's motivation in making God's self known not only to our ancestors in faith but also to all human beings from the very origin of our species. Once again there is an implication for where preachers can discover God's word. As writers since the time of the early church, notably Justin Martyr, have recognized, "the seeds of the Logos"—traces of the word of God—are to be found in every human person and community as well as in creation itself. This insight helps considerably in overcoming what too often becomes a false dichotomy between revelation and human experience.

Although *Dei Verbum* does not explicitly discuss that issue, the model it offers of revelation as genuine communication and an offer of friendship suggests that revelation is necessarily made known to us through human experience, but it is not identical with human experience. This insight is more fully developed in *Fulfilled in Your Hearing*, which emphasizes that the purpose of the homily is "to point to the presence of God in people's lives" (FIYH 23). In our ordinary lives, something deeper is going on: God is at work.

To return to the theology of revelation that is explicit in *Dei Verbum*: after affirming God's presence in creation and God's offer of friendship to all human beings, the document attends specifically to the human rejection of that offer in sin, a reality that has marked all of human history from the beginning. Focusing on God's response to that human rejection of the offer of love, rather than to the origins of the reality of sin, *Dei Verbum* states that God "buoyed them up with hope of salvation, by promising redemption" and that God "has never ceased to take care of the human race, in order to give eternal life to all who seek salvation by persevering in doing good" (see Rom 2:6-7). That final phrase includes a belief that is echoed in the words of Eucharistic Prayer IV when we pray for "those whose faith is known to God alone." In other words, *Dei Verbum* recognizes that the search for salvation for some persons is demonstrated by their faithful ethical lives, their "perseverance in doing good." This possibility that some people respond to God's offer of love and salvation outside of explicit religious faith had already been confirmed a year earlier in the other dogmatic constitution from the Council, *Lumen Gentium: The Dogmatic Constitution on the Church,* when it stated: "Those who, through no fault of their own, do not know the Gospel of Christ or his church, but who nevertheless seek God with a sincere heart, and moved by grace, try in their actions to do his will as they know it through the dictates of their conscience—these too may attain eternal salvation" (LG 16). In other words, as Aquinas once wrote, "God's grace is not limited by our sacraments,"[8] much less by our preaching. Some fear that these claims undercut missionary or evangelical zeal, but from another perspective, it can be a source of encouragement to preachers to realize that God's grace always goes ahead and prepares the way for preachers.

Although *Dei Verbum* turns next to the faith of Israel and our Jewish ancestors, we also need to remember that *Nostra Aetate*, the *Declaration on the Relation of the Church to Non-Christian Religions*, was a separate document that was approved only a few weeks before the vote on *Dei Verbum*.[9] That declaration addresses the religious awareness and beliefs of those who belong to religions other than Christianity and Judaism, stating that "throughout history, to the present day, there is found among different peoples a certain awareness of a hidden power, which lies behind the course of nature and the events of human life. . . . The Catholic Church rejects nothing of what is true and holy in these religions" (NA 2). Once again, we might ponder what this means for Christian preaching and the church's mission of evangelization, which cannot be identified with the church's commitment to interreligious dialogue if we are to have, in dialogue, genuine respect for the faith of others and a true *dialogue*.

Dei Verbum does not take up that issue, although both of the later apostolic exhortations on evangelization do. Instead, *Dei Verbum* moves from a discussion of what has traditionally been called "natural or general revelation," the kind of knowledge that is accessible to all persons through fidelity to conscience, to the Jewish covenant where the offer of friendship with God was explicitly recognized and responded to in faith by the people of Israel, represented here by Abraham, the patriarchs, Moses, and the prophets who "recognized the only living and true God" (DV 98).

The implications for a theology and spirituality of preaching here are more evident and have been richly explored by Abraham Heschel and Walter Brueggemann, among others.[10] The role of the prophet, under the guidance of the Holy Spirit, is to articulate the word of God in the concrete challenges and new contexts of Israel's ongoing history. Among the crises that the prophets and prophetic figures faced—and that we and our communities face as well—were the call to move into an unknown future, a crisis of leadership within the community, betrayal and infidelity to the covenant, the failure of the community to see the connection between its religious practice and the social and political crises of the time, or the despair and fear of a community in exile. Whatever the social or religious challenge of the day, the task of the prophetic preacher—then and now—is to speak a word of God by reinterpreting the people's authentic tradition of faith in light of the contemporary crisis.

Jesus' preaching of the reign of God followed this very pattern as he reinterpreted Jewish messianic hopes for the reign of God in his own first-century context. But the Christian community also believes that Jesus was more than a prophet. He not only proclaimed the future reign of God, he embodied it. In his person and his actions, as well as in his words, he announced the good news of salvation. Jesus preached God's reconciling mercy not only by words of forgiveness but also by sharing a table with sinners. He announced God's healing power by touching lepers. He challenged the limited social roles and the restrictions of his culture and of many of the dominant voices in his own tradition by talking with Samaritans, entering into friendships with women, choosing a tax collector as a disciple, curing the sick on the Sabbath. Jesus did not just speak God's word of compassion; he was God's compassion in the flesh.

Thus *Dei Verbum* cites the Letter to the Hebrews: "After God had spoken many times and in various ways through the prophets, in these last days [God] has spoken to us by . . . [sending God's Son] (Heb 1:1-2) . . . the eternal Word who enlightens all humankind, to live among them and to tell them about the inner life of God" (DV 4). Here we begin to see that *Dei Verbum*'s theology of revelation is not only trinitarian and christological but also sacramental. The American author Andre Dubus once defined sacraments simply as "grace made physical"[11]—or, as we say, "visible signs of invisible grace." In *Dei Verbum*'s language, "the works performed by God show forth and confirm the doctrine and realities signified by the words; and the words, for their part, proclaim the works and bring to light the mystery they contain" (DV 2). God's word is made known to us not only in words but also in actions as well as in personal presence and in the witness of the communities we form in Jesus' name (see DV 4).[12]

What does all of this say to preachers about the word of God that we are called to announce? And about how we as a church are to hand on this word of God that we believe is "living and active" today? If the "word of God" refers to this entire mystery of God's self-communication and offer of friendship that culminates in God's becoming one with history and with matter itself in the incarnation, then what we are asked to hand on is more than church teaching and even more than the written Scriptures, which are the church's primary witness to the founding events of Christian faith. Each of these is essential to the church's preaching ministry, but the second chapter of *Dei Verbum*, titled "The Transmission of Divine Revelation," reminds us that the fullness of our apostolic heritage, the treasure that has been entrusted to us, is more than that. It is the very mystery of Christ that has been entrusted to "the entire holy people, united to its pastors. It is *that* mystery that we are we are called to hand on not only in words but as a lived reality, by being the body of Christ, by being that sign of salvation in and for the world (DV 8, 10). But if the church's authentic tradition includes the entire life of the church, as *Dei Verbum* proclaimed in a passage that it took largely from Congar's *Tradition and Traditions*,[13] the way that we hand on this mystery of Christ includes "everything that serves to make the people of God live their lives in holiness and increase their faith. In this way the church, in its doctrine, life and worship, perpetuates and transmits to every generation all that it itself is, all that it believes" (DV 8).

Although the good news of salvation cannot be identified with the Scriptures, why do *Dei Verbum* and *Sacrosanctum Concilium: the Constitution on the Sacred Liturgy,* among other documents from the Council, put such a large emphasis on the importance of restoring the Scriptures to the center of the life of the church? *Dei Verbum* draws attention to the special nature of the biblical texts by highlighting the influence of the Holy Spirit on both the authors and the text, referring to each as "inspired." Further reflection on the question of inspiration in relation to the Scriptures by biblical scholars and theologians includes the impact of the Spirit on the biblical authors and acknowledges the text as capable of mediating an encounter with God when read and heard in faith. That reflection also offers a broader theology of revelation that recognizes the role of the Spirit throughout the history of the community that gave rise to the text, as well as in the oral interpretation of faith that preceded the written text, especially the apostolic preaching. Moreover, as Scripture scholar Sandra Schneiders suggests in *The Revelatory Text*, Christians believe that the church's Scriptures have the power to function not only as a record of past revelation, even our founding revelation, but also as a present sacrament of encounter with God.[14] In other words, we believe that God's invitation to life is extended again here and now when the Scriptures are read, heard, and proclaimed in faith. That too is part of the process of inspiration. This is one reason that the church extends the Johannine reference to Jesus as the "bread of life" not only to the Eucharist but also to the Scriptures. Benedict XVI, in *Verbum Domini*, cites the concern of Jerome on this same point. He says: "When we approach the [Eucharistic] Mystery, if a crumb falls to the ground we are troubled." Yet, Jerome lamented that "when we are listening to the word of God, and God's Word and Christ's flesh and blood are being poured into our ears yet we pay no heed. . . ."[15]

The final chapter of *Dei Verbum* returns to this imagery of being fed by the biblical word of God, stating that all of the preaching of the church, as indeed, the entire Christian religion, should be nourished and ruled by Sacred Scripture (DV 22, 23). This nourishment enlightens the mind, strengthens the will, and fires the hearts of men and women with the love of God. Here *Dei Verbum* refers to diverse "ministr[ies] of the word," including "pastoral preaching, catechetics, and all forms of christian instruction, among which the liturgical homily should hold pride of place, [all of which] gain healthy nourishment and holy vitality from the word of scripture" (DV 24). The constitution ends on the hopeful note that "a new impulse of spiritual life" might be expected in Catholic spirituality thanks to this return to "veneration of the word of God," just as the church draws life from the Eucharist (DV 26).

Much more could be said about *Dei Verbum* and its significance for preachers, but my intent has been to highlight two things: First, the richness and breadth of the theology of the word of God found there. Benedict refers to it as a polyphonic hymn or a symphony to draw attention to the multiple meanings of the word of God. And second, the privileged place that the Scriptures hold in the church's handing on of the good news of salvation.

If we had time to consider the implications of the other documents of Vatican II for the church's preaching mission, we might draw up an agenda for that future conference to celebrate the fiftieth anniversary of the Council and include the following:

1. From *Gaudium et Spes: The Pastoral Constitution on the Church in the Modern World*, an extension of the theology of revelation in *Dei Verbum* that calls for reflection on "the signs of the times" in light of the Gospel, taking as its starting point the "joys and hopes, the grief

and the anguish of the people of our time, especially of those who are poor or afflicted." The opening preface of that constitution states that "nothing genuinely human fails to find an echo in the hearts of the followers of Christ" (GS 1).

2. From *Nostra Aetate: The Declaration on the Relation of the Church to Non-Christian Religions* and *Ad Gentes Divinitus: The Decree on the Church's Missionary Activity*, the question of how the church's missionary activity relates to interreligious dialogue, with specific attention to the uniqueness of Jewish-Christian dialogue and the irrevocability of God's covenant with the Jewish people (which Benedict emphasizes in *Verbum Domini*).

3. From the *Decree on Ecumenism, Unitatis Redintegratio*, the claim in the opening paragraph that the lack of unity among all Christians "openly contradicts the will of Christ, scandalizes the world, and damages the sacred cause of preaching the Gospel to every creature" (UR 1).

4. From *Sacrosanctum Concilium: The Constitution on the Sacred Liturgy*, the centrality of the liturgy in the life of the church, the presence of Christ in the Word and the assembly as well as in the Eucharist and the priest; the call for "full, active, and conscious participation of all of the baptized"; the claim that the Liturgy of the Word and the eucharistic liturgy form "one sacred act of worship"; the call to "open up the treasures of the Bible more lavishly so that richer fare may be provided for the faithful at the table of God's word"; and the importance of the restoration of the liturgical homily. The theologies of revelation in *Dei Verbum* and *Gaudium et Spes* taken together suggest that the conciliar definition of the homily as the "proclamation of God's wonderful works in the history of salvation, the mystery of Christ ever made present and active in us" (SC 35, 20) and the definition of the homily offered by our bishops in 1982 in *Fulfilled in Your Hearing* as "a scriptural interpretation of human existence which enables a community to recognize God's active presence, and to respond to that presence in [worship and in life]" (FIYH 29, cf. 26) are not in conflict but rather two sides of a single mystery. In other words, the question of whether the homily is a proclamation of God's wonderful works *or* "a scriptural interpretation of human existence" is a false dichotomy.

5. A celebration of the diverse ministries of preaching would include *Christus Dominus: The Decree on the Pastoral Office of Bishops in the Church*, emphasizing that bishops are called to give to the preaching of the Gospel pride of place among all of their important duties. They are called to be "heralds of the faith . . . who listen to the word of God devoutly, hand on what has been entrusted to them, serve the word of God, and guard that treasure reverently" (CD 11–35).[16]

6. From *The Decree on the Life and Ministry of Priests, Presbyterorum Ordinis*, we also hear that it is "the first task of priests, as co-workers of the bishops, to preach the Gospel of God to all" (PO 4).

7. *Lumen Gentium* and *The Decree on the Apostolate of Lay People, Apostolicam Actuositatem*, both emphasize the share of all of the baptized in the priesthood and prophetic office of Christ, the charisms bestowed on all of the baptized and the responsibilities that flow from those gifts of the Spirit for the sake of the building up of the body of Christ and for the church's mission in and for the world. As Cardinal Suenens appealed to his brother bishops at the time of the Council: "Does not each one of us know lay people, both men and women, in his own diocese who are truly called by God? These people have received various different charisms from the Spirit, for catechesis, evangelization, apostolic action of various types. . . . Without these charisms, the ministry of the Church would be impoverished and sterile."[17]

Rather than turning to any of those topics directly in the concluding section, I want to highlight how the two later apostolic exhortations of Paul VI and Benedict XVI have built on and extended *Dei Verbum*, and how the language of evangelization can expand our understanding of both how vast and how central the preaching ministry of the church is.

Evangelii Nuntiandi

The opening question in Paul VI's apostolic exhortation conveys the concern behind the entire document and the 1974 Synod of Bishops from which it was derived: "In our day, what has happened to that hidden energy of the Good News, which is able to have a powerful effect on the human conscience?" (EN 4). Although the document recognizes the complexity of defining the very term "evangelization," it does not limit it to preaching that is directed toward those who have never heard the Gospel, but rather speaks of multiple ways of "bringing the Good News into all the strata of humanity." A good part of the document is spent exploring the multiple forms of evangelization to which the entire church is summoned, including such diverse forms of ministries of the Word as catechesis, teaching, and multiple forms of preaching with the homily remaining the preeminent form of Christian preaching since it maintains the unbroken relationship of word and sacrament (EN 43). But evangelization also includes the witness of lay Christians, not only in "the vast and complicated world" of politics, economics, culture, science, art, and the mass media as well as in relationships, family life, education, and professional work (EN 70) but also in many forms of lay ecclesial ministries, which Paul VI notes may appear to be new but actually have a "real history in the church."

The pope also mentions the preaching that occurs in the "domestic church" of the family. Here he goes beyond *Lumen Gentium*'s claim that parents are the "first preachers" of their children to suggest that children can evangelize their parents as well (EN 71). He calls for special attention to youth. He speaks of them as agents of evangelization and "apostles of youth." They are not only those in need of being evangelized (EN 72); they *are* evangelizers. Noting that the whole church has the mission of evangelizing, Paul VI states the most obscure preacher, catechist, or pastor is exercising an ecclesial act (EN 60). He affirms the evangelization that occurs in base communities that gather to reflect on their lives in light of the Gospel (EN 58), and he reiterates that work for social justice and liberation is not foreign to evangelization (EN 21–22).

Throughout the document there is a strong emphasis on witness as the church's first form of proclaiming the Gospel. The "silent proclamation" of those whose lives are clearly rooted in the Gospel inevitably raises the questions, the pope says, of "Why are they like this? Why do they live this way? What or who is it who inspires them? Why are they in our midst?" (EN 21)[18]—the very questions that many point to as the reason for the great interest in the award-winning movie, *Of Gods and Men*.[19]

In a new note, Paul VI also speaks of the church's own need to be evangelized—the church's need to listen and constantly to be converted by the Gospel if it is to announce the Gospel to the world with credibility (EN 15). Stating that the church's conduct and life is its first means of evangelization, he draws out the implications for the reception of the

Word, the hearing of the Gospel, stating that modern persons "listen more willingly to witnesses than teachers, and if [they] do listen to teachers, it is because they are witnesses" (EN 41). Other notable aspects of the document are to be found in a fuller emphasis on the role of the Holy Spirit as the principal agent of evangelization (EN 75), the call for preaching to be a proclamation of hope, and a greater stress on Jesus' ministry to the poor and suffering, including the reminder that the poorest were often the most receptive to his message (EN 6).

One final observation related to the church's missionary activity: Paul VI states clearly that the preaching of the Gospel is not an optional contribution for the church; it is the very reason for the church's existence and the heart of its mission (EN 14). He also states explicitly that this is a question of people's salvation. But the meaning of that claim is not as clear as it may sound at first. On the one hand, the pope speaks of responding to the command of the Lord Jesus to preach the Gospel "so that people can believe and be saved" (EN 5). He argues that people have a "right to hear the proclamation of the good news of salvation" and insists that it is the evangelizer's duty to proclaim it. But the document also speaks of the difference between proposing and imposing the Gospel and the need for total respect for the freedom of the consciences of others. Near the end of the document, the pope gives this concern about salvation a new twist when he recommends that every evangelizer pray about the following thought: "[Others] can gain salvation in other ways, by God's mercy, even though we do not preach the Gospel to them, but as for us, can we gain salvation . . . if we fail to preach it?" (EN 80).

Finally, we might note that the phrase "new evangelization" appears already in Paul VI's exhortation where he calls for evangelizing culture. He expresses confidence that "the Gospel and evangelization are not necessarily incompatible with [culture]," but rather remain capable of permeating cultures without being subject to them (EN 20). Yet he is convinced that the church is called to challenge the aspects of culture in conflict with the word of God (EN 19), a theme that became even more prominent in the writings of both Pope John Paul II and Pope Benedict XVI.

Verbum Domini

Thirty-five years after *Evangelii Nuntiandi*, Benedict XVI also celebrated *Dei Verbum* as a milestone in the history of the church. Following the

2008 Synod of Bishops on the Word of God in the Life and Mission of the Church, he remarked on *Dei Verbum*'s contributions to a theology of revelation and the study of Scripture as well as its revival of interest in the word of God in the Church (DV 3). *Verbum Domini* is a rich and complex document that is written more in the style of a theological text than that of a pastoral exhortation. Its accomplishments and challenges, especially the treatment of biblical hermeneutics and the call for specific forms of theological and spiritual exegesis, go beyond the scope of the present article.

Instead, I want to highlight a few points of new emphasis in this document that have particular significance for preachers. Benedict speaks of a God who not only speaks and invites us to friendship but also who "wants to enter into *dialogue,* a term never used in *Dei Verbum* and only once in *Evangelii Nuntiandi* (in a brief reference to pastoral dialogue)." He recognizes clearly that we are not equal partners with God but reminds us that God's grace in fact makes us partners with God and capable of response (VD 22). Benedict points to the psalms, rooted in the context of daily life and struggle, as expressing the full range of human emotions in response to God. He mentions "joy and pain, fear and hope, distress and trepidation" as included in the prayer of the church and thus as human feelings to which preachers should give expression. Given the literary forms of the psalms, we might also include "lament" as an important form of the church's preaching that could help to facilitate human and ecclesial conversion. Benedict likewise reminds us that the word of God does not stifle authentic human desires but rather illuminates, purifies, and brings them to fulfillment (VD 23). He expresses concern about homilies that are generic and abstract as failing to bring the scriptural message to life in a way that helps the faithful to recognize that God's word is present and at work in their everyday lives (VD 59).

Although Benedict does not refer to revelation as mediated by experience, he affirms the ancient wisdom that the preachers should be the first to hear the word of God that they proclaim, and cites Augustine as describing as "barren" those who preach the word of God outwardly without hearing it inwardly. There is a strong emphasis in the document on the spirituality of the preacher, the importance of the interrelationship of study and prayer in preparing to preach, and the value of spiritual practices such as *lectio divina* to keep those called to evangelization rooted in the word of God they preach. Further, the pope advises the preacher to ask what these words say to him personally and to the community in light of the concrete situation. That suggests that we are called to trust that God's Spirit continues to transform the fragments that we can offer and to use those fragments to nourish hungry crowds with abundance.

But we can't offer others a word that hasn't nourished us. As preachers we need to "eat the scroll" ourselves if we are to speak words that carry conviction. Perhaps part of the contemporary crisis in preaching is a crisis of faith at some level for preachers. In discouraging times in both church and world, do we believe that the word of God will not return void but will accomplish God's purposes (Isa 55:11)? Are we convinced that the Spirit of God can transform communities of dead bones (Ezek 37)? Do we dare to hope that the Creator God can speak a word of life again in the void and the chaos of our times? Those convictions are deepened and sustained in the silence of prayer. They are the gifts of the Spirit that no amount of work or study can replace, and no human eloquence can match. When preachers are engaged in their own ongoing relationship with God, which like all intimate friendships includes both communion and struggle, their words come from a deeper place.

In one particularly valuable section of *Verbum Domini*, Benedict highlights the role of the Holy Spirit in preaching. He reminds us of two ancient prayers in the liturgy. The first was an invocation of the Spirit before the proclamation of the readings so that the one who proclaims them might interpret them worthily and in a way that touches the hearts of the hearers. The second prayer, after the homily, implored God to send the Spirit upon all those who heard the word since only the Holy Spirit can transform merely human words into the word of God (VD 15).

Benedict affirms the singular importance of the liturgical homily, but like Paul VI, he recommends creativity in discovering and creating multiple alternative opportunities for preaching, including celebrations of the Word, the Liturgy of the Hours, *lectio*, Sunday celebrations of the Word in the absence of a priest, pilgrimages, feasts, missions, retreats, and occasions for the celebration of forms of popular piety (EN 75). He notes that the Bible should be at the center of all pastoral work, that catechesis should be biblically inspired, and that the word of God should be central to all forms of church meetings and congresses, World Youth Days, and formation programs for ordained and lay ministers.

In his reaffirmation of Paul VI's call for a "new evangelization" as an "evangelization of culture," Benedict recognizes that the Gospel and proclamation are always inculturated and affirms that God always communicates in concrete history. He confirms that there are positive values in every culture, identifying the internet, for example, as a new forum for making the Gospel heard today. He describes the word of God as a leaven that has a profoundly *intercultural* character that is capable of enhancing the positive elements within culture and opening it to the values of the Gospel. Yet in other parts of the document, Benedict's assessment of culture is decidedly more critical. After stating that the light of Christ needs to illumine every area of human life, including the family, schools, culture, work, and leisure, he remarks that "it is not a matter of preaching a word of consolation, but rather a word which disrupts, which calls to conversion . . ." (VD 93).

Benedict highlights his particular concern and the focus of the upcoming synod on the "new evangelization" as directed not only toward those who have never heard the Gospel preached but, even more so, toward those who have been baptized but still not heard the Gospel proclaimed persuasively in such a way that they can "concretely experience the power of the Gospel" (VD 96).

He reaffirms the connection between preaching the Gospel and work on behalf of justice and peace, citing Matthew 25, and proclaiming that "denouncing injustice, and promoting solidarity and equality are essential elements of evangelization" (VD 102), a theme that has been emphasized since the time of the 1971 Bishops Synod *Justice in the World*. That earlier synod text provides another resource as we reflect on the importance of the church's witness as its first form of evangelization. As *Justice in the World* stated: "While the Church is bound to give witness to justice, [it] recognizes that anyone who ventures to speak to people about justice, must first be just in their eyes. Hence we must undertake an investigation of the modes of acting and of the possessions and lifestyle within the Church [itself]."[20]

Conclusion

One way that we as church will come to recognize the conversion that Paul VI reminded us is essential to our evangelizing mission is by listening to the many voices in our communities, especially, as *Gaudium et Spes* reminded us, to "those who are poor or who suffer in any way" (GS 1). In that regard, Benedict's apostolic exhortation reminds us that those who are poor are not only the recipients of evangelization but also "agents of evangelization."

If the Word has been entrusted to the entire community, there are many voices we have yet to hear. We all might ask: who are the voices who remain silent or unheard in our own communities? The poet Denise Levertov offers an image of the supper at Emmaus in her reflection on a painting by Diego Velasquez in the National Gallery of Art in Dublin called *Kitchen Maid with the Supper at Emmaus*. The young Moorish woman in the forefront of the painting of that feast remains at the margins of the meal, with her back to the table, but she is clearly attending to the words that are being spoken. As Levertov imagines her,

> But she is in the kitchen, absently touching the winejug she's to take in,
> a young Black servant intently listening,
> swings round and sees
> the light around him
> and is sure.[21]

What words of hope and conviction have we yet to hear at the margins of our own tables? Whose sure faith can nourish our own? Finding ways to listen to the proclamation of what these witnesses have seen and heard—the word of life that they have touched with their own hands—is surely part of the new evangelization by which the word of God can transform both the church and the world.

Endnotes

1. Lucien Deiss, "Wisdom Has Built Herself a House," in *Biblical Hymns and Psalms*, vol. 2 (Cincinnati: World Library Publications, 1940), 14.

2. Yves Congar, "Sacramental Worship and Preaching," in *The Renewal of Preaching: Theory and Practice*, Vol. 33 of *Concilium* (New York: Paulist, 1968), 62.

3. Timothy Radcliffe, "The Road to Emmaus" in *I Call You Friends* (New York: Continuum, 2001), 173–175 at 174.

4. Mary Catherine Hilkert, *Naming Grace: Preaching and the Sacramental Imagination* (New York: Continuum, 1997).

5. On this point, see Edward Schillebeeckx, *Christ: The Experience of Jesus as Lord*, trans. John Bowden (New York: Seabury Press, 1980), 64.

6. Bsp. Dupanloup, cited by Edward Schillebeeckx in "Priest and Layman in a Secular World," in *World and Church*, trans. N. D. Smith (New York: Sheed & Ward, 1971), 32–76 at 39.

7. My thanks to Jude Siciliano, OP, and the Evangelization Team for the Diocese of Wheeling, WV, in 1979, for this insight.

8. Thomas Aquinas, *Summa Theologiae* III, q. 68, a. 2, reply.

9. *Nostra Aetate* was approved on 28 October 1965; *Dei Verbum* was approved on 18 November 1965.

10. See Abraham Heschel, *The Prophets*, Vols. 1 and 2 (New York: Harper & Row, 1962); Gerhard von Rad, *The Message of the Prophets* (New York: Harper & Row, 1962); and Walter Brueggemann, *The Prophetic Imagination* (Philadelphia: Fortress, 1978), and numerous later texts, in particular, *Finally Comes the Poet,* in which Brueggemann develops the connections for preachers.

11. Andre Dubus, "Sacraments," in *Meditations from a Movable Chair* (New York: Alfred A. Knopf, 1998), 85–99 at 85.

12. In the well-known words of Augustine, a sacrament is a "visible word" (*verbum visibile*) and the word of faith is an "audible sacrament" (*sacramentum audibile*).

13. New York: Macmillan, 1966.

14. See Sandra M. Schneiders, *The Revelatory Text* (San Francisco: Harper SanFrancisco, 1991), especially chapter 2.

15. *In Psalmum* 147: CCL 78, 337–338, as cited in *Verbum Domini* 56, n. 199.

16. This is also delineated in LG 25 and DV 10. See also EN 68 where Paul VI addresses bishops and priests in a similar way: "What identifies our priestly service, gives a profound unity to the thousand and one tasks which claim our attention day by day and throughout our lives, and confers a distinct character on our activities, is this aim, ever present in all our action: to proclaim the Gospel of God."

17. As quoted by Albert Vanhoye, SJ, "The Biblical Question of Charisms after Vatican II," in *Vatican II: Assessment and Perspectives Twenty-Five Years After (1962–1987)*, Vol. I, ed. Rene Latourelle (New York: Paulist, 1988), 439–468, esp. 442–443.

18. See also the section on religious life as communal witness to the Gospel, EN 69.

19. Directed by Xavier Beavois, Sony Pictures, 2010.

20. Synod of Bishops, *Justice in the World* (Washington, DC: United States Catholic Conference, 1971), #40.

21. Denise Levertov, "The Servant-Girl at Emmaus (A Painting by Velasquez)" in *Breathing the Water* (New York: New Directions, 1987), 66.

Chapter 3

New Perspectives on Preaching from *Verbum Domini*

Jeremy Driscoll, OSB

At first glance readers and commentators of *Verbum Domini* who were looking for significant new directions in homiletics were disappointed. True, there is one paragraph (59) devoted to the question. Even so, it can seem that nothing especially new or insightful is said about homilies there. Paragraph 60 suggests the preparation of a Directory on Homiletics "in which preachers can find useful assistance in preparing to exercise their ministry." No one, of course, would be against "useful assistance," but in these several paragraphs nothing more specific is said, it would seem, about homilies.

I carefully began my observation, however, with the phrase "at first glance." Looking more carefully, *Verbum Domini* can bring something new to how we conceive the homilist's task. In fact, its contribution lies in its whole vision of what the word of God is and can be in the life and mission of the church. This whole vision was the topic of the synod and consequently the topic of Pope Benedict's post-synodal apostolic exhortation. It is for us to draw conclusions for preaching from the document's wider vision. (Presumably a Directory on Homiletics would do the same.)

I draw your attention to the richness of *Verbum Domini*'s theological vision of the word of God and, as I do so, draw some conclusions about the consequences for preaching. In this process we can "sneak up," as it were, on paragraph 59 in its broader context and see that, brief as it is, something quite significant is said about the homily. It could go without saying, perhaps, that it will not be possible for me to be exhaustive. I have picked and chosen some sections to concentrate on. There would be more.

The exhortation is divided into three major parts: the Word of God, the Word in the Church, and the Word [Addressed] to the World. I have selected from the first two parts, for these are the parts that directly bear on our topic. It is from the Word preached within the church that the Word goes out to all the world. Part 1, the Word of God, presents a concise theological summary of the reality of God's word. Let us look at one of the developments within this part.

Christology of the Word

Some rich theological paragraphs are grouped together under the title "Christology of the Word" (VD 11–13). In fact, these paragraphs help us to take the theological measure of a claim that is made later in the document, in the paragraph on homilies, namely, that Christ must stand at the center of every homily (VD 59). Why? A Christology of the Word can answer this question.

This section begins and bases itself in the well-known opening of the Letter to the Hebrews: "In many and various ways God spoke of old to our fathers by the prophets; but in these last days he has spoken to us by a Son . . ." (Heb 1:1-2 as in VD 11). God's word and God's speaking does not begin in Jesus Christ, but it does arrive at a qualitatively different level in the incarnation of the Word. For in the mystery of the incarnation, we come to see that the expression and very concept "word of God" does not refer to actual words coming somehow from out of the sky and booming down upon us. Nor does it refer ultimately to words written in a book. No, to use the words of *Verbum Domini*, "Here we are set before the very person of Jesus. His unique and singular history is the definitive word which God speaks to humanity." Such a claim cannot be made without expressing wonder. The document does so eloquently, calling the incarnation "an unprecedented and humanly inconceivable novelty" (VD 11).

The novelty of the incarnate Word is developed in the next paragraph, (12). "Now the word is not simply audible; not only does it have a *voice*, now the word has a *face*, one which we can see: that of Jesus of Nazareth." The whole life of Jesus is, of course, this word with a face. Furthermore, his is a life in which his humanity shows its uniqueness precisely in his own relation to the word of God, for Jesus is the one who constantly hears his Father's voice and obeys it. As such then, "In a perfect way, he hears, embodies and communicates to us the word of God (cf. Luke 5:1)."

This perfect expression of the word of God that Jesus is in his whole life reaches its climax in the paschal mystery. This is strikingly expressed by the document: "here we find ourselves before the 'word of the cross' (1 Cor 1:18). The word is muted; it becomes mortal silence, for it has 'spoken' exhaustively, holding back nothing of what it had to tell us." This would be the strongest example of what I said earlier in stressing that the expression "word of God" does not mean words booming down upon us from out of the sky. I point to the silent dead body of Jesus on the cross. I point to the "word of the cross" (1 Cor 1:18), where God has spoken exhaustively.

The word of the cross, of course, includes the resurrection; and in fact all the Scriptures bring us again and again to this central and exhaustive expression of God. Paragraph 13 makes this point forcefully, and it is full of consequences for anyone who wants to think about how the hom- ilist is meant to understand the Scriptures that are to be preached: "The New Testament thus presents the paschal mystery as being in accordance with the sacred Scriptures and as their deepest fulfillment." The funda- mental creedal statement of St. Paul from 1 Corinthians 15:3-4 is cited. Jesus' death for our sins is "in accordance with the scriptures" (NABRE). And that he rose on the third day is likewise "in accordance with the scriptures." What are the consequences of this brief creedal statement of Paul's, which he himself presents as already being a traditional formula- tion? It means that the death of Jesus "is an event containing a *logos*, an inner logic." Because it happened "in accordance with the scriptures," it means that there is a hidden providence in this "word." It means that this death "says" something, "expresses" something. It expresses God. It is God's word. Something similar is true of resurrection. It too is "in accordance with the scriptures." This means, to use the words of the document, "that Christ's victory over death took place through the crea- tive power of the word of God."

At the end of this development of a Christology of the Word, Pope Benedict offers a beautiful image that expresses the centrality of Christ's death and resurrection in the whole of the Scriptures. We have already mentioned the beginning of the Letter to the Hebrews in which the "many and various ways" in which God speaks are mentioned. We may consider this a symphony, the pope suggests, in which many voices or instruments sound. But then he offers this striking development. He says, "In this symphony one finds, at a certain point, what would be called in musical terms a 'solo,' a theme entrusted to a single instrument or voice which is so important that the meaning of the entire work depends on it. This 'solo' is Jesus. . . . The Son of Man recapitulates in himself earth and heaven, creation and the Creator, flesh and Spirit. He is the centre of the cosmos and of history, for in him converge without confusion the author and his work."

Nothing explicitly has been said about homilies in anything summarized here from *Verbum Domini.* Nonetheless, there are significant conclusions to be drawn. The death and resurrection of Jesus is the central deed of God for our salvation. The homilist, then, must again and again put into relief this "according to the scriptures" of the death and resurrection of Jesus. Every scriptural text on which one preaches leads to that center and sheds light on the mystery of that central deed of God from a particular perspective—from the perspective of some foreshadowing event in Israel's history (the first reading), from the perspective of an apostle's theological reflections (the second reading), from the perspective of a particular evangelist (the gospel reading) who does what all the evangelists do, namely, speak of the life of Jesus in such a way as to show its climax in his death and resurrection. We have here nothing less than the fundamental hermeneutical key to all the Scriptures. With this key "Christ can stand at the center of every homily," as paragraph 59 urges; and we see that such urging is far more than a pious flourish of the document. It is a theological necessity.

The Church as the Primary Setting for Biblical Hermeneutics

It is clear that someone prepares to preach by knowing the Bible well, by studying, by continually increasing one's understanding. But how? Naturally a synod on the Word of God in the life and mission of the church will have taken up the question of proper interpretation of the Bible. Let us see now how the pope uses the work of the synod to shed light on this critical question. We can begin with a section of several paragraphs (VD 29–30) grouped under the title "The Church as the Primary Setting for Biblical Hermeneutics."

The exhortation clearly states that "authentic biblical hermeneutics can only be had within the faith of the Church. . . ." Or again, "the primary setting for scriptural interpretation is the life of the Church." Some people will hear such claims as an attempt of church authority to keep control over biblical interpretation. They will see it as interference in what should be freely open debate and discussion by any and all. The document, however, wants to forestall such a possible reaction by immediately explaining the deeper sense of this context of interpretation. It says, "This is not to uphold the ecclesial context as an extrinsic rule to which exegetes must submit, but rather is something demanded by the very nature of the Scriptures and the way they gradually came into being." I appreciate the document's wanting to rule out the objection that this would be merely an "extrinsic rule" imposed without any real relation to the biblical text. In fact, the Scriptures are themselves the testament of faith, evidence for faith, produced at the service of faith within communities of faith. How could they be properly and sensitively understood outside this context of faith? And so the document urges, "Exegetes, theologians and the whole people of God must approach it [Scripture] as what it really is, the word of God conveyed to us through human words (cf. 1 Th 2:13). . . . The Bible is the Church's book, and its essential place in the Church's life gives rise to its genuine interpretation."

Anyone who knows the work of Joseph Ratzinger before his election as pope is aware of how much thought he has devoted to this critical question. Naturally, then, in this exhortation he is not satisfied with only making the point from one angle. He usefully quotes the Pontifical Biblical Commission's 1994 document *The Interpretation of the Bible in the Church:* "Access to a proper understanding of biblical texts is only granted to the person who has an affinity with what the text is saying on the basis of life experience" (p. 20). And what the text is saying is always "faith" in the context of the communities of faith. Again, we should check in ourselves a negative reaction to the document's insistence on this point. Understood rightly, this ecclesial context leads to "the growth of genuine understanding," and it leads to communion with others. "Listening to the word of God introduces and increases ecclesial communion with all those who walk by faith."

Paragraphs 31, 32, and 33 speak about a specific concern of the synod. "The Synod likewise felt a need to look into the present state of biblical studies and their standing within the field of theology." The key word in this deceptively simple paragraph is the word *within*. What is at issue is a fruitful relationship between exegesis and theology. It must be admitted that the relationship has not always been peaceful or fruitful. So, how to make it so is naturally a concern of this synod. The pope begins by unequivocally acknowledging "the benefits that historical-critical exegesis and other recently-developed methods of textual analysis have brought to the life of the Church." This is not merely a *pro forma* nod required before going on to say that these methods are not enough. The pope exposes the deep theological roots of the historical-critical method when he says, "For the Catholic understanding of sacred Scripture, attention to such methods is indispensable, linked as it is to the realism of the Incarnation: 'This necessity is a consequence of the Christian principle formulated in the Gospel of John 1:14: *Verbum caro factum est.* The historical fact is a constitutive dimension of the Christian faith. The history of salvation is not mythology, but a true history, and it should thus be studied with the methods of serious historical research.'"

After this the Holy Father recalls several of the significant interventions around this question of his predecessors in the last several centuries. He mentions Leo XIII, Pius XII, and John Paul II. Pope Benedict's description of Leo XIII's contribution nicely expresses the balance that he himself is concerned to preserve: "Pope Leo XIII's intervention had the merit of protecting the Catholic interpretation of the Bible from the inroads of rationalism, without, however, seeking refuge in a spiritual meaning detached from history. Far from shunning scientific criticism, the Church was wary only of 'preconceived opinions that claim to be based on science, but which in reality surreptitiously cause science to depart from its domain.'" Science departs from its domain if it attempts to interpret texts authoritatively for communities of faith. Once again the Pontifical Biblical Commission's 1994 document is usefully cited: "In their work of interpretation, Catholic exegetes must never forget that what they are interpreting is the *word of God*. Their common task is not finished when they have simply determined sources, defined forms or explained literary procedures. They arrive at the true goal of their work only when they have explained the meaning of the biblical text as God's word for today" (p. 30). This last expression—"God's word for today"—shows the relevance of this discussion on proper interpretation for the task of preaching. Obviously the homilist must be concerned about putting into relief "God's word for today." But such a word comes to us from a text created in concrete historical circumstances considerably different from our own. Interpretation bridges this gap, and it is critical that it be properly conceived.

The next section carries a title that is itself a significant part of the text of the exhortation. It is called, "The Council's biblical hermeneutic: a directive to be appropriated." This is the synod—and the Holy Father affirming the synod's work—noting that the work of the council is not yet finished. In effect the claim is that there is something in what the council said about biblical interpretation that still needs to be appropriated in the present day. The pope refers especially to the conciliar document *Dei Verbum* and notes that this document "indicates three fundamental criteria for an appreciation of the divine dimension of the Bible: 1) the text must be interpreted with attention to *the unity of the whole of Scripture*; nowadays this is called canonical exegesis; 2) account is be taken of the *living Tradition of the whole Church*; and, finally, 3) respect must be shown for *the analogy of faith*. 'Only where both methodological levels, the historical-critical and the theological, are respected, can one speak of a theological exegesis, an exegesis worthy of this book.'"

The task of attending to these three fundamental criteria belongs also to the homilist since the homilist's exegesis must be a theological one. Both *Dei Verbum* and *Verbum Domini* only mention the three criteria but without elaboration. Where the *Catechism of the Catholic Church* has occasion to speak of them, quoting *Dei Verbum,* it elaborates slightly. These brief elaborations can indicate to the homilist the direction for developing an understanding of what bearing they might have on preaching.

For example, concerning the first, the unity of the whole of Scripture, the *Catechism* says, "Different as the books which compose it may be, Scripture is a unity by reason of the unity of God's plan, of which Christ Jesus is the center and heart, open since his Passover" (cf. Lk 24:25-27, 44-46; CCC 112). Here, once again, is stressed that center of Scripture, which is Jesus Christ in his paschal mystery. Surely then it is part of the preacher's task to help the Christian people read the Scriptures in such a way as to come always to this center and heart.

Concerning the second criterion, understanding the Scriptures within the living tradition of the whole church, the *Catechism* says, "Sacred Scripture is written principally in the Church's heart rather than in documents and records, for the Church carries in her Tradition the living memorial of God's Word, and it is the Holy Spirit who gives her the spiritual interpretation of the Scripture" (CCC 113). Certainly the liturgy represents an important manifestation of the relationship between Scripture and tradition. During the long centuries in which the Sacred Scriptures were being written and the biblical canon was taking shape, the people of God gathered regularly to celebrate the liturgy; indeed, the writings were created in good part for such gatherings. The preacher must take account of these liturgical origins of the Scriptures and look to them for clues on how to open a text in the new context of the community where the ancient text is still alive and ever new in the moment of its proclamation.

The third criterion is defined by the *Catechism* in this way: "By 'analogy of faith' we mean the coherence of the truths of faith among themselves and within the whole plan of Revelation" (CCC 114). This in fact raises a very important question about homilies, namely, the way in which doctrine might properly be treated in the course of a homily. The core of our faith is the mystery of the Trinity and the invitation for us to participate in this divine life. This reality is revealed and effected through the paschal mystery. And so the homilist must interpret the Scriptures in such a way that the paschal mystery is revealed in them and, at the same time, lead the people to enter into participation in this mystery through the celebration of the Eucharist.

It is clear that the bishops of the synod and the Holy Father with them consider the relationship between Scripture and theology to be an important one. *Verbum Domini* summarizes the concern in this way: "While today's academic exegesis, including that of Catholic scholars, is highly competent in the field of historical-critical methodology and its latest developments, it must be said that comparable attention needs to be paid to the theological dimension of the biblical texts, so that they can be more deeply understood in accordance with the three elements indicated by the Dogmatic Constitution *Dei Verbum*."

Let us return to the question raised about doctrine in homilies. The great positive achievement in Catholic preaching in these recent decades is that preaching has been centered on the scriptural texts read in the liturgy, and these texts themselves present a much richer exposure to the biblical world. Preaching in this way, however, has for the most part been pursued with little or no reference to doctrine and with little or no teaching on the Eucharist or other sacraments. Some theories of preaching claim that it would be out of place to do so, that preaching is not to be confused with a classroom and with rarefied discussions of doctrine. I personally have long thought that we need to conceive the homily in such a way as to allow for an appropriate teaching of doctrine and sacramental—or mystagogical—teaching. *Verbum Domini* is challenging us to revisit this question.

Plainly, doctrine is not meant to be propounded in a homily in the way that it might unfold in a learned treatise or in a speculative lecture in the academy. Nonetheless, doctrines guide the homilist and ensure that preaching arrives at what is in fact the deepest meaning of Scripture and sacrament. Doctrines simply formulate with accuracy what the church has come to know through the Scriptures proclaimed in the believing assembly and through the sacraments that are celebrated on the foundation of these Scriptures.

The most central doctrines of the church (the analogy of faith is concerned to identify these)—the divine and human natures of Christ and the mystery of the Trinity, which Christ reveals in his paschal mystery—were discovered and formulated precisely when the Scriptures were proclaimed in the liturgical assembly and when the Scriptures became sacrament in the eucharistic rite. These doctrines were formulated to keep the communities that read the Scriptures and celebrated the Eucharist in a same communion of right understanding and right worship (orthodoxy) about these things, a communion that was to hold across the whole world and through the centuries. For that same reason these doctrines ought to be seamlessly introduced and articulated still today in the course of our celebrations in order to ensure that by reading the Scriptures and celebrating the Eucharist we understand ever more deeply the essential beliefs of the church. It is not that one would first speak of Scripture and then of doctrine. Doctrine is the deepest sense of Scripture and sacrament.

With these reflections on the role of doctrine in preaching, I hope I have given an example of what I suggested at the very beginning, namely, that the consequences for preaching in *Verbum Domini* must be drawn out of the document and developed by us who are directly interested in preaching. In any case, I hope our discussion has illustrated why the pope's apostolic exhortation finds it so important to insist that "authentic biblical hermeneutics can only be had within the faith of the Church. . . ." Or again, "the primary setting for scriptural interpretation is the life of the Church."

Now, let us turn to those paragraphs of *Verbum Domini* that have the most direct bearing on how we might conceive the homilist's task.

The Liturgy, Privileged Setting for the Word of God

The paragraphs I have in mind are grouped under the title "The Liturgy, Privileged Setting for the Word of God" (VD 52–60). They occur in the second major section of the document, called "The Word of God and the Church." This section opens with two beautiful paragraphs that lead directly into the discussion of the liturgy. These paragraphs want to introduce a key concept, that of the vital importance of receiving the word of God. Yes, God speaks a word. The whole first section was a meditation on various dimensions of this reality. But God's speaking introduces the dramatic possibility of our receiving his word or rejecting it. To receive the Word is, the document says, "the beginning of a new creation; a new creature is born, a new people comes to birth" (VD 50). This is the church. "Here we can glimpse the face of the Church as a reality defined by acceptance of the Word of God . . ." (ibid.). This is a powerful way to define the church. The church is the gathering of all those who accept the word that God speaks. It is not difficult to see how this will lead naturally to a discussion of liturgy.

The other key concept of these opening paragraphs is an insistence on what we could call the "today" of the Word. "The relationship between Christ, the Word of the Father, and the Church cannot be fully understood in terms of a mere past event; rather, it is a living relationship which each member of the faithful is personally called to enter into. We are speaking of the presence of God's word to us today: 'Lo, I am with you always, to the close of the age' (Mt 28:20)" (VD 51). The formulations of these paragraphs are concerned not only to establish the reality of the church in relationship to the word of God but also to emphasize the need for each individual personally to accept the Word. This is beautifully stated just before the document opens its direct discussion on the liturgy. "In the word of God proclaimed and heard, and in the sacraments, Jesus says today, here and now, to each person: 'I am yours, I give myself to you'; so that we can receive and respond, saying in return: 'I am yours' " (ibid.).

If someone were to say to me, "Show me that. Show me that happening. Show me where Jesus says today, here and now, 'I am yours, I give myself to you,' " I would point to the liturgy. I would point to the liturgy, and I would speak about it in such a way that this beautiful possibility of a relationship with Jesus is clearly seen as the liturgy's deepest sense. And if I were a homilist, I would recognize that I have here the framework that defines my basic task: to show in the Scriptures proclaimed in the liturgy and in all the other actions of the liturgy that Jesus here and now offers himself to each one of us and that each one of us and all of us together can say in return to Jesus, "I am yours."

I said I would point to the liturgy. The document does the same now. As we enter the particulars of what these paragraphs say, we would do well to remind ourselves that a homily is *part* of the liturgical action. It too is a liturgical moment. There are more implications in this than first meet the eye. It means that a homily must be constructed as a part of the whole, that it ought not stick out as a different moment, that liturgy doesn't stop for a while for the homily and start up again when it is over. So, everything that *Verbum Domini* says about Scripture and the liturgy is something to which the homilist should be especially sensitive. Let's look at some of that now.

The first paragraph in the liturgical section establishes some important claims. "The liturgy is the privileged setting in which God speaks to us in the midst of our lives; he speaks today to his people, who hear and respond. Every liturgical action is by its very nature steeped in sacred Scripture" (VD 52). Again, we see that key word "today" and the insistence on the structure of hearing and responding. These points are developed in what follows by citing several important passages from Vatican II's document on the liturgy and the valuable and often overlooked theological introduction to the church's post-conciliar Lectionary. With such citations the synod continues to drive home the original intentions of the council, which naturally can be more firmly and broadly established as the years and decades pass. The concern of these citations is to show that "The word of God, constantly proclaimed in the liturgy, is always a living and effective word through the power of the Holy Spirit."

In the paragraphs just examined on the ecclesial context of interpretation, we saw the concern of the synod to promote a faith-filled reading of the Scriptures. Now such a reading is related to the liturgy in a foundational way. *"A faith-filled understanding of sacred Scripture must always refer back to the liturgy*, in which the word of God is celebrated as a timely and living word . . ." (emphasis in original).

Reference to the Lectionary is critical here because in effect it is by means of the Lectionary that most Catholics have access to Scripture. This is more, not less. It is not as if, had we the time and energy, we would read the whole Bible straight through. No, the structure of the Lectionary holds a key to understanding the whole of the Bible. The Lectionary is, in effect, a way of reading the whole Bible. And so Pope Benedict notes, "Here one sees the sage pedagogy of the Church, which proclaims and listens to sacred Scripture following the rhythm of the liturgical year. . . . At the centre of everything the paschal mystery shines forth, and around it radiate all the mysteries of Christ and the history of salvation which become sacramentally present."

Here, once again, we encounter this insistence on the center, on the paschal mystery. The homilist should habitually refer to this center, always aware of it when treating all that radiates around it. And something else should be noted in the text just cited, namely, that what is read becomes sacramentally present. What is read is summarized with the phrase "mysteries of Christ and the history of salvation." These become present! The homilist must say so. The homilist must teach that and proclaim it. It is a wonderful claim, and by the preaching the assembly should be awakened to this wonder. The word of God, precisely as it comes to be understood and savored in the liturgy, becomes, the document says, "the basis for a correct approach to sacred Scripture." This final statement is of fundamental importance. It is an implicit evocation of the principle *lex orandi, lex credendi.* The Scripture understood in the liturgy is Scripture with a clear paschal center, and Christ and his mysteries become present sacramentally within the liturgy where they are proclaimed. All Scripture must be approached in this light.

The next paragraph, 53, urges a new effort at connecting Scripture and the sacraments. It cites yet again the Pontifical Biblical Commission: "It is the task of priests and deacons, above all when they administer the sacraments, to explain the unity between word and sacrament in the ministry of the Church" (p. 28). Obviously, the homily would be the primary place where such explanation can take place. It is nothing less than a call for the kind of mystagogical preaching of which we have such splendid examples in the patristic church.

In this paragraph the document also usefully puts forward the concept of what it calls "the performative character of God's word." It explains, "In salvation history there is no separation between what God *says* and what he *does*" (emphasis in original). The relationship between *word* and *sacrament* is the liturgical expression of this performative character. This fact is a framework that a homilist could usefully keep in mind. What God *says* in the Liturgy of the Word, God *does* in the sacramental action. This is what one would preach about.

Paragraphs 54 and 55 are a specific development on the word of God and the Eucharist. "The profound unity of word and Eucharist is grounded in the witness of Scripture (cf. Jn 6; Lk 24), attested to by the Fathers of the Church, and reaffirmed by the Second Vatican Council." An ample footnote is attached to this statement with references to some nine texts of the council. So, once again in this point, we see the synod and the pope pushing forward the council's agenda, always urging a deeper appropriation. The citation mentioned John 6, Jesus' discourse on the Bread of Life, and Luke 24, the story of the risen Lord's encounter with the two disciples on the road to Emmaus. Both texts are examined in what follows.

The document shows us, however briefly, that a homilist would do well to become imbued with the profound sense of these two passages, for their implications spread out and cover virtually any text of Scripture in relation to a eucharistic celebration in which it might be proclaimed. At issue throughout the whole Bread of Life discourse is the true "bread come down from heaven" as being at one and the same time a reference to teaching (word) and Eucharist (sacrament). Within this framework the document concludes, "The mystery of the Eucharist reveals the true manna, the true bread of heaven: it is God's *Logos* made flesh, who gave himself up for us in the paschal mystery."

The well-known Emmaus account is developed in what follows. Of course, the church and preachers have long had no difficulty in seeing in this story the two halves of the eucharistic liturgy, the Liturgy of the Word corresponding to Jesus' discussion with the disciples about the Scriptures, the Liturgy of the Eucharist corresponding to the breaking of the bread by Jesus. But *Verbum Domini* summarizes this very effectively: "The two disciples began to look at the Scriptures in a new way in the company of this traveler who seemed so surprisingly familiar with their lives. What had taken place in those days no longer appeared to them as failure, but as fulfilment and a new beginning. And yet, apparently not even these words were enough for the two disciples. The Gospel of Luke relates that 'their eyes were opened and they recognized him' (24:31) only when Jesus took the bread, said the blessing, broke it and gave it to them, whereas earlier 'their eyes were kept from recognizing him' (24:16)."

What is striking in this summary is the phrase "and yet." It is a way of saying that in some sense it is not enough simply to hear the Scriptures and have them explained. The breaking of the bread, the Eucharist, is necessary not only for the ultimate recognition of Jesus but also for the ultimate understanding of the Word. Only after the breaking of the bread are the disciples able to appreciate in a new way what they experienced in the encounter with the Word: "Were not our hearts burning [within us] while he spoke to us on the way and opened the scriptures to us?" (Luke 24:32, NABRE).

The document makes an important claim as it draws the strands of these two gospel accounts together. It is that "Scripture itself points us towards an appreciation of its own unbreakable bond with the Eucharist"

(VD 55). And then it cites a very strong text from what earlier I called the often overlooked theological introduction to the Lectionary. We read, "It can never be forgotten that the divine word, read and proclaimed by the Church, has as its one purpose the sacrifice of the new covenant and the banquet of grace, that is, the Eucharist." All of Scripture finds its culmination in Eucharist. But the dynamic does not move in one direction only. Eucharist causes us to look back to the Scriptures with greater understanding, just as the Scriptures culminate in the banquet of grace. In the precise words of the document: "The Eucharist opens us to an understanding of Scripture, just as Scripture for its part illumines and explains the mystery of the Eucharist."

We have reached a point in the apostolic exhortation *Verbum Domini* where the vision of Scripture in the life and mission of the church that it presents can be understood to be suggesting a new emphasis, a new dimension in Catholic preaching. Virtually every homily preached during the Mass should make some connection between the Scriptures just heard and the Eucharist about to be celebrated. Depending on what opportunities the texts in question provide, such a connection might be very brief or even only implicitly indicated, but at other times a firm connection should be established and drawn out. In any case, the connection can always be made by following a fundamental pattern. The center of the Scriptures is the death and resurrection of Jesus. The Eucharist is a memorial of the Lord's death, during the course of which we recognize that "the Lord has truly been raised" (Luke 24:34, NABRE) and is present to us and recognized by us in the breaking of the bread. When this connection is consistently made clear to the Christian people, then they will understand the Scriptures ever more deeply, and they will be ever more admiring of the mystery of the Eucharist. They will understand the inextricable connection between Scripture and Eucharist as part of the wise design of Providence, and the liturgical celebration itself will be their glad thanksgiving, *their* Eucharist. This is what the council fathers were speaking about when they said, "The Church has always venerated the divine Scriptures just as she venerates the body of the Lord, since, especially in the sacred liturgy, she unceasingly receives and offers to the faithful the bread of life from the table both of God's word and of Christ's body." (DV 21. See also PO 18 and SC 51, 56.)

After this intense development, several more paragraphs intervene before we arrive at paragraph 59, which bears the specific title "The Importance of the Homily." These intervening paragraphs treat in turn the sacramentality of the Word, the Lectionary, the actual proclamation of the word, and the ministry of Reader. If one just consults *Verbum Domini* to see what it says about homilies, it can be at first glance disappointing. But then I described the reflection I have conducted here as a sneaking up on paragraph 59, that is, discovering it and reading it in its fuller context. In this fuller context it becomes clear that the paragraph is offering some important directives that involve letting homilies be very much influenced by this fuller vision of Scripture that the entire document is anxious to promote.

First, Pope Benedict repeats something he said in the Exhortation that followed the previous synod on the Eucharist: "The quality of homilies needs to be improved." People have complained that in paragraph 59, he said no more than that, offered no direction. But surely the direction of improvement lies in absorbing the vision of Scripture and sacraments and the whole ecclesial context of interpretation that we have been discussing here. The pope reminds us also that "The homily is part of the liturgical action." This tells us a great deal about the tone and style of a homily, about the atmosphere it is meant to create and be a part of. The way a preacher speaks ought not to stick out as a different moment that makes it seem like liturgy is stopping for a while and will start up again when the homily is over.

After this, four important things that a homily ought to achieve are delineated. "[1] The homily is a means of bringing the scriptural message to life in a way that helps the faithful to realize that God's word is present and at work in their everyday lives. [2] It should lead to an understanding of the mystery being celebrated, [3] serve as a summons to mission, and [4] prepare the assembly for the profession of faith, the universal prayer and the Eucharistic liturgy" (numbers, my addition). Read by itself, this text may not be especially striking. But read in the context of the whole document, we can see that it summarizes many of the key themes we have examined. This citation gains its strength by reference to the treatment of those themes elsewhere in the document.

The first point recalls the stress on the "today" of the Word to which I had occasion to draw our attention a number of times. The second point stresses the mystery of Christ himself and salvation history being actually present by means of the liturgical celebration. The summons to mission, the third point, will in fact be dealt with in the third major part of the document, and we have not had the time to treat it here. Obviously it is of critical importance as that part of the document makes clear. The fourth point speaks of the homilist's responsibility to build bridges from what is said about Scripture to the rest of the liturgy, mentioning specifically the profession of faith, where the doctrinal dimensions of the Scripture are seen; mentioning the universal prayer, where the Scriptures give shape to what we pray for and how; and mentioning finally the eucharistic liturgy, whose intimate link to the Scriptures we have examined at length, just as the document itself does.

Finally, throughout this discussion I have pointed frequently to what the document itself frequently emphasizes, namely, the center in Christ and in his paschal mystery. And we see this theme also distinctly mentioned in this short paragraph on the homily. "The faithful should be able to perceive clearly that the preacher has a compelling desire to present Christ, who must stand at the centre of every homily."

Conclusion

My task here has been to treat new perspectives on preaching from *Verbum Domini*. I hope I have been able to indicate that *Verbum Domini* actually offers some very fresh new perspectives on Catholic preaching or that, at the very least, it offers timely reminders of what we have tended to lose sight of. I have only been able to indicate some of the kinds of reflections for homilies that could be developed from this apostolic exhortation. There could certainly be more.

By way of conclusion, let me try now to draw the strands of our discussion together into what could be called "giving the homily its basic shape."

First, Jesus Christ must stand at the center of every homily—or more precisely, Jesus Christ in his death and resurrection. It must be shown that his death is "in accordance with the scriptures." And it must be shown that his resurrection is "in accordance with the scriptures."

Second, every homily must clearly be a profoundly ecclesial homily, seamlessly uniting Scripture and doctrine. The faith community of the church is given expression by the homilist's preaching. It should be preaching that leads to growth of genuine understanding and that increases ecclesial communion with all those who walk by faith and who have walked by faith before us.

Third, this ecclesial dimension is essential precisely because the homily is a part of the liturgy, and the liturgy is the privileged setting for the word of God. The whole manner of celebration throughout the entire celebration displays the homilist's understanding of all that is happening, and this is rendered explicit in the words of the homily. What is happening in the liturgy? God speaks and so urges the people's response. God speaks and says, "Jesus Christ." God speaks, and his word is deed—that is, his word becomes sacrament, his word becomes Eucharist.

In hundreds of ways and in many styles and cultures and with hundreds of different texts from many parts of the Scriptures, the homilist explains and teaches and points out and lifts up these things for the Christian people. But in all the different ways this *core* should be discernible: Jesus Christ crucified and risen is God's definitive word to the world, a word given in the very flesh and blood in the Eucharist. This word begs a response, which it is the homilist's duty to elicit. The response is given here and now in the liturgy that follows the homily. In a particular community's acceptance of the Word, in a particular church's acceptance of the Word, the church is transformed through the eucharistic liturgy into the new world, the new creation, which the word of God creates. The church becomes Body of Christ, word of God, where *word* becomes *deed*. The church becomes God's word to the world and for the sake of the world.

Chapter 4

Preaching from and for the Liturgy:
A Practical Guide

Jan Michael Joncas

While it is certainly true that homiletic preaching is usually inspired by the Scriptures proclaimed at the liturgy at which that preaching takes place, the *General Instruction of the Roman Missal* (GIRM) indicates that other sources of inspiration exist:

> 65. The Homily . . . should be an explanation of some aspect of the readings from Sacred Scripture or of another text from the Ordinary or the Proper of the Mass of the day and should take into account both the mystery being celebrated and the particular needs of the listeners.

Thus in addition to the Scriptures proclaimed, a homilist might find inspiration in the liturgical texts themselves, whether invariant (the "Ordinary" of the Mass) or variable (the "Proper" of the Mass). I would extend this to the other sign systems the liturgy employs since so often a liturgical text explicates a rite (as when the *"Agnus Dei"* chant explicates the meaning of the Fraction Rite). A third source of inspiration would be the "mystery being celebrated," whether that might be the lives of saints on their feast days, the sacrament being conferred at ordination, matrimony, or confirmation, or encounter with the paschal mystery at a funeral.

The focus here is on the second of these three sources of inspiration for a homily: the texts and ceremonies of the liturgy. To that end, I will first offer a short definition of liturgical preaching. I will then try to model a process by which preachers might prepare a homily inspired by the major euchology (such as a eucharistic prayer or a preface), the minor euchology (such as the collect, the prayer over the offerings, or the post-Communion prayer), the liturgical chants, and liturgical gestures and objects.

1. A Definition of Liturgical Preaching

Some years ago I devoted a chapter of my book, *Preaching the Rites of Initiation,* to describing a liturgical homily.[1] The following is a slight modification of what I wrote there, in the light of further years of experience as a preacher.

Liturgical preaching is *oral communication*:

Spoken from faith. The preacher does not offer disinterested observations from some neutral height but self-implicates as one who passionately believes the message he offers.

Addressed to believers. Believers sometimes preach to nonbelievers, but that form of preaching is properly called "evangelical" or "conversionary." The goal of evangelical preaching is to reach those who have not encountered the message and person of Christ in a compelling way and to invite them to respond if God is calling them to Christian faith. "Evangelical/ conversionary" preaching contrasts with "liturgical preaching" since the latter aims to reach those already converted to Christ. With the exception of non-baptized visitors (usually unknown to the preacher) and the catechumens/elect, all of those whom the preacher addresses at liturgy are believers, though usually exhibiting widely differing ways of actualizing their belief. The preacher must then address them from a stance of shared discipleship rather than treating them as "baptized pagans."

Contextualized by worship. Treating "The Sunday Homily as Integral to the Eucharist" in chapter 1 of *Preaching the Mystery of Faith: The Sunday Homily,* the U.S. episcopal conference beautifully articulates how liturgical preaching, unlike some other forms, is always contextualized by worship.[2] One of the most important teachings of Vatican II in regard to preaching is the insistence that the homily is an integral part of the

Eucharist itself [see *Sacrosanctum Concilium* 52]. As part of the entire liturgical act, the homily is meant to set hearts on fire with praise and thanksgiving. It is to be a feature of the intense and privileged encounter with Jesus Christ that takes place in the liturgy. One might even say that the homilist connects the two parts of the Eucharistic liturgy as he looks back at the Scripture readings and looks forward to the sacrificial meal.[3]

Inspired by the Scriptures proclaimed, the liturgical texts recited, and/or the celebration enacted. I have treated this issue above in relation to GIRM 65.

Proximately intended to assist the worshipers to do the liturgical act called for. In the short run, the goal of liturgical preaching is to draw listeners into the mystery being celebrated in the liturgy. Preaching at a wedding should lead the assembly to pray for the couple making matrimonial covenant. Preaching at a funeral should declare the power of the paschal mystery as manifest in the dead person's life, allowing the living to commend the deceased to God and to confront death with Christian hope. Similarly, preaching in the context of the Eucharist should assist the participants to receive and maintain a holy communion with the Lord Jesus and his Abba God, with the angels, with the saints who have gone before us in faith, and with fellow worshipers in the Holy Spirit.

Ultimately intended to help the worshipers to live the gospel in daily life. In the long run, the goal of liturgical preaching is to draw people ever more deeply into the mystery of Christ so that their lives are transformed in holiness as they live out their baptismal commitment in the world. This goal will appear strongly articulated in the offering of the Eucharistic Prayer considered below.

Having presented this short sketch of what liturgical preaching is, I now turn to explore that preaching inspired by the texts and ceremonies of the liturgy itself.

2. Liturgical Preaching from Presidential Euchology

The term *euchology* is formed from two Greek words, *euchē* (prayer) and *logos* (structure, discourse, word). Liturgists use the term to refer to appointed prayer texts (as opposed to spontaneous prayers) employed in a liturgy, usually spoken or chanted by an ordained minister. Presidential euchology normally divides into two categories: major and minor.

Liturgical Preaching Inspired by Major Presidential Euchology

Major presidential euchology comprises the lengthier and more ritually important prayers recited or chanted by the officiating minister. In the Roman Rite examples of major presidential euchology would include:

- Blessing of Baptismal Water at Baptism
- Prayer for the Laying on of Hands in Confirmation + Concluding Blessing
- Eucharistic Prayers + Prefaces at Mass
- Solemn Blessings at Mass
- Formula of Absolution in Reconciliation
- Nuptial Blessings at Weddings
- Prayers of Ordination

A simple method for preparing a liturgical homily based on presidential euchology could include the following three steps:

1. Determine from official church teaching the intended function of a particular presidential text.
2. Study the structure and content of the liturgical text, exploring its original formulation and history of transmission if necessary.
3. Decide how the knowledge gleaned from this study will be communicated as catechetical (i.e., aimed at catechumens/elect) or mystagogical (i.e., the baptized) preaching, or both, in the context of a particular liturgy.

Liturgical Preaching Inspired by a Eucharistic Prayer

The major presidential text I consider first is the Eucharistic Prayer for Masses for Various Needs and Occasions. (Note that I will treat the Preface of the eucharistic prayer as a separate topic below.) While a simple overview of the eucharistic prayer might occupy a single homily, the density and richness of this text suggests a series of homilies. While it could be possible to preach on particular elements of the eucharistic prayer at scattered celebrations during the year (e.g., treating the epiclesis on Pentecost or the intercession for the dead on All Souls), a sermon series (perhaps when the Johannine Bread of Life discourse forms a series of successive gospels during Year B) might be the most effective way of doing this preaching.

The Preface Acclamation

Fortunately the GIRM offers us a succinct précis of the structure of this major prayer and gives insight into its progress of thought and content. The first element we will consider is the preface acclamation, also known as the *Sanctus-Benedictus*, or the Holy, Holy, Holy:[4]

> 79. The main elements of which the eucharistic prayer consists may be distinguished from one another in this way:
>
> . . .
>
> b) The acclamation, by which the whole congregation, joining with the heavenly powers, sings the "*Sanctus*" ("Holy, Holy, Holy"). This acclamation, which constitutes part of the Eucharistic Prayer itself, is pronounced by all the people with the Priest.

Here is the Latin text of the preface acclamation with a slavishly literal English translation not intended for liturgical use:

> *Sanctus, Sanctus, Sanctus, Dominus Deus Sabaoth.*
> Holy, Holy, Holy, Lord God of hosts.
> *Pleni sunt caeli et terra gloria tua.*
> Full are the heavens and earth with your glory.
> *Hosanna in excelsis.*
> Come and deliver us from on high.
> *Benedictus qui venit in nomine Domini.*
> Blessed is he who comes/has come in the name of the Lord.

The following insights might help a preacher prepare catechetical or mystagogical preaching on just the beginning of this text.

The first two sentences modify the cry of the seraphim in Isaiah 6:1-4 (and the preacher might want to proclaim that text for the assembly). He could then ask the question: "Why is God acclaimed three times as holy?" The direct answer is that Hebrew grammar often expresses a superlative by repetition; if one wanted to say "This Big Mac is gigantic," the grammatical structure would be "Big, big, big is the Big Mac." But the rabbis were not content with such a prosaic insight and offered multiple *midrashim* (explanatory stories based on the biblical text) to illuminate its meaning. One midrash holds that the triple "Holy" is to give the effect of an echo, thus indicating just how enormous the heavenly sanctuary is. Another midrash suggests that the two seraphim are outdoing each other in crying out God's greatness: the first declares "Holy," and the second in effect says "Holy? I'll see your 'holy' and raise you one— 'Holy, Holy.'"

When Christians adapted this text for their own worship, they saw in the triple "Holy" a mystical anticipation of the revelation of God as triune, with the statement that God the Father, God the Son, and God the Holy Spirit are all equal in holiness. That Christian interpretation might be furthered by considering the musical character of the text, with each "Holy" considered as a note in a triad sounding with root, fifth, and third: each note has its distinct relation to the others, no matter in which octave the notes appear, yet the three together comprise a single chord (and without all three there is no triad).

Similar kinds of catechetical and mystagogical insights can be gleaned from the other phrases and sentences of the preface acclamation. The preacher might even conclude his homily by inviting the congregation to sing the "Holy, Holy, Holy" that they will chant later in the Mass.

The Epicleses

A second element of the eucharistic prayer is the *epiclesis*, a request made by the praying community that God the Father would send forth the Holy Spirit. As GIRM 79c teaches:

> The epiclesis, in which, by means of particular invocations, the Church implores the power of the Holy Spirit that the gifts offered by human hands be consecrated, that is, become Christ's Body and Blood, and that the unblemished sacrificial Victim to be consumed in Communion may be for the salvation of those who will partake of it.

Notice that a peculiarity of Roman Rite eucharistic prayers is the so-called split epiclesis. The request that the Holy Spirit descend to sanctify the eucharistic elements occurs before the narrative of the Last Supper while the request that the Holy Spirit descend to sanctify those who partake of the consecrated elements occurs after the institution narrative. Here are the two epicletic texts from the Eucharistic Prayer for Masses for Various Needs and Occasions:

> Therefore, Father most merciful, we ask that you send forth your
> Holy Spirit, to sanctify these gifts of bread and wine, that they may
> become for us the Body and Blood of our Lord, Jesus Christ. . . .

> [Look with favor on the oblation of your Church, in which we show
> forth the paschal Sacrifice of Christ that has been handed on to us,
> and] grant that, by the power of the Spirit of your love, we may be
> counted now and until the day of eternity among the members of
> your Son, in whose Body and Blood we have communion.

How might a preacher be inspired by these texts to offer liturgical preaching? First, he might clarify for the congregation that the consecration of
the bread and wine is never an act of magic. No one has the power to
manipulate God. The prayers and gestures the priest recites and enacts
during the eucharistic prayer do not force God into the hosts lying on
the paten and the wine within the chalice. Rather, we believe that God
freely and graciously responds to the request of the community made
through the priests' prayers and gestures by the action of the Holy Spirit.

Second, he might explore how the members of the liturgical assembly
are made "members" of the Mystical Body of Christ through baptism
and sustained in their membership by Holy Communion. As members
of his Body, moreover, we are given the task of "showing forth" the
paschal sacrifice of Christ, i.e., to be engaged into his redemptive work
of the transformation of the world.

The Institution Narrative and Consecration

In a very dense paragraph, GIRM 79d limns a central element of the
eucharistic prayer, when, among all the great deeds of God that we re-
count, we especially hallow the actions of Christ at his Last Supper:

> The institution narrative and Consecration, by which, by means of
> the words and actions of Christ, that Sacrifice is effected which Christ
> himself instituted during the Last Supper, when he offered his Body
> and Blood under the species of bread and wine, gave them to the
> Apostles to eat and drink, and leaving with the latter the command
> to perpetuate this same.

The actual text of the institution narrative corresponds very closely to
the description given in the GIRM:

> On the day he was to suffer, on the night of the Last Supper, he took
> bread and said the blessing, broke the bread and gave it to his dis-

ciples, saying: "Take this, all of you, and eat of it, for this is my Body which will be given up for you."

In a similar way, when supper was ended, he took the chalice, gave you thanks, and gave the chalice to his disciples, saying: "Take this, all of you, and drink from it, for this is the chalice of my blood, the blood of the new and eternal covenant, which will be poured out for you and for many, for the forgiveness of sins. Do this in memory of me."

What catechetical and mystagogical insights might a preacher share by preaching from this text? If he wished to further the grand theme of Gregory Dix's *The Shape of the Liturgy*,[5] he could show how the shape of our present eucharistic worship relates to the biblical accounts of Jesus' Last Supper. Notice that the institution narrative doesn't reproduce any of the biblical accounts *tout court*; rather it highlights the following structure. Before the meal, Jesus did four actions with bread: taking it, blessing it, breaking it, and giving it to those at table for consumption. After the meal, Jesus did three actions with wine: he took up a cup, said a thanksgiving, and gave the cup of wine to be shared by those at table.

Dix's theory holds that these seven actions before and after Jesus' last meal became ritually commemorated quite early in Christian practice as four actions without a meal: the taking of bread and wine (corresponding to the offertory or presentation and preparation of gifts), the blessings of bread and wine (corresponding to the eucharistic prayer), the breaking of bread [and pouring out of the cup?] (corresponding to the Fraction Rite), and the giving of consecrated bread and wine for consumption (corresponding to Communion).

The Anamnesis

Anamnesis is the technical term used by liturgists to refer to liturgical memorial. Unlike most acts of memory, which simply call to mind the mental residue of a past event or at most its effects, liturgical anamnesis makes a worshiper present to the event and its power. GIRM 79e describes the liturgical anamnesis proper to the Eucharist:

The anamnesis, by which the Church, fulfilling the command that she received from Christ the Lord through the Apostles, celebrates the memorial of Christ, recalling especially his blessed Passion, glorious Resurrection, and Ascension into heaven.

In this text from the Eucharistic Prayer for Masses for Various Needs and Occasions, the formal liturgical anamnesis of the paschal mystery is placed in the context of the assembly's recalling of the many *mirabilia Dei*:

> Therefore, holy Father, as we celebrate the memorial of Christ your Son, our Savior, whom you led through his Passion and Death on the cross to the glory of the Resurrection and whom you have seated at your right hand, we proclaim the work of your love. . . .

To highlight the catechetical and mystagogical riches of this text, the preacher would have to make sure that the congregation understood what liturgical anamnesis is, and that is not easy in our culture with its "thin" understanding of memorial. The preacher might want to make it clear that, when we celebrate the liturgy, we are not "historical enactors" like those who dress up in Civil War costumes to refight the Battle of Gettysburg. Instead, we are actually encountering the living risen Lord Jesus, who is the only Jesus actually available to us. We don't pretend that he is dead on Good Friday, entombed on Holy Saturday, and "re-risen" (whatever that might mean) on Easter Sunday. Rather, Jesus' resurrection is best understood as a disclosure of Jesus' ultimate future, permanently victorious over death in the reign of God, a future that has been retrojected into our history and that we thus experience as past and present.

Liturgical anamnesis is quite literally "remembering the future," becoming present to the saving events disclosed in Jesus' life, death, deeds, and destiny. Thus (as Thomas Aquinas taught) the Eucharist is a memorial of past events, a present celebration of the ultimate significance and reality of those events, and a foretaste of the fulfillment of those events all at once.

The Oblation

GIRM 79f highlights the intimate connection between liturgical anamnesis and sacrificial offering:

> f) The oblation, by which, in this very memorial, the Church, in particular that gathered here and now, offers the unblemished sacrificial Victim in the Holy Spirit to the Father. The Church's intention, indeed, is that the faithful not only offer this unblemished sacrificial

Victim but also learn to offer their very selves, and so day by day to be brought, through the mediation of Christ, into unity with God and with each other, so that God may at last be all in all.

It is a bit surprising to discover that the rich liturgical spirituality found in this article of the GIRM finds such curt expression in this eucharistic prayer:

and we offer you the Bread of life and the Chalice of blessing.

Clearly the preacher needs to unpack the catechetical and mystagogical richness of what offering "the Bread of life and the Chalice of blessing" means for the assembly. One technique might be to trace the processes by which grain becomes bread (the interaction of "natural" processes in soil, seed, and sky with "cultural" processes of human ingenuity and decision-making) and then becomes nourishment (with "natural" processes of eating and digestion interacting with "cultural" processes of dining as markers of group identity, kinship, etc.).

A similar reflection could consider how grapes become wine become nourishment. Perhaps by making reference to the *berakah* prayers said aloud over the bread and wine when there is no chant sung during the presentation and preparation of the gifts, the preacher can highlight the divine-human partnership in offering, not nature "raw" as grain and grapes but nature "transformed" by human thought and will as bread and wine. To give it to be further transformed as Christ's Body and Blood so that we who consume it might become more deeply incorporated as Christ's Body and Blood is to pledge ourselves in symbol to be willing to be sacrificed as was Christ to nourish a needy world.

The Intercessions

The anamnesis-offering leads the assembly to exercise its baptismal priesthood (much as it has in the universal prayer, but now at the very heart of the Eucharist) in prayer for various needs for the church itself and for the wider world. GIRM 79g teaches the following concerning this element of the eucharistic prayer:

The intercessions, by which expression is given to the fact that the Eucharist is celebrated in communion with the whole Church, of both heaven and of earth, and that the oblation is made for her and

for all her members, living and dead, who are called to participate
in the redemption and salvation purchased by the Body and Blood
of Christ.

In the Eucharistic Prayer for Masses for Various Needs and Occasions
there are five topics for intercessory prayer. The preacher could easily
fashion a homily about "what do we get out of Mass" by exploring the
intercessions. Here I will reproduce the text of each topic and then suggest a catechetical and mystagogical insight for preaching.

1) *Bring your Church, Lord, to perfect faith and charity, together with N., our
   Pope, and N., our Bishop, with all Bishops, Priests, and Deacons, and the
   entire people you have made your own.*

The unity that the church seeks is not so much that of a primary sociological community as it is a global unity of faith and love. We should not
be surprised, then, when people of differing political opinions, economic
ranks, ethnic heritages, and cultural formations comprise our assemblies.
The unity of the church can serve as a sacramental sign to the wider
world that it is possible to live in mutual respect and encouragement
beyond the divisions this world holds so important.

2) *Open our eyes to the needs of our brothers and sisters; inspire in us words
   and actions to comfort those who labor and are burdened. Make us serve them
   truly after the example of Christ and at his command.*

Direct service of others (charity) is not an "optional extra" in the Christian life but a constituent part of life as a baptized human being. The
preacher might help to "open the eyes" of his assembly by naming some
of the concrete areas in which charitable activity needs to take place.

3) *And may your Church stand as a living witness to truth and freedom, to
   peace and justice, that all people may be raised up to a new hope.*

Interestingly, Christians are called not only to charitable activities but to
offer witness on social issues, i.e., to act to create a more equitable and
humane world. As in the first of the intercessions, the church is seen as
offering the world an effective sign of hope for the transformation of
those structures that undercut human dignity. Very importantly, intercessions two and three teach that the church cannot opt for either charitable
activity or work for justice, although individuals may be drawn more to
one than the other.

4) *Remember our brothers and sisters, [N. and N.,] who have fallen asleep in the peace of your Christ, and all the dead, whose faith you alone have known. Admit them to rejoice in the light of your face, and in the resurrection give them the fullness of life.*

After a set of intercessions whose focus is the transformation of this world under grace, the assembly's prayer now turns to the world beyond this one. One of the truly great advances in contemporary Roman Rite euchology is the formula of prayer for the dead. Where the traditional Roman Canon really only prayed for those who were members of the church, the newer eucharistic prayer also prays for "all the dead" whose faith only God can know. At every Mass we commend not only our coreligionists but all the dead to God's mercy and abundance of life in the world to come.

5) *Grant also to us, when our earthly pilgrimage is done, that we may come to an eternal dwelling place and live with you forever; there, in communion with the Blessed Virgin Mary, Mother of God, with the Apostles and Martyrs, [with Saint N.] and with all the Saints, we shall praise and exalt you through Jesus Christ your Son.*

Finally, with great realism, we recognize that we, too, will pass from this world to the next and pray that the Holy Communion we have come to know with the Lord and each other in a partial yet real way sacramentally here on earth may be fully realized in heaven. The preacher might want to explore how communion sanctorum means both "communion of the holy things" (i.e., Eucharist) and "communion of saints," with both being ordered to each other.

The Concluding Doxology

The last element of the eucharistic prayer to be considered for a homily might also be the hardest for a preacher, but it is absolutely vital that congregations have a lively understanding and experience of doxology. GIRM 79h highlights how doxology concludes the progress of thought in the eucharistic prayer:

> The concluding doxology, by which the glorification of God is expressed and which is affirmed and concluded by the people's acclamation Amen.

The invariable text of the eucharistic prayer's doxology makes it easily held in people's memory:

> Through him, and with him, and in him, O God, almighty Father, in the unity of the Holy Spirit, all glory and honor is yours, for ever and ever. Amen.

A preacher might want to note that the eucharistic prayer begins with giving God "thanks and praise" because it is "right and just" and ends by giving each of the Divine Persons "all glory and honor." In effect the prayer ends where it began, in rapturous praise of God. Since doxology is formed from two Greek words—*doxa* (clarity [of light, of thought]) + *logos* (order, structure, discourse, word)—it might be helpful to explore with the congregation biblical understandings of God's glory, whether as "weightiness" (*kabod* in Hebrew), thus as significance, or "radiance" (*doxa* in Greek), thus as guiding light.

Preaching Inspired by the Preface of the Eucharistic Prayer

Although technically part of the eucharistic prayer, the preface because of its variability is usually treated as a separate category of major presidential euchology. GIRM 79a gives a clear description of the content and function of the preface in today's Roman Rite Eucharist:

> a) The thanksgiving (expressed especially in the Preface), in which the Priest, in the name of the whole of the holy people, glorifies God the Father and gives thanks to him for the whole work of salvation or for some particular aspect of it, according to the varying day, festivity, or time of year.

It's helpful to note that, in addition to the six-part dialogue that introduces it and the preface acclamation that concludes it, the preface itself is structured in three parts: (1) the protocol (a stereotypical opening making a transition from the conclusion of the dialogue to the central concerns of the preface); (2) the body (a more or less lengthy recounting of what prompts the community's praise of and thanksgiving to God at the particular liturgy); and (3) the *eschatocol* (a stereotypical conclusion aligning the praise of the worshiping assembly with that of the heavenly liturgy in a transition to the preface acclamation). Thus, to uncover the central insights of the preface for a homily, the preacher turns to the body of the preface rather than the protocol or the eschatocol.

The following is a slavishly literal translation of the text of the preface for the Solemnity of the Nativity of John the Baptist,[6] not intended for liturgical use. I have chosen to number sections of the body of the text to make discussion easier:

Vere dignum et iustum est, æquum et salutáre,
Truly it is right and just, proper and life-giving,
nos tibi semper et ubíque grátias ágere:
for us always and everywhere to give thanks to you:
Dómine, sancte Pater, omnípotens ætérne Deus:
Lord, holy Father, almighty eternal God:
per Christum Dóminum nostrum.
Through Christ our Lord.
In cuius Præcursóre beáto Ioánne tuam magnificéntiam collaudámus,
In whose Forerunner, the blessed John, we together praise your
    magnificence,
quem inter natos mulíerum honóre præcípuo consecrásti.
[John] whom you have consecrated with extraordinary honor among
    those born of women.
Qui cum nascéndo multa gáudia præstitísset,
Who, [1] while by his being conceived had brought many joys,
et nondum éditus exsultásset ad humánæ salútis advéntum,
and [2] while not yet exited [from the womb] he had exulted/leapt at
    the coming of human salvation,
ipse solus ómnium prophetárum Agnum redemptiónis osténdit.
[3] he himself, alone of all the prophets, revealed the Lamb of redemption.
Sed et sanctificándis étiam aquæ fluéntis ipsum baptísmatis lavit auctórem,
Yet also [4] he even bathed the author of baptism himself by means of the
    water which was to make the stream holy,
et méruit fuso sánguine suprémum illi testimónium exhibére.
And [5] he [John] merited to manifest the supreme testimony to him
    [Jesus] by his blood outpoured.
Et ídeo, cum cælórum Virtútibus,
And therefore, with the Virtues of the heavens,
in terris te iúgiter prædicámus,
on earth we proclaim you constantly,
maiestáti tuæ sine fine clamántes:
crying out to Your Majesty without end:

This preface revels in multiple scriptural allusions as it lifts up the particular reasons why the Christian community makes liturgical anamnesis of the Birth of John the Baptist. Notice first of all how the text blends Eastern ("Forerunner"), Western ("Blessed," i.e., "saint"), and biblical ("greatest of those born of women") in the titles it assigns to John. A preacher could then point out how important John is, not only to Christians, but to Jews (he is mentioned in Josephus' *Jewish Antiquities*) and Muslims (with mosques dedicated to him). Like Abraham, John is a figure shared by the three monotheistic religions. The preface then extracts from the Scriptures five reasons for rejoicing at the birth of John:

1. his parents' delight in conceiving in their old age manifests a God who will do surprising acts of generosity to those who believe in him;

2. John's leaping in Elizabeth's womb indicates that, even prior to physical birth, he was responsive to the promptings of the Spirit (a fact that the preacher may want to raise in terms of respect for the unborn);

3. moving beyond John's birth to his ministry, the preface recounts John's pointing out Jesus to his own disciples under the mysterious title of "Lamb of God," prophesying his role in redemption;

4. the preface also recalls John's great act of baptizing Jesus, highlighting the Eastern tradition in which the waters of the Jordan (and by extension all the waters of the earth, which in the Hebrew mind were associated with the *tohu-wa-bohu*, the primordial chaos of Genesis 1) are made holy by contact with Jesus' body;

5. John's testimony about the scandal of Herod Antipas' marriage to his brother's wife Herodias that earned him beheading. The preacher might follow the preface's lead in developing the idea that anyone of conscience witnessing with their lives to the truth is implicitly witnessing to the Truth Personified in Jesus the Christ.

Preaching Inspired by Minor Presidential Euchology

Minor presidential euchology consists of the shorter and less ritually important prayers recited or chanted by the officiating minister. Traditionally in Roman Rite Eucharist they include:

- Opening Prayer (*Collecta/Oratio*)

- Prayer over the Offerings (*Super oblate/Secreta*)

- Prayer after Communion (*Post communionem/Ad complendum*)

The structure of these Roman Rite orations can be conveniently recalled by an English-language mnemonic: "you/who/do/through":

- You = direct address, usually to the Father (although sometimes to Christ) as "God" with one or two modifying adjectives (typically "*Deus omnipotens et sempiterne*," "Almighty and eternal God")

- Who = appositive phrase(s) or a relative clause, articulating some divine attribute or recounting a divine action

- Do = request that God would act in a way related to the appositive phrase(s) or relative clause

- Through = stereotyped Trinitarian ending

Here is the text of the collect for the Solemnity of the Nativity of John the Baptist. I have added numbering to make the progress of thought clearer.

> *Deus,*
> God,
> *qui beátum Ioánnem Baptístam suscitásti,*
> Who [1] have raised up blessed John the Baptist
> *ut perféctam plebem Christo Dómino preæparáret,*
> so that [2] he might prepare a perfect/complete people for Christ the Lord,
> *da pópulis tuis spiritálium grátiam gaudiórum,*
> [3] give to your peoples the grace of spiritual joys,
> *et ómnium fidélium mentes dírige in viam salútis et pacis.*
> and [4] direct the minds of all the faithful into the way of salvation and peace.
> *Per Dóminum nostrum Iesum Christum, Fílium tuum,*
> Through our Lord Jesus Christ, your Son,
> *qui tecum vivit et regnat in unitáte Spíritus Sancti,*
> who lives and reigns with you in the unity of the Holy Spirit,
> *Deus, per ómnia saécula sæculórum.*
> God, through all the ages of ages.

Since the prayer is simply addressed to "God," its address could be to the Triune God or any of the three Divine Persons, but the concluding "*Per Dominum*" makes it clear that here "God" is "God the Father." The relative clause directly credits God the Father with commissioning John the Baptist to prepare a people for Christ; the preacher might suggest that, in the light of the New Evangelization, such a task still calls out for generous folk who would emulate the Baptist in bringing people to Christ. The request of the collect might seem generic until we remember the joys of the Baptist's parents at his conception (joys that might be paralleled by those serving to bring faith to birth in others) and the canticle of Zechariah (Luke 1:68-79) in which the Baptist's father not only declares that his son will prepare the way of the Lord by giving his people "knowledge of salvation" but that the "dawn from on high" would guide our feet into the "way of peace." The ending sentence is the usual stereotyped trinitarian conclusion, but could serve the preacher as a way to talk about the typical stance in liturgical prayer: directed to the Father, through the Son, in the Holy Spirit.

Preaching Inspired by Liturgical Chants

In addition to the presidential texts, preaching might be inspired by liturgical chants. In traditional Roman Rite practice, these chants are divided into two categories: the Ordinary (nearly invariant chants sung at most Masses, such as the *"Kyrie eleison," "Gloria in excelsis," "Credo in unum Deum," "Sanctus-Benedictus,"* and *"Agnus Dei"*) and the Proper (variable chants sung at particular Masses, such as the *"Antiphona ad Introitum," "Graduale,"* "Tract," "Alleluia," "Sequence," *"Antiphona ad Offertorium," "Antiphona ad Communionem"*).

Here I would like to consider the proper liturgical chants appointed for the Solemnity of the Nativity of John the Baptist as a source for liturgical preaching. There is no Tract, Sequence, or Offertory[7] appointed for this celebration, and the Gradual/Responsorial Psalm is really to be considered one of the biblical proclamations of the Liturgy of the Word rather than a liturgical text, so we will consider only the verse before the gospel and two processional antiphons.

Preaching from the Proper Chants

Gospel Alleluia and Verse

Alleluia. Alleluia.
You, child, will be called prophet of the Most High,
for you will go before the Lord to prepare his way. (Luke 1:76)
Alleluia. Alleluia.

Entrance Antiphon

>A man was sent from God, whose name was John.
>He came to testify to the light,
>to prepare a people fit for the Lord. (John 1:6-7; cf. Luke 1:75)

Communion Antiphon

>Through the tender mercy of our God,
>the Dawn from on high will visit us. (cf. Luke 1:78)

These texts might encourage the preacher to explore both the synoptic and the Johannine traditions about John the Baptist in preaching about his significance for contemporary worshipers. If the three texts were taken in order, the preacher could construct a homily on John as prophet (clarifying the biblical role of the prophet and presenting John as last of the Jewish and first of the Christian prophets), as witness (with an exploration of the Johannine theme of testimony with John testifying to Jesus, Jesus testifying to his Abba, and the believers' call to testify to both), and as herald of the dawn (perhaps connecting with the Old Testament image of the city watchman).

The Hymn of the Day as a Form of Liturgical Preaching

The Hymn of the Day (HOD) is a congregational hymn centered on the Lectionary readings appointed for a particular liturgy. Originally generated in the Lutheran tradition as a congregational reclaiming of the choral Gradual sung after the epistle, the HOD appears today as part of the Liturgy of the Word in some Lutheran, Episcopalian/Anglican, Methodist, Presbyterian, and Congregationalist traditions, employed before or after the sermon, sometimes in relation to the recitation of a creed. Placing the HOD after the proclamation of all the Scripture readings and the sermon allows the congregation to internalize and claim the read and preached word of God in a full, conscious, and active fashion.

There is no provision in the present Roman Rite Order of Mass for the HOD as part of the Liturgy of the Word, but since according to the *General Instruction of the Roman Missal*, one of the functions of the opening liturgical song is to lead the thoughts of the faithful to the feast or season being celebrated, an HOD might appropriately be sung as part of the Introductory Rites. Another (better) possibility would be for the preacher to incorporate an HOD as the conclusion of the preaching. The HOD might also possibly appear as the congregational hymn after the Communion processional, especially since many of the Communion antiphons hearken back to the gospel proclaimed.

Here is an example of an HOD appropriate for the Solemnity of the Nativity of John the Baptist. Written by Thomas Troeger, it is yoked with the hymn tune TERRA BEATA, but could be sung to any SMD ("Short Meter Doubled") hymn tune (i.e., 66.8.66.86):

> The moon with borrowed light
> Gives witness to the sun,
> Discreetly fading with the night
> When morning has begun.
> John's borrowed light was drawn
> From heaven's vibrant rays,
> His life a witness to the dawn
> Of Christ's approaching blaze.
>
> When temple Levites asked
> What title did John claim;
> He said he had a single task,
> A simple goal and aim:
> To redirect their sight
> Beyond what he had done
> To Christ the pure and primal light
> That lightens everyone.
>
> The clouds of sin yet mask
> Earth's tangled, stubbly ground,
> And O how many hearts still ask
> Where God's clear path is found.
> For borrowed light we pray
> So we may be a sign
> That point to Christ, the truth, the way,
> The life, the light divine.[8]

Preaching Inspired by Liturgical Gestures and Objects

The final form of liturgical preaching to consider is that inspired by non-textual sources. One might preach on the organization of liturgical space and its adornment, exploring with the congregation the multiple meanings of the church building, altar, ambo/lectern, presidential chair, tabernacle, processional cross, font, stained glass, candles, etc. One might preach on the organization of liturgical time and its adornment, exploring with the congregation the multiple meanings of yearly festivals (Advent/ Christmastide, Lent/Triduum/Eastertide, commemorations), weekly (Lord's Day Eucharist, Friday observances), daily (dawn, noon, dusk, midnight in the Liturgy of the Hours).

One might preach on how the liturgy hallows life (baptism with birth, confirmation with maturity, reconciliation with excommunication and reinstatement, anointing of the sick with illness and recovery, viaticum and funeral rites with death, matrimony and holy orders as specifying one's baptismal character in service to the church and world) with special attention to the central and secondary ("explanatory") rituals that make up the rite. The preacher must always take care that such preaching never devolve into simple instruction but that it remain catechetical and mystagogic in tone, drawing believers into a deeper encounter with Christ through these signs.

To that end, I would like to offer a short mystagogical reflection on the sign of the cross. The preacher might first consider the gesture itself without any accompanying words. By means of the sign of the cross, Christian believers claim space for Christ; the vertical connects the depths of the earth (traditionally the dwelling place of the dead) with the sky above (traditionally the dwelling place of God), while the horizontal encompasses all on earth stretching from horizon to horizon. Thus all space is brought under the protection and lordship of the cross. By means of the sign of the cross, Christian believers claim time for Christ; the gesture quadrates the year with its two solstices and two equinoxes into four seasons; and it quadrates the day with four milestones: dawn, midday, dusk, and midnight. Thus all time is brought under the protection and lordship of the cross. The sign of the cross without text also expresses a theological anthropology: the vertical both places the human being on his/her own two feet on the good earth (not crawling on his/her belly like the Genesis serpent) and with his/her head under heaven (but not with his/her "tongue in heaven" so as to look down one's nose at all terrestrial realities while claiming divine status); the horizontal places one in solidarity with all other upright human beings standing side by side on the good earth beneath heaven.

When a text is added to this gesture, further meanings ensue. By touching their forehead when speaking "In the name of the Father," human beings acknowledge their relationship with the Begetting God (Father, associated with the seat of thought and will in the mind). When they trace a vertical from forehead to breast while reciting "and of the Son," they acknowledge the relationship of the Begetting God with the Begotten God (Son, associated with the descent into the enfleshment of the heart). And when they trace a horizontal from shoulder to shoulder while reciting "and of the Holy Spirit," they confess their indwelling by the Spirated God (Holy Spirit) who elevates them with holiness and equips them for mission (as symbolized by the work of their hands).

Notice then how this fundamental trinitarian, christological, and anthropological sign enriches nearly all the church's sacramental rites. Following the example of the deacon before proclaiming the gospel, we trace a sign of the cross on forehead, lips, and heart when hearing the gospel proclaimed that we might receive the word of God in heart, proclaim it with our lips, and believe and cherish it in our hearts. At the Rite of Entry into the Catechumenate, we claim inquirers for Christ with an elaborate set of signs of the cross marking their senses. At the Rite of Baptism of Infants, after learning from the parents the child's name and their intention that their child be baptized, Christ and the church claim the child through signs of the cross traced on its forehead by priest and/or deacon, parents, godparents, other family members, and friends. A sign of the cross is implicit in the laying on of hands and anointing at confirmation, in the anointing of forehead and hands of the sick, and in the anointing of hands and head in ordination. In every case it recalls and intensifies the signing begun at baptism.

I hope these few reflections encourage preachers to attempt preaching inspired by liturgical texts and ceremonies. While I believe preaching from the Scriptures should be the regular default mode for preaching, this kind of preaching may be helpful when the preacher is blocked in the attempt to preach from the biblical texts or with a seasonal or ferial focus. It can also be helpful from time to time to deepen the participants' own experience of the worship they offer with the priest through Christ in the Holy Spirit in the holy church to God the ever-living and ever-loving Father.

Endnotes

1. Jan Michael Joncas, *Preaching the Rites of Initiation*, Forum Essays #4 (Chicago, IL: Liturgy Training Publications, 1994).

2. United States Conference of Catholic Bishops, *Preaching the Mystery of Faith: The Sunday Homily* (Washington, DC: USCCB Publishing, 2012 [first printing 2013]).

3. *Preaching the Mystery of Faith,* 17.

4. I could have treated the preface acclamation below as an example of preaching from a liturgical chant, but I chose to treat it here as an invariant part of the major presidential euchology, even though the assembly recites or chants this text with the priest celebrant.

5. Gregory Dix, *The Shape of the Liturgy* (London: Dacre Press, 1945). It must be said that subsequent liturgical scholarship has shown some of Dix's understandings of liturgical history to be inaccurate. His claims regarding the offertory in his four-fold shape of the Eucharist theory have also been criticized as Pelagian, though there have been defenders as well.

6. While this article is being put into final form in February 2013 (thus allowing reference to *Preaching the Mystery of Faith*), it was originally presented at the Notre Dame preaching conference in the week after the celebration of the Solemnity of the Nativity of John the Baptist on Sunday, June 24, 2012. I deliberately chose to use the liturgical texts from that celebration for my examples, both because they would be immediately familiar to those who had gathered and to avoid any sense that I had cherry-picked liturgical texts easily adaptable to liturgical preaching.

7. Actually an *Antiphona ad Offertorium* with suggested psalm verses does appear in the *Graduale Romanum*, but no offertory antiphon appears in the Roman Missal 2011.

8. Thomas H. Troeger, "The Moon with Borrowed Light," in Thomas H. Troeger and Carol Doran, *New Hymns for the Lectionary: To Glorify the Maker's Name* (New York: Oxford University Press, 1986).

Chapter 5

Preaching and Catechesis: Mending the Rift between Scripture and Doctrine

John C. Cavadini

"At the heart of catechesis we find, in essence, a Person, the Person of Jesus of Nazareth, the only Son from the Father . . . who suffered and died for us and who now, after rising, is living with us forever" (CT 5). To catechize is "to reveal in the Person of Christ the whole of God's eternal design reaching its fulfillment in that Person. It is to seek to understand the meaning of Christ's actions and words and of the signs worked by him" (CT 5). Catechesis aims at putting "people . . . in communion . . . with Jesus Christ: only he can lead us to the love of the Father in the Spirit and make us share in the life of the Holy Trinity" (CT 5).

In catechesis, "Christ, the Incarnate Word and Son of God . . . is taught—everything else is taught with reference to him" (CT 6; cf. Jn 7:16) (CCC 426–27).

Isn't it interesting how these words, from the *Catechism of the Catholic Church*, citing John Paul II's *Catechesi Tradendae*, could just as easily be spoken of preaching? Wouldn't it be just as true to say that, "At the heart of preaching we find, in essence, a Person, the Person of Jesus of Nazareth, the only Son from the Father . . . full of grace and truth [the CCC omits that part of John 1:14], who suffered and died for us and who now, after rising, is living with us forever?" Or, preaching "aims at putting people not only in touch but in communion, in intimacy, with Jesus Christ" [to use the full sentence from CT itself]?

Here is another sentence from the same sections of CT from which the *CCC* has been quoting, only following our temporary conceit of replacing the word "catechesis" with "preaching":

> The primary and essential object of [preaching] is, to use an expression dear to Saint Paul and also to contemporary theology, "the mystery of Christ." [Preaching] is in a way to lead a person to study this Mystery in all its dimensions: *To make all people see what is the plan of the mystery . . . comprehend with all the saints what is the breadth and length and height and depth . . . know the love of Christ which surpasses knowledge . . . [and be filled] with all the fullness of God* (Eph 3:9, 18-19). (CT 5)

I am not claiming, of course, that preaching and catechesis are identically the same enterprise, but I am sure you would agree that the preacher could do worse than to have the aim of helping anyone listening to "comprehend with all the saints what is the breadth and length and height and depth . . . the love of Christ which surpasses all knowledge." Not a bad objective for starters, anyway. But if that is so, it seems that there could not possibly be a conflict between preaching and catechesis. It would seem that catechesis would be one of the intrinsic aims of preaching, if it is what John Paul II describes here in *Catechesi Tradendae.*

Further, just like the catechist, shouldn't the preacher, again in the words of *Catechesi Tradendae,* be able to apply to himself the mysterious words of Jesus, "My teaching is not mine, but his who sent me" (John 7:16 NRSV; CT 6)? And wouldn't it be equally true for the preacher that, again in the words of *Catechesi Tradendae,* "This teaching is not a body of abstract truths. It is the communication of the living mystery of God" (CT 7)? How then could there possibly be any conflict perceived between preaching and catechesis, such that to preach with a catechetical intent would be contrary to the essential intention and motivation behind preaching? It seems as though the preacher would have to work hard to *avoid* being catechetical if the aim of catechesis is to teach "Christ, the Incarnate Word and Son of God," and "everything else . . . with reference to him."

I wonder if the perceived conflict between liturgical preaching and catechesis may come from a misunderstanding of what catechesis actually is. Perhaps, though, one may object at this point, that preaching is essentially exposition of Scripture, and it accomplishes the aims it admittedly has in common with catechesis by breaking open the scriptural word. But even here, I think, we have to look closer. We can read in *Catechesis Tradendae* that "catechesis must be impregnated and penetrated by the thought, the spirit and the outlook of the Bible and the Gospels through assiduous contact with the texts themselves." Catechesis is meant to be a thoroughly scriptural enterprise from start to finish, and yet John Paul II reminds us that "catechesis will be all the richer and more effective for reading the [scriptural] texts with the intelligence and the heart of the Church and for drawing inspiration from the two thousand years of the Church's reflection and life" (CT 27). John Paul II reminds us here that catechesis is not a matter of choosing to be scriptural or to teach according to tradition, but that these, properly understood, are one and the same activity because Scripture and tradition are intrinsically related to each other, as *Dei Verbum* states it and John Paul quotes, "Sacred Tradition and Sacred Scripture make up a single sacred deposit of the word of God, which is entrusted to the Church" (DV 10, CT 27, also cited by the CCC 84, cf. 80, which quotes DV 9). The source of catechesis is thus "the living word of God transmitted in Tradition and Scripture," and it is this "living word" that is presumably the "source" for all of the ministries of the Word in the church. To catechize in an authentically scriptural way will inevitably be to catechize in an authentically traditional way, and the same is true for preaching because the two are not accidentally but intrinsically related. The opposite is true, too, I think: to catechize, and to preach, in an authentically traditional way must also be to have one's catechesis or preaching "impregnated and penetrated by the thought, the spirit and the outlook of the Bible and the Gospels through assiduous contact with the texts themselves."

The intrinsic connection between Scripture and tradition, reflected in the intrinsic connection between preaching and catechesis, is made more explicit in *Catechesi Tradendae* in the section on homiletics itself:

> The homily takes up again the journey of faith put forward by catechesis, and brings it to its natural fulfillment. At the same time it encourages the Lord's disciples to begin anew each day their spiritual journey in truth, adoration and thanksgiving. Accordingly, one can say that catechetical teaching too finds its source and its fulfillment in the Eucharist, within the whole circle of the liturgical year. Preaching, centered upon the Bible texts, must then in its own way make it possible to familiarize the faithful with the whole of the mysteries of the faith and with the norms of Christian living. (CT 48)

This passage, cited in full, three years later, in Note 10 of *Fulfilled in Your Hearing*, preserves the special purpose of the liturgical homily, which is in part to prepare people for the celebration of the Eucharist by helping them to see the work of God in their lives. Preaching, then, and here specifically liturgical preaching, is once again seen to be intrinsically, and not accidentally, catechetical. Such preaching will be "centered upon the Bible texts," and as such "*must* . . . make it possible to familiarize the faithful with the whole of the mysteries of the faith and with the norms of Christian living" (emphasis added), because otherwise it is impossible to know fully what God *has* done for us in Christ, and to be invited to see how *that* work, and not something imagined as God's work, can be found in the lives of the faithful. If we are to encounter "Christ, the Incarnate Word, and Son of God," and everything else "in reference to Him," then neither the catechist nor the preacher is fulfilling the job description if there is never any clarification about what is meant by the phrase "Incarnate Word," and the phrase "Son of God." Again from *Catechesi Tradendae*,

> What kind of catechesis would it be that failed to give their full place to the creation of human beings and to sin, to God's plan of redemption and its long, loving preparation and realization, to the Incarnation of the Son of God, to Mary . . . the Mother of God . . . and to her role in the mystery of salvation, to the mystery of lawlessness at work in our lives and the power of God freeing us from it, to the need for penance and asceticism, to the sacramental and liturgical actions, to the reality of the Eucharistic presence, to participation in divine life here and hereafter, and so on. (CT 30)

It is worth noting that *Fulfilled in Your Hearing*, published three years after *Catechesi Tradendae*, itself is in substantial agreement, when, albeit in somewhat more general terms, it notes:

> It is the faith of the church that the preacher must proclaim, not merely his own. Consequently, the more familiar the preacher is with the history of scriptural interpretation and the development of the church's doctrine, the more capable he is of bringing that word into dialogue with the contemporary situation. Church doctrine is nourished by profound meditation upon the inspired Word, the exegesis of the fathers, conciliar documents and the teaching of the Magisterium. Therefore, the qualified preacher will lead his people to ever greater unity of faith among themselves as with prior generations of believers. (p. 13; cf. p. 26, first full paragraph)

Finally, to bring it down to our own time, Benedict XVI, in the apostolic exhortation *Sacramentum Caritatis*, notes that, "Given the importance of the word of God, the quality of homilies needs to be improved" (46). Noting that the homily is "meant to foster a deeper understanding of the word of God, so that it can bear fruit in the lives of the faithful," he reminds us that "the catechetical and paraenetic aim of the homily should not be forgotten." He goes on to say that "during the course of the liturgical year it is appropriate to offer the faithful, prudently and on the basis of the three-year lectionary, 'thematic' homilies treating the great themes of the Christian faith," that is, I imagine, such themes as John Paul II listed in the passage from *Catechesi Tradendae* 30 cited earlier.

It should be clear by now, then, that there is no conflict between liturgical preaching and catechesis, and that, in fact, the two activities, though certainly not coincident with each other, are intrinsically related. In fact, a homiletic practice that failed to be catechetical, that is, that failed at "putting people not only in touch but in communion, in intimacy, with Jesus Christ," and that failed "to make all people see what is the plan of the mystery . . . comprehend with all the saints what is the breadth and length and height and depth . . . know the love of Christ which surpasses knowledge . . . (and be filled) with all the fullness of God" (CT 5), would be a failed homiletics. So, the failure to see that there is not only no conflict between catechesis and liturgical homiletics, such that the latter should be catechetical by its very nature, is a failure either in the understanding of catechesis or in the understanding of liturgical homiletics, or both. For example, if one preaches catechetically without regard for the readings from the Lectionary, one has not really grasped the essence of liturgical homiletics.

One suspects, however, that the issue may be more basic, namely, that one imagines that to preach scripturally means avoiding Christian doctrine, or to preach doctrinally means avoiding the exposition of Scripture, as though these two activities were essentially different activities, the one "catechetical" and the other "scriptural." In turn, this arises from a misconception about Christian doctrine, namely, that it is a self-enclosed system of teaching that has abstracted the essence of Scripture, with some additions from tradition, and that it can be propagated and mastered independently, apart from Scripture or the various elements of tradition that it incorporates.

In other words, it is to treat Christian doctrine as though it were merely "information" and the mastery of this "information" an end in itself.

But, as the *Catechism* states, "We do not believe in formulas, but in those realities they express, which faith allows us to touch," and then, citing Thomas Aquinas, " 'The believer's act [of faith] does not terminate in the propositions, but in the realities [which they express]' " (St. Thomas Aquinas, *STh* II-II, 1, 2, *ad* 2) (CCC 170). That means that Christian doctrine, while propositional and formulaic, and necessarily so, is not simply a body of propositions and formulae that exist for their own sake. They exist because mystery cannot be handed on without a reliable and precise way of speaking that ensures we are handing on the mystery in question and not a reasonable or unreasonable facsimile thereof. As the *Catechism* puts it, "All the same, we do approach these realities with the help of formulations of the faith which permit us to express the faith and to hand it on, to celebrate it in community, to assimilate and live on it more and more" (ibid.).

The formulae and propositions are like little valises or briefcases or suitcases for carrying mystery. You need something to help you "grasp" a mystery, itself ungraspable, in order to hand it on—the essence of "tradition" is the "handing on"—so this is a necessary part of catechesis, nowadays sometimes overlooked, that is, the mastery of the propositions and formulae. Yet the heart of catechesis is to *use* the propositions and formulae in order to nurture an encounter with the Person who is at the "heart of catechesis" and of preaching, too, the one Person of Christ, that Person that *is* the mystery hidden from all ages in God and now revealed in its length, depth, height, and breadth. The catechist's job is to open up the carrying cases, as it were, so that people can "assimilate" the faith expressed and to "live on" its mystery "more and more."

But this "opening up" of the carrying cases, if I can continue this somewhat crude analogy, is impossible without the use of Scripture. Scripture is filled with the life of the Holy Spirit who inspired it. It is filled with vivid images that are part of revelation just as much as the more discursive statements. A good example of this is the image from John 19 of Jesus hanging dead on the cross, his side pierced with a lance and blood and water flowing out. This is the image used as the basis for Benedict's first encyclical, *God is Love* (2005). The image appeals, and is meant to appeal, to the imagination, and we can think of so many more whose beauty and nobility are unsurpassable: the image of the Suffering Servant in the four Servant Songs in Isaiah, especially the fourth; the image of the throne chariot in the opening chapters of Ezekiel, and of the Temple flowing with the waters of the Holy Spirit at the end of the that book. Scripture is full of stories, of powerful exhortations, and even of propositions, such as, for example, "God is Love," which cannot be confined to the limits of a doctrinal system, and overflow its banks, helping the catechist or the homilist allow the faith of the hearer to touch, however tentatively, the reality expressed in the formulas. A system of doctrine left on its own tends to close in on itself and to present the temptation to equate "understanding" with mastery of the system, instead of with encounter with the Mystery the system is meant to render communicable.

So, doctrinal instruction, if it is to be true to the intention of Christian doctrine itself, cannot over the long term be accomplished apart from recourse to the text of Scripture. At the same time, the exposition of Scripture *as Scripture*, that is, as the word of God, cannot be accomplished over the long term apart from recourse to the formulae and propositions of Christian doctrine that have been developed to clarify and safeguard scriptural teaching. The "rule of faith" evolved in part as a way of summarizing the essentials of scriptural teaching so that someone about to be baptized could be questioned in a meaningful way. Scripture on its own is a kind of flood of images and stories and teachings, and the rule of faith, progressively honed in precision as questions came up, is a way of bringing out the intrinsic teaching of Scripture itself. It is a way of giving form to scriptural teaching. This is an important point to grasp, namely, that the rule of faith, and subsequent doctrinal clarifications, are not overlays on top of Scripture, obscuring its teaching, but attempts to articulate and defend what is revealed in Scripture. Therefore, understanding Scripture and understanding Christian doctrine are intrinsically related enterprises.

If this were not true, *Dei Verbum* could not have said that "Sacred Tradition and Sacred Scripture are bound closely together and communicate one with the other," and that "both of them, flowing out from the same divine well-spring, come together in some fashion to form one thing and move towards the same goal" (DV 9, cited at CCC 80). Scripture itself, as canonized Scripture, bears the imprint of the church's discernment. Practices of public, liturgical reading of Christian texts, such as the letters of Paul, were made in part because the documents were seen to be compatible with the "rule of faith." Decisions about what documents were canonical were made not simply on the basis of the claim that an apostle wrote them, but that they conformed to apostolic teaching. In fact, that was one way to verify that an apostle, or someone in the school of an apostle, wrote them.[1] Scripture was only preserved because it was judged to be in conformity with the apostolic preaching, and documents purporting to be written by apostles, such as the Gospel of Peter, were rejected on the grounds of their content. This means that in interpreting Scripture, if we mean interpreting it *as Scripture* and not simply as an artifact of antiquity, we are at the same time deepening our encounter with the mind of the church. We are coming to discern ever more clearly the tradition by which the church intuited and judged that particular literary compositions merited canonization. The interpretation of Scripture *as Scripture* is thus inseparable from the explication of the traditional teaching, the rule of faith, by which Scripture was accepted as Scripture, just as, on the other hand, the specific formulations of doctrine that attempt to capture the essence of this traditional teaching cannot be understood properly divorced from scriptural exposition.

For example, Gregory of Nazianzus, in his fifth theological oration, takes up the question of the divinity of the Holy Spirit. "Time and time again," he tells his opponents, "you repeat the argument about *not being in the Bible*." Of course, Gregory must admit that it does not anywhere say in Scripture that the Holy Spirit is God.

> Yet we are dealing here not with a smuggled-in alien, but with something disclosed to the consciousness of people past and present. The fact stands already proved by a host of people who have discussed the subject, all people who read the Holy Scriptures not in a frivolous, cursory way, but with penetration so that they saw inside the written text to its inner meaning. They were found fit to perceive the hidden loveliness; they were illuminated by the light of knowledge. (21)

Gregory is not saying that the divinity of the Holy Spirit is based on an allegorical or spiritual, as opposed to literal, understanding of the text. He is saying that careful attention to the literal sense of Scripture discloses the doctrine of the divinity of the Holy Spirit as something essentially biblical and that to deny it would be a rejection of scriptural faith.

Of course, he has to show what he means. He shows that the Holy Spirit is always part of the triad, Father, Son, and Holy Spirit, and there are never any other names used for members of this triad, while biblical usage does not assign the Holy Spirit membership in any other grouping. The Bible also mentions true worship and true prayer as the work of the Spirit. Would we worship God in any Spirit that was not God? The Holy

Spirit, though, dwells in us and teaches us all things (27), but no one but God can reveal the things of God. There follows a remarkable passage, which can be cited here only partially:

> I shudder to think of the wealth of titles, the mass of names, outraged by resistance to the Spirit. He is called "Spirit of God," "Spirit of Christ," "Mind of Christ," "Spirit of the Lord" and "Lord" absolutely; "Spirit of Adoption," "of Truth," "of Freedom"; "Spirit of Wisdom," "Understanding," "Counsel," "Might," "Knowledge," "True Religion" and of "The Fear of God." The Spirit indeed effects all these things, filling the universe with his being, sustaining the universe. His being "fills the world," his power is beyond the world's capacity to contain it. It is his nature, not his given function, to be good, to be righteous and to be in command. He is the subject, not the object, of hallowing, apportioning, participating, filling, sustaining; we share in him and he shares in nothing. He is our inheritance, he is glorified, counted together with Father and Son; he is a dire warning to us. The "finger of God," he is, like God a "fire," which proves, I think, that he is consubstantial. The Spirit it is who created and creates anew through baptism and resurrection. The Spirit it is who knows all things, who teaches all things, who blows where, and as strongly as, he wills, who leads, speaks, sends out, separates, who is vexed and tempted. He reveals, illumines, gives life—or rather, is absolutely Light and Life. He makes us his temple, he deifies. . . . All that God actively performs, he performs. (29)

I cited this passage at length because it comes from a sermon. Is it doctrinal? Certainly it is doctrinal because Gregory is arguing that it is appropriate to call the Spirit "God" in a way that is proper, such that the Spirit is "consubstantial" with Father and Son. Is the sermon scriptural? Speaking for myself, I feel moved at the depth of the scriptural teaching contained in this passage. I feel as though I love the Scriptures more and want to read them more. This is the seamless conjoining of doctrinal catechesis and scriptural exegesis, or scriptural catechesis and doctrinal exposition. The doctrine of the divinity of the Holy Spirit is demonstrated as something that makes Scripture speak more as itself, as Scripture, and the scriptural exegesis makes it so that we understand the meaning of the term *consubstantial*, we do not stop at the formula, but we penetrate to the reality of faith it contains. We see the word *consubstantial* as a word that lets Scripture *be* Scripture and calls attention to itself only as such.

Finally, since this is an excerpt from a sermon, we see the sermon exhibited as almost the privileged place for a doctrinal exposition that is scripturally infused, and a scriptural rhetoric that is spoken as clearly as it is because it is doctrinally shaped. Which is it? Scriptural or catechetical? It is both, at one and the same time. And, as a result of listening, aren't we all a little more aware of the work that God has done in our lives, in the life of prayer, of worship, of baptism? And this not *in spite* of its being doctrinal, but because it is, though in the way just described, not as the communication of an isolated and self-enclosed system or formula preached as an end in itself.

I can't resist one more example from Gregory Nazianzus. Before offering it, I want to note that I am not proffering Gregory's homilies as an example whose second sophistic style is one we can take over today. That is a culturally limited art form that can't be reproduced today without sounding hopelessly artificial and striving for effect. Rather, I offer these passages as examples to replenish our own imaginations about what preaching both scripturally and doctrinally can mean. Here is the second passage from Gregory. It comes from the third theological oration, where Gregory is making a very technical argument, far more technical than one in good conscience could recommend for any homilist today. And yet that is why I bring it up, as a kind of limiting case. In a way, the whole point of the sermon, much more than in the fifth oration just cited, is the meaning of the term *consubstantial* when applied to the Father and the Son. The oration makes the crucial doctrinal distinction that enabled the settlement at Constantinople, namely, that the Father and the Son are not distinguished by anything on the level of substance, but rather, Gregory says, addressing his critics, "My expert friends . . . 'Father' designates neither the substance nor the activity, but the relationship, the manner of being, which hold good between the Father and the Son" (16). So, the Son is not the same Person as the Father, and yet is just as fully God. But this is not just specialized theological or doctrinal "information," an end in itself, an argument won, a fine point of logic argued. It means that the incarnate Son, fully divine, is also fully human, for he is not allowed the special privilege (which I myself would have insisted on if I were divine and incarnate) of praying to himself when he is in trouble. He really does have to pray to someone else, just like we do, when we are in need, and there is no farce or falsehood involved, as though the human being Jesus were praying to the nonhuman part of the same Jesus. His prayer is a true prayer, uttered by one subject, someone the gospels present as praying and yet hearing prayers: "He prays, yet he hears prayers." Here is the mystery of this Person. The doctrinal precision that Gregory argues for is meant to further the proclamation of the gospel mystery, the mystery of the Person who

> prays, yet . . . hears prayers. [Who] weeps, yet . . . puts an end to weeping. . . . He is sold, and very cheaply, thirty pieces of silver, yet he buys back the world at the mighty cost of his own blood. . . . A lamb, he is dumb—yet he is the "Word," proclaimed by "the voice of one crying in the wilderness." . . . He is given vinegar to drink, gall to eat—and who is he? Why, one who turned water into wine, who took away the taste of bitterness, who is all sweetness and desire. He surrenders his life, yet he has power to take it again. . . . He dies, but he vivifies and by death destroys death. (20)

Here is a moving evocation of the Person who is found at the heart of catechesis completely in scriptural terms, and yet it is the same Person that is evoked or described in the exquisitely precise doctrinal formulations Gregory has preached. The two types of exposition work together. We feel the power of the evangelical language even more, the awesomeness of the mystery revealed, when we realize that the one who is so human that he was sold for thirty pieces of silver is also so divine that it is also God who is sold, who has allowed himself to be sold into death, and in that act of love, turns bitterness into sweetness, just as the water in the desert was turned from bitter to sweet by the work of God. The doctrinal exposition increases our appreciation for the biblical proclamation.

And, in a complementary fashion, the exquisite fabric of scriptural allusions and quotations fills our imagination, informing us of what is at stake in the doctrinal formula, and, far from allowing that formula to be the terminus of our attention and understanding, catapults us to a contemplation of the mystery of the Person it was formulated to define.

Once again, we have a scriptural exposition that is doctrinally shaped, and a doctrinal exposition that is scripturally infused. There is no seam and no division of intention, one doctrinal, one scriptural. For, we can hear the Second Vatican Council saying, "Sacred Tradition and Sacred Scripture . . . are bound closely together and communicate one with the other [and] . . . flowing out from the same divine well-spring, come together in some fashion to form one thing and move towards the same goal." We can continue with the gloss of the *Catechism*, "Each of them makes present and fruitful in the Church the mystery of Christ" (DV 9, cited, with gloss, at CCC 80).

Now, to explore this theme just a little bit more fully, I want to turn to St. Augustine, to offer a Western example. The birthday of John the Baptist is an ancient feast. It is ranked as a solemnity, which means it is still to be celebrated when it falls on a Sunday. It might be interesting to go back about sixteen hundred years and listen to the homily preached sometime before 410, perhaps at Hippo Regius, by Bishop Augustine. We can tell that the gospel read was similar to the one provided in the modern Lectionary, a passage from the Gospel of Luke.

Augustine begins by reminding the assembly of the feast day and of the gospel reading: "The reason for our large and festive gathering today," he says, "is to celebrate the birthday of John the Baptist, whose marvelous conception and birth we heard about when the gospel was read" (Sermon 289).[2] Augustine calls the hearers' attention to the mystery the text proclaims: "It's a great and significant mystery, my brothers and sisters," meaning that the conception of John in a barren older woman and of a father who was an old man, is not only "marvelous" but precisely as "marvelous" as "significant." The miracle is a sign pointing to the mystery of God's plan. "Meanwhile," Augustine goes on, "the virgin also conceived, and this was a sublime miracle and far and away more remarkable. A barren woman conceives the herald, a virgin the judge. John is born of man and woman, Christ of woman only. Can John perhaps be compared with Christ? Perish the thought."

Augustine comments on how difficult it will be to explain the mystery that is invoked here, by the parallelism the gospel sets up between the two miraculous births, one a greater wonder than the other, but neither of them just wonders meant to dazzle us, but wonders that are signs of the greater wonder of God's economy of salvation in Christ.

Augustine continues: "Elizabeth conceived a human being, and so did Mary. . . . But the one Elizabeth conceived was only a man, the one Mary conceived was God and man. It's a marvelous thing, how a creature could conceive the creator. So what is to be understood by it, my brothers and sisters, but that it was the same one making flesh for himself from a mother alone, who had made the first human being without father and mother" (2), and Augustine then invokes the typology of Christ and Adam and Mary and Eve. Of course at this point, we can see that Augustine is speaking, as he himself recommends in the *De doctrina*, from the rule of faith, invoking the formulaic account of the Christ as both

"God and man." Note that the formula is brought in to help us under-stand, and to be moved by, the scriptural account, not to serve as a puzzle or a random piece of information independent of the scriptural account. Yet we also begin to understand this part of the "rule of faith" better precisely in its use to help us understand the significance of the wonder recounted in Scripture.

Then, as though anticipating the thoughts of the "large and festive gathering" in front of him, who might be wondering if he will get to the point, he says, "So what does John the Baptist mean? Why was he in-serted into the story, why was he sent ahead? I will tell you, if I can," Augustine somewhat confidently, somewhat cautiously, advises them. Note how Augustine uses his own person to magnify the mystery of the scriptural text, since he rhetorically advertises himself as possibly not able to explain it. "Our Lord Jesus Christ," he continues, "said about John, 'Among those born of women, none has arisen greater than John the Baptist' (Matt 11:11)," and Augustine comments that "the only one who beats him is the God-man." "So greatly did he excel, such was the grace evident in him, that he himself was thought to be the Christ" (3).

The original passage from the Gospel of Luke invited the comparison between John and Jesus, and now Augustine finds elaboration of that comparison in Matthew and in the other gospels and spins it out in a beautiful fabric of scripturally infused rhetoric until he gets to the Gospel of John, who says, as Augustine notes, "He was a burning and shining lamp, and you were willing for a time to exult in his light" (John 5:35, cited at sec. 4). But his light is only the light of a "lamp." John the evan-gelist draws a comparison between the light of this lamp and "the true light which enlightens every man coming into this world" (John 1:9, ibid.), and Augustine cites these passages in a very effective question-and-answer format that is meant to ensure that his "large and festive gathering" hears the beautiful words in which the Gospel of John states the contrast. "What, though, does John the evangelist say about him? 'There was a man sent by God, whose name was John; this man came for witness, to bear witness about the light; that man was not the light' (John 1:6-8)." Who? John the Baptist. Who says this? John the evangelist. "That man was not the light." We can note that the repetition helps the assembly memorize the words of Scripture (and I have reproduced here only part of the repetition in the passage).

Now Augustine returns to the "mystery" that Scripture and the rule of faith simultaneously—that is, simultaneously in the homily—state.

He says, "So if we have understood the mystery, my brothers and sisters, John is a man, Christ is God. Let the man be humbled, and God be exalted. . . . A great and significant sacrament indeed. That's why we celebrate John's birthday, like Christ's, because the very birth is full of mystery. What mystery? The mystery of our heights and depths." The mark of our weakness as humanity is that "we need a lamp to look for the daylight" (5). And yet this is also a mark of the humility of God, of the depth of the vulnerability of the Word made flesh; who is the Day, and yet who must be pointed out by a lamp; who is the Word, and yet who must be pointed out by a voice, the one "crying in the wilderness"; who is Truth, and yet must be borne witness to. There is no more characteristic passage in the preaching of Augustine for helping his hearers to grasp the immensity of the mystery of the incarnation than the one used here, of the Sun, the Light itself, emptying himself to the point where he cannot be recognized without a "lamp."

My point is simply that the listener does not notice when the homily is "doctrinal" and when it is "scriptural" because it is seamlessly both. The formulaic phrases that come from the rule of faith as elaborated in the creeds are used to help evoke the magnificence of the scriptural revelation of the humility, not only of John but of the Son. And the scriptural exegesis serves to help the hearer understand the propositions set out by the rule of faith, so that our faith, to invoke the words of the *Catechism*, "does not terminate in the propositions, but in the realities [which they express]" (St. Thomas Aquinas, *STh* II-II, 1, 2, *ad* 2) (CCC 170). Yet we can also see that, again in the words of the *Catechism*, "we do approach these realities with the help of the formulations of the faith which permit us to express the faith and to hand it on, to celebrate it in community, to assimilate and live on it more and more."

And Augustine does not miss the opportunity to provide, in his homily, an opportunity to assimilate and live on the faith. He ends the homily on a dramatically stark note, in an exhortation to humility, directed especially at the rich:

> After all, what were you, man? Everyman, notice how you were born; even if you were born a noble, you were born naked. What's nobility, anyway? At birth, poor and rich alike are equally naked. Or perhaps because you were born a noble, you can live as long as you like? You came in when you didn't know, you go out when you don't want to. Finally, let the graves be examined, and the bones of the rich told apart. (6)

That is where the homily ends. Perhaps the "large and festive crowd" did *not* see that coming. What a spoil sport the bishop is, some in the crowd may be thinking. But note that this stark ending is not mere moralism, as though Augustine were reducing the Scripture to a moral common-place. Rather, because we have been treated to a homily on the humility of John, as itself a pointer to the greater humility of the Word made flesh, the stark evocation of the human condition is also a parting echo of the humility of the Word, who descended to this condition, born just as naked as any of us. No one going away from this homily is going to look at a naked baby in the same way, because now that nakedness is an indi-cation of the humility of the Word made flesh even as it is a reminder of our common humanity, our solidarity in nakedness and death.

Perhaps few of the homilies we hear or give on Sunday, as the case may be, were really quite up to this level, but we can learn something from studying the homilies of the great preachers. One thing we can learn is, as already noted, how seamless can be the exposition of Scripture and the exposition of doctrine. Perhaps then, the so-called rift between Scrip-ture and doctrine was one very much of our own making. Perhaps there never was such a rift in the first place, at least not if the doctrine is au-thentically traditional and the Scripture genuinely canonical.

I bring this reflection to a close by way of a suggestion that goes beyond the non-problem as to whether homilies can be doctrinal and scriptural at the same time. On Augustinian grounds, I would like to suggest that the homily is the most privileged venue for such a combination. Recall the passage from John Paul II, cited above, namely, that "The homily takes up again the journey of faith put forward by catechesis, and brings it to its natural fulfillment." Why is the homily able to do this?

Augustine's work *De doctrina Christiana*, whose title is almost untrans-latable, envisions the process of interpreting and explaining Scripture as having two phases, or "modes," the first one a "research mode" of "discovering what is to be understood" (*modus inveniendi*), and the second a "mode of speaking forth that which has been understood" (*modus proferendi*). "What has been understood" does not fully exist as a "doc-trina," as teaching, apart from its being "spoken forth" or proclaimed by the preacher. It is that which is proclaimed that is "understood." It is in this sense that Augustine will sometimes say that he learns by writing or by speaking.

In any event, isn't Augustine saying here, that far from preaching being a kind of secondary form of discourse, derivative from the real exegesis that goes on in commentaries or classrooms, it is the privileged locus for interpreting Scripture, because the Word is not fully interpreted until it is proclaimed, in fact, in the act of proclaiming it? This is because Scripture is, for Augustine, itself a record of preaching, the preaching of the apostles, and so it arises from proclamation and is *intended* to be proclaimed. We do not fully grasp the intention of Scripture until it is, in fact, proclaimed. Hearing the Word proclaimed means experiencing its original intention, continuous with the intention of the apostles and of the incarnation itself.

But what about the exposition of doctrine? How does that come in? For Augustine, this is simply impossible to express in Latin as something separate from the interpretation of Scripture. The word *doctrina* means "teaching." Scripture and the rule of faith both contain this *doctrina*. The attempt to explain what Scripture teaches will naturally be facilitated by the invocation and use of expressions drawn from the rule of faith, since they are both expressions of the same *doctrina*.

In like manner, the exposition of Scripture will be a way of helping people understand what is meant by these formulations such that the rule of faith becomes something we cannot only "confess" but also "practice and make progress in," as he puts it in a homily on the handing over of the Creed (212.2). The rule of faith guides the exposition of Scripture so that the mystery at the heart of Scripture may be fully appreciated in its awesomeness; in turn, Scriptural exposition infuses the rule of faith with an understanding that does not end in the knowledge of the formula, but in the life of the baptized as a kind of practice of the *doctrina* and a making progress in it.

Thus, the homily, far from simply being tolerant of the combination of scriptural interpretation and doctrinal exposition, is the privileged locus for this combination. The *doctrina* that Scripture itself is, and which is summarized in the rule of faith, is not fully interpreted until it is proclaimed, and the rule of faith, which summarizes the *doctrina* of Scripture, is not fully understood until the proclamation of Scripture has directed us through the formulae and beyond into life in the mystery, until in our very living we ourselves begin to "comprehend with all the saints what is the breadth and length and height and depth . . . to know the love of Christ which surpasses knowledge . . . (and to be filled) with all the fullness of God" (CT 5).

Endnotes

1. See, for example, Jaroslav Pelikan, *The Christian Tradition: A History of the Development of Doctrine*, vol. 1 (Chicago: University of Chicago Press, 1971), 114.

2. Augustine, Sermon 289, in *The Works of Saint Augustine* III/8: *Sermons 273–305A*, trans. Edmund Hill (Hyde Park, NY: New City Press, 1994).

Chapter 6

The New Evangelization
and the New Media

Robert Barron

Over the last several years, much has been published, posted, tweeted, and spoken about the new media, by both Christian and secular experts.[1] Opinions differ about what is effective, what doesn't work, and what more could be done. But amidst this speculation, I'd like to turn our attention to the *content* side of the new media. That's what I've been doing at Word on Fire over the years—providing evangelistic content through videos, articles, podcasts, and blog posts—and I've learned much from working with the new media and its new expressions. I've learned mainly by just digging in and experimenting, mostly with my YouTube video commentaries on culture.

When YouTube emerged on the scene, I noticed how videos of cats jumping off of roofs would get a million views. I thought, couldn't this work for spiritual and religious content, too? So I posted some commentaries, starting with an eight-minute commentary on Martin Scorsese's *The Departed*. That video quickly drew in thousands of views. I continued posting more, and while my colleagues and I didn't know who would watch these video commentaries, we've discovered to our delight and surprise that millions of people have watched them over the years.

From the demographic data on YouTube we've determined that our videos are mostly viewed by men in their 20s, 30s, and 40s—a group that, coincidentally, the church is not very good at reaching. How else would the church reach out to disaffected, maybe non-believing, men of that age group?

For this reason and more, I'm an excited fan of YouTube. I must admit that I enjoy a bit of what the French call *joie de guerre* ("the joy of battle"). I love entering into the comment boxes on my videos and conversing with the folks who engage me online. In doing so, I've learned an awful lot not only about what gets in the way of the proclamation of faith. From these YouTube comments—of which about ninety percent are negative—I've learned what really concerns folks and challenges their thinking and behavior. I've then been able to use these comments as starting points for other videos and projects—and, of course, in preaching.

In this essay I will share what I've learned from my engagement in new media, beginning with a brief introduction to the new evangelization, and show how these insights can fuel your own preaching.

What Is the New Evangelization?

To understand the new evangelization, perhaps it's best to return to that iconic image of John XXIII announcing the Second Vatican Council. He's in a room with a huge globe next to him, and at that press conference he uses, for the first time, a lovely, lyrical phrase: *lumen gentium*. Of course this later became the title of one of the council's principle constitutions, as that constitution opened with the assertion that Christ is the *Lumen Gentium*.

It's the church's job to illuminate or enlighten the *gentes*, to bring that light to the nations. John XXIII wanted, it seems to me, a missionary council that would make the church a more appropriate vehicle for the proclamation of Christ. *Aggiornamento*? Yes, indeed, in the measure that the church should be brought up-to-date so as to make it a more effective vehicle for evangelization. *Aggiornamento*, it seems to me, but not in the sense of using the modern world as the norm by which the church is measured.

It is well known that many non-Catholics were invited as observers to the Second Vatican Council. One of these was the Swiss Reformed theologian Karl Barth. Barth was deeply honored by that invitation. At the end of the council, one of the key questions the theologian brought to the council fathers with whom he met was "What does *aggiornamento* mean? "Accommodating and updating" he was told. But he replied: "Accommodating to what?"[2] In effect, Barth questioned when they would know that the church was sufficiently updated.

Now this was a question with a sting in its tail. Barth was asking, "Are you using the modern world as the *norma normans*?" Is the modern world the norm by which the church is measuring itself? Is the project modernization in that sense? Or is the project the Christification of the world and the modernization of the *vehicle* aimed at that end?

The idea and impetus of Vatican II was to bring Christ out from the church into the world. Several years before the council, Hans Urs von Balthasar wrote a book entitled *Razing the Bastions*.[3] He believed that the church was crouching or sequestering itself behind medieval walls and that those walls needed to be knocked down to allow the life of the church to flood the world—to get the *Lumen Gentium* out to the *gentes*. He wasn't advocating a program of modernization, as if the church must get itself up-to-date. He was, rather, focused on knocking down the walls that prevented us from evangelizing well.

Moving forward to 1975, we receive that outstanding document by Pope Paul VI: *Evangelii Nuntiandi*. People often appeal to John Paul II for the new evangelization, as they should, but prior to that pontificate stands this extraordinary text of Paul VI, where he states, in effect: "The church doesn't have a mission. The church is a mission." That is a deeply John XXII and Vatican II idea. The church's very identity is to bear the light to the nations.

It's no coincidence that in attendance at the synod that produced *Evangelii Nuntiandi* was the archbishop of Krakow, Karol Wojtyla. In fact, he wrote one of the preliminary drafts of *Evangelii Nuntiandi*. Therefore it's no surprise that when he becomes John Paul II just three years later, the new evangelization becomes one of his principal concerns. It came out of his experience at Vatican II and of producing *Evangelii Nuntiandi*.

In 1983, not yet five years into his pontificate, John Paul II gave a now-famous speech in Port-au-Prince, Haiti, where he characterized the new evangelization as basically the same old evangelization (at least in content)—the declaration of Christ risen from the dead. But he added that we need new ardor, new expressions, and new methods. That little triplet, repeated often in documentation and speeches thereafter, is my organizing principle for the remainder of this essay: new ardor, new expressions, new methods.

New Ardor

Vatican II was a missionary council. At the end of the day, this is the take-home from Yves Congar's detailed journal of the council.[4] It's one of the most entertaining books I've read. At 1,100 pages, it's an enormous tome and, to be sure, not every page is compelling. It's more a diary than a novel. But Congar is such an entertainingly caustic observer. For instance, he will talk about meeting with a certain bishop and say, "What a bore." Or about some famous theologian, he'll write, "He talks too much." While very entertaining, the book awakened for me that whole wonderful sense of what the council was about—this missionary enthusiasm now to bring the church to the world.

I went to first grade in 1965 and came of age in the 70s, right after the council. Was the church of that time characterized by this deep passionate ardor to proclaim the Christian faith to the world? I'm afraid it was marked more by fussy, internal questioning and inward turn toward questions of sexuality and authority. Those are of course good questions, and serious people entertain them. But it was certainly not the agenda of the council for the church to turn inward and question itself.[5] The council was about the church going out into the world with a confident message.

At the end of his book *Principles of Catholic Theology,* Joseph Ratzinger has a fascinating epilogue dealing with the aftermath of Vatican II. Of course we are all aware of the polemics regarding how to interpret the council—hermeneutics of continuity versus hermeneutics of rupture, etc.—but in this epilogue Ratzinger makes a simple but profound point: "From time to time, councils are a necessity, but they always point to an extraordinary situation in the Church and are not to be regarded as a model for her life in general or even as the ideal content of her existence. They are medicine, not nourishment."[6] In other words, we should not aim to perpetuate the spirit of the Second Vatican Council, indeed, the spirit of *any* council!

There have only been twenty councils in the two thousand-year history of the church, and thereupon hangs a tale. Only twenty—why? Because councils are dangerous moments when the church throws itself into question to resolve something of great importance. Necessary? Yes. Nicea, Chalcedon, Trent, etc. Vatican II? They were all needed by the church during which the church puts itself in suspense. But then, Ratzinger argues, we're meant to move from a council out into the world with our mission. What is undesirable is a perpetual council, that is to say, the church perpetually in suspense, perpetually questioning even its most basic doctrines. In short, that is Ratzinger's critique of the early days of the journal *Concilium,* that it aimed to be "a permanent organ for the perpetuation of [the spirit of the council's] influence."[7]

We see this proper attitude, advocated by Ratzinger, in many twentieth-century giants of spiritual literature. In his recent book *Bad Religion,* Ross Douthat argues that, across the Protestant-Catholic divide, you've got outstanding figures such as Thomas Merton, Dorothy Day, T. S. Eliot, W. H. Auden, C. S. Lewis, and Graham Greene. What characterizes all of those figures? They passionately believed in classical Christianity, and they felt it was the message the world needed to hear. What wasn't found in those figures was a sort of fussy, hesitant, questioning quality.[8]

That's the ardor we need to be truly evangelical. Does that mean we need to be unintelligent? Far from it. We want the church to be resourcing its rich intellectual tradition at all times. We want it questioning, in that sense, but it can't be undermining itself or else the ardor of that message is lost.

But now we come to the most important question: what is the source of the church's ardor? Simply put, it is its belief in the resurrection of Jesus Christ from the dead.

Several years ago I spoke on the third day of an evangelization conference, and I got up and said, "Evangelization is the proclamation of Jesus Christ risen from the dead," and the whole room broke into applause. I responded, "On behalf of the risen Jesus, thank you for that!" Afterward audience members explained to me their applause: "Father, we've heard three days of talks and conferences, and no one has ever mentioned the resurrection."

That's a problem if we want to be evangelical, because the *euangelion*, the good news, is the resurrection of Jesus from the dead. It's not a myth, not a legend, not a symbol, not a literary device. When you refer to some of the books, some of the extremely influential theology of the 1970s, you'll find accounts of the resurrection such as: "Jesus died. His disciples gathered, felt forgiven or felt his spirit, and then told evocative stories about empty tombs and appearances." In more recent years you'll find exactly the same thing repeated: the disciples sat in a memory circle, recalled how powerful he was, how he mediated God to them, and then in symbolic language they spoke of resurrection from the dead. If that's all it is, then, to quote Flannery O'Connor, "to hell with it." There's no evangelical power in that.

I have a theory about Christology: if you're saying something about Jesus that I could just as well say about my grandmother, then it's not a good Christology. My grandmother mediated to me the presence of God more than anyone when I was a kid. When she died, I did indeed feel, "Boy, there were probably things I did that offended her, and I wasn't as responsive as I should have been, and she was so good to me and I wasn't always." But I really did, as a little kid, feel forgiven. I knew that Grandma, now in heaven, of course forgives me. No one mediated to me the unconditional love of God more than my grandmother. When a teacher in grade school explained what "unconditional love" meant, right away I thought of my grandmother. But if that's *all* we're saying about Jesus, our message lacks evangelical power.

What strikes me is that in going through the New Testament, every page has a distinct "grab you by the lapels" quality. The apostles are not merely trading generic, spiritual teachings, with Jesus as just one more mystical guru among others. Jesus is indeed a great spiritual teacher, and there are, in fact, points of contact between him and the other great spiritual traditions. But the New Testament authors want to grab the whole world by the lapels and say, "Jesus Christ is risen from the dead!"

First-century Jews weren't dualists. When Paul said Jesus rose from the dead, he never meant that only Jesus' soul went to heaven, but that his body remained. Paul never meant that Jesus had risen into the *kerygma* or that he was a myth or a legend or a symbol. First-century Jews wouldn't talk that way. They'd say, "I saw him, I saw him! Jesus, who was crucified—that same Jesus—I saw him alive through the power of the Holy Spirit and everything changes because of it!"

What does this mean for preaching? Truly evangelical preaching, the kind that has this new ardor of which John Paul II spoke, is preaching that is *on fire*. It's preaching that neither forgets nor domesticates the resurrection. That is key to the new ardor.

New Expressions

I've learned a lot about new expressions through my work with Word on Fire, the media evangelization ministry I founded, and especially through my YouTube dialogues. It is true that this age-old message of the risen Jesus needs to be said in a new way because of a new cultural situation. With that in mind, I'd like to focus on three distinct elements of the cultural milieu which I've detected through my online engagement: confusion about what we mean when we say "God"; the disenchantment of the world; and a combination of the cultural forces of relativism, subjectivism, and indifferentism.

1. *A Deep Confusion about "God"*

In the twentieth century huge parts of the earth came under officially atheist regimes. Today, much of the West is dominated by what John Paul II called "practical atheism"—we act as though God doesn't exist.

On top of all of that, we now have the aggressive New Atheism coming in, fueled by the writings of Richard Dawkins, Sam Harris, and the late Christopher Hitchens. Atheists are challenging us that speaking about God is simply propagating childish superstitions, projecting our fearful needs, backed up by no scientific evidence, and in fact running *counter* to the sciences. God is, if you will, a threat to human flourishing: intellectually, morally, and otherwise.

Much of this increasing atheism, however, is built on a faulty conception of God. There's a great scene in Thomas Merton's *The Seven Storey Mountain*, where as a non-believing twenty-something, Merton comes across Etienne Gilson's *The Spirit of Medieval Philosophy* in the window of the Scribner's bookstore on Fifth Avenue in New York City.[9] He thought, "Well, I'm studying French and medieval literature, so maybe I should get a sense of what the medievals were about." So he bought the book, boarded a train to Long Island, opened the book, and as soon as he saw the *Nihil Obstat* on the copyright page, he wanted to throw the book out the window. He had no interest in reading a Catholic book! But then, by some strange grace, he actually read on. And what did he find? He found Gilson's articulation of Aquinas's great sense of God as *ipsum esse subsistens*—not *en summum*, or "highest being," but *ipsum esse subsistens*, "the sheer act of to-be itself." Merton was utterly fascinated by this refined intellectual discussion of God. He had always thought of God as a noisy, mythological being, but here he was confronted with an entirely different God.

In my YouTube forums almost any day, you'll find lots of evidence that people today think that God is nothing more than a noisy, mythological being. For example, perhaps you've heard about the Flying Spaghetti Monster. In a tongue-in-cheek letter to the Kansas State Board of Education, Bobby Henderson wrote that there's as much evidence for a Flying Spaghetti Monster as there is for God.[10] God is indistinguishable from some wild, fantastical, creation of your imagination. But this is merely what Terry Eagleton critiques as the "Yeti" theory of God—where some say there is a Yeti, or Bigfoot, and some say there is not. So the only way to determine the truth, such a theory presumes, is to gather and weigh the evidence.[11]

The problem with this theory is that it construes God as a fussily competitive being along with everything else. When God is construed that way, inevitably God comes into conflict with us. God's supreme power and supreme freedom will come up against my limited freedom. God will compete with me for the same ontological space.

I would argue that many Enlightenment philosophies wrestled with such a competitive God until, finally, with Feuerbach, Marx, and company, people said, "Well, let's just get rid of Him. Let's just get rid of this God who is threatening my freedom." Jean Paul Sartre says that if God exists, I can't be free. But I am free; therefore, God doesn't exist.[12] It's a good argument, a perfect syllogism. But the assumption behind it is that God's freedom competes with ours. God is not a supreme being among others but *ipsum esse*, the sheer act of to-be itself. He does not compete with me but rather *grounds* me.

Meister Eckhart, who held Aquinas's chair of theology in Paris for a short time, said that we *sink* into God.[13] That's right out of Thomas's metaphysics. God is the very source and deepest ground of one's being, and therefore the surrender to God is not a surrender to a competitive freedom but rather the discovery of *one's own deepest freedom*. Irenaeus presents us with the opposite of Sartre when he writes in the fourth book of *Against Heresies: "Gloria Dei vivens homo."* The glory of God is the human being fully alive! God competes with neither our freedom nor our flourishing, but his glory is when we come fully to life.

Contrast the image of the burning bush with theophanies in the Greek and Roman mythological traditions. In those latter cases, gods come crashing into human affairs and people are incinerated. Things have to give way when Zeus decides to come barreling in. But the burning bush is different: on fire, it's not consumed. When God comes close, we become luminescent, ardent, and we are not consumed but enhanced in the process.

We Christians have not always done well articulating what we mean by "God." The great Dominican theologian Herbert McCabe often engaged atheists publicly. He always allowed the atheist to give his argument at great length, and then McCabe would get up to the microphone and say, "I completely agree with you"—because, in every case, the atheist was rejecting some competitive, fussy supreme being. And McCabe agreed: we Christians don't believe in that God either.

Good preaching speaks of God, and it speaks of the God of the burning bush. It speaks of the God of Jesus Christ. We see this in the Council of Chalcedon. The Christological statements of that council evoke the burning-bush: two natures coming together without mixing, mingling, or confusion. God doesn't come destructively barreling in, but rather enhances that which he touches. As preachers, *that's* what we need to speak about.

2. *The Disenchantment of the World*

A second roadblock to faith today is "the disenchantment of the world," a phrase Max Weber uses to describe a process that began around the time of the Reformation, bringing about the Enlightenment and Modernity.[14] Charles Taylor used it again in his classic book on the secular age.[15] Disenchantment is a state of being with no spiritual dimension, no spiritual reference at all. It's a firm belief only in the world that you can see, measure, and control. It's the belief that you will find your joy completely in and only through that world.

I encounter this constrictive worldview all the time online. Almost every day someone tells me on an Internet forum, "Father, I don't need what you're talking about. I'm perfectly happy." In response, I tease the person: "I don't believe you."

Despite what my interlocutor may suggest, Augustine was right: all of us are wired for God. "Lord . . . you have made us for yourself," he wrote, "and our heart is restless until it rests in you."[16] There's no better statement in the whole tradition of Christian anthropology: Lord, by our very nature we are ordered to you, which is why our hearts are restless.

When I encounter disenchanted moderns, I say, "I know you're not telling me the truth because no matter how much truth your mind attains, your mind is still hungry. You can't deny that. No matter how much justice you attain, and we have indeed attained great works of justice like the Civil Rights Movement, you are never satisfied. We've attained great beauty and artists that we celebrate up and down the centuries, but it's still not enough."

St. John of the Cross understood this well. In *The Living Flame of Love*, he recounts a spectacular vision in which he sees memory, intellect, and will as "deep caverns of feeling." So deep are these caverns that "anything less than the infinite fails to fill them" because it is God alone who comprises their object.[17] The central tragedy of our human life is that we throw the petty goods of the world into those caverns thinking they are going to fill them up. We throw pleasure, power, money, and honor down those caverns, and when those caverns don't fill up, the inevitable result is addiction. We must throw more pleasure, more money, more power, and more honor down into those caverns. And when that still doesn't work, the addictions become stronger and harder to kick.

There's a noteworhty scene from 1 Kings in which Elijah stands in spiritual battle against the priests of Baal (18:21-40). It's much more than "My god is bigger than your god." It is a very telling spiritual story. The priests of Baal, with their altars erected to their god, stand for this errant human longing. They stand for all of our attempts to fill up the infinite hunger with something less than God, be it wealth, pleasure, power, or honor. They hop around the altar, begging, wheedling, and cajoling Baal to appear. However no one responds. No one comes to satisfy the deepest longing of their hearts. The telling moment arrives when the prophets of Baal begin to cut themselves and bleed as they hop around the altar. They are wounded in this process, which is not a harmless one. After the false prophets spill their blood in service of their god, Elijah calls upon the true God, who answers with fire. The response affirms that it is only the true God who can answer with fire, who can meet that ardent longing of our hearts.

Good evangelical preaching is one that names these deep caverns and points to the only being who can fulfill them. Walk through the gospels, and you will find encounters between Christ and someone with this infinite longing in some form—whether it is Peter, the woman at the well, the man born blind, Zacchaeus, or anyone else whom Jesus meets. They all come with some version of this longing. As preachers, we must articulate that desire, stir it up, and make people uncomfortable with all the false ways they've tried to fill it.

3. *Relativism, Subjectivism, and Indifferentism*

A third cultural barrier to faith is the relativism, subjectivism, and indifferentism that have been lamented by both John Paul II and Benedict XVI. Together these "isms" suggest, "My will determines value. What you believe, that's up to you. But my truth is not your truth, and your truth is not mine. We all make up our own minds."

In the *Purgatorio,* Dante punishes the slothful by making them run around, almost as in a gym. There is a Marian admonition on every stage of purgatory, and the one for slothful is, "She went in haste." It was after the Annunciation, and Mary went in haste up into the hill country. She was going somewhere. She knew what she was about.

The trouble with these "isms" is that they've produced a culture that doesn't go in haste—in fact it doesn't go *anywhere.* It's sort of stuck in its own subjectivism, relativism, and indifferentism.

The great philosopher Dietrich von Hildebrand distinguished between the merely subjectively satisfying and the objectively valuable. As an example, I like spaghetti and meatballs. Spaghetti and meatballs is subjectively satisfying to me. I don't like to eat fish, and it seems to me that

98 percent of the specials at restaurants are always fish. Fish is not subjectively satisfying to me. But have I ever in my life felt the need to evangelize on behalf of spaghetti and meatballs? Or against eating fish? No, it is just a matter of my own tastes.

Now compare spaghetti or fish with Beethoven's Ninth Symphony. Whether you understand it or even enjoy it, the Symphony has a power of immense objectivity. The saints have the same effect. There is something about Saint Francis or Mother Teresa of Calcutta of such extraordinary, objective value that you are seized, changed, and sent by those figures.

Or take golf as another example. Golfers know how demanding the sport is, and golf doesn't care whether you can play or not. I can hit a bad shot, and I can hit a good shot that ends up in a sand trap or the rough, and sometimes I hit the ground with my club. But golf itself doesn't care; I am not hurting it. It is just there in all of its objective golfness.

My point is that until we come to that moment of a real encounter with the Good, until we break out of our little subjective spaces and into some very clear objective values, we have not begun to live. Evangelical preaching is preaching that raises up this great objective value of the Gospel, overcomes our cultural tendency toward the merely subjectively satisfying, and puts forward the great value of God and His objective laws and demands.

Now of course, in America we are uneasy with law. The law is great because you need it to survive, but deep down we prefer that there were not any laws. I would like to drive 120 miles per hour on the expressway, but I cooperate with the law and drive 70, and I have to go through those toll plazas even though I don't want to. The law is an affront to my freedom. But when you are dealing with the objectively good, the objectively valuable, you learn to love the laws associated with the process of being drawn into that value.

About ten years ago I went to a golf instructor, who asked me to adopt a new line up for a shot and then told me that in this new orientations, I was prepared to hit a perfect slice every time, which is what happened. Now, the first time I assumed that stance I felt like Frankenstein. But as I began swinging under his guidance, and after a lot of painful adjustment, I began hitting the ball in a way I had never hit it before. During that experience I was reminded of the Psalmist who describes finding joy in the law of the Lord, meditating upon it day and night (1:2).

Recently one night while lying in bed, I read in *Golf Digest* a collection of stories on how to improve your game, stance, and swing. What was

I doing? I was meditating upon the law, day and night, thinking about what I need to do with my golf game.

If the law is just an affront to freedom one cannot find joy. One might tolerate it but not enjoy it. But if I am dealing with the objectively valuable, and I want to be drawn into its power, I indeed learn to enjoy the law.

Good evangelical preaching raises these great objective values of God, Jesus Christ, the Word made flesh, and the church as the mystical body of Jesus, and it proclaims the laws of the church not as a fussy interruptions to our freedom but as the condition for the possibility of moving into that world of value. That is preaching with new ardor and new expressions.

New Methods

Six years ago I was teaching at Mundelein Seminary and Cardinal George came to me and said, "I would like you to jump-start evangelization," and I said, "Great! But what does that mean, Your Eminence?" And he said, "I don't know, but I want you to do it." He had been in Rome with John Paul II, who asked him: "What are you doing to evangelize the culture?" Cardinal George didn't know what to say. So that was what Cardinal George wanted me to help with, evangelizing the culture.

For several years I gave talks in Chicago at business clubs, union league clubs, university clubs—the idea was for the church to go out to the people in the business world. We invited people on their lunch hours, we gave them lunch, and I would give a short talk. The events were generally well-received. But at the end of the process, I said to Cardinal George, "You know it's great what we're doing here, Your Eminence, but there is something charmingly nineteenth-century about it, like something John Henry Newman might have done. Today, with the new technologies around us, there is another world opening itself up to us."

That is what spurred my work through Word on Fire. We have tools today that Fulton Sheen would have given his right arm for. He had to rely on people taking a particular time to listen to the radio or watch a particular television show. Now, you put a YouTube video up, and it is available online 24/7 all over the world. I love the fact that I can do a video commentary on culture, and within ten minutes I can get emails from Nepal, the Philippines, and an American sailor off the coast of Japan. I love the range the Internet gives. What I have tried to do is make commentaries on culture: on books, movies, music, what is going on in the news, and to do so usually in a positive way. I'm looking for what the Church Fathers called the *semina verbi*, the seeds of the Word, small touch points of faith scattered throughout the culture.

That is why I took up Martin Scorsese's *The Departed* in my very first video. Scorsese is deeply Catholic in sensibility, which you can spot easily in this film. I've also sought to reveal depictions of Christ in explicitly non-religious films. Who would have guessed, for example, that the most compelling Christ figure in contemporary film would appear in Clint Eastwood's *Gran Torino*? That movie contains a shockingly beautiful rendition of the "Christus Victor" theory of salvation. By referencing these films, and exploring their spiritual themes, I can reach groups of people the church otherwise has great difficulty connecting with.

Several years ago I received an email from nineteen-year-old who began the email with "Dear Father, I hated the Catholic Church, and I hated the priests," but went on to say he loved Bob Dylan. One night he was googling Bob Dylan and "up came one of your videos. It came up, and I saw the Roman collar, and I just wanted to close the window. But I watched it, and I liked it and so I watched another one of your Bob Dylan commentaries, and then a third one. That led me to lots of your other videos and that led me back to your website, and then I got drawn into it." Then he added, "And now I am in the RCIA program."

What I love about this story is that the sowing of the seeds is what the new media gives us—that possibility to evangelize new people in new ways. How would that kid ever have come into a church? He's not going to visit the rectory or one of our institutions. But in that weird virtual world of the web I was able to sow this seed.

Today we are in a time of extraordinary power akin to the days of Gutenberg. We are in the midst of a technological revolution that has enabled us to reach out to a culture that I have described in a cursory but truthful way. It is a time to use these new media tools and engage the culture with this massively objective value that we call the Gospel of Jesus Christ. When we allow that Gospel to change us and draw us into its power, then we catch on fire just like the burning bush—on fire, luminous, but not consumed. Then we can become bearers of that *lumen gentium* to the wider world.

Endnotes

1. See Brandon Vogt, *The Church and New Media: Blogging Converts, Online Activists, and Bishops Who Tweet* (Huntington, IN: Our Sunday Visitor, 2011).

2. Karl Barth, *Ad Limina Apostolorum: An Appraisal of Vatican II*, trans. Keith R. Crim (Richmond, VA: John Knox Press, 1968), 20.

3. Hans Urs von Balthasar, *Razing the Bastions: On the Church in this Age* (San Francisco: Ignatius Press, 1993).

4. Yves Congar, *My Journal of the Council* (Collegeville, MN: Liturgical Press, 2012).

5. In other places I've characterized this era as "beige Catholicism." See my "Beyond Beige Catholicism," *Church* 16 (2000), 5–10; and in *Bridging the Great Divide: Musings of a Post-liberal, Post-conservative Evangelical Catholic* (Lanham, MD: Sheed & Ward, 2004), 11–21.

6. Joseph Cardinal Ratzinger, *Principles of Catholic Theology: Building Stones for a Fundamental Theology*, trans. Mary Frances McCarthy (San Francisco: Ignatius Press, 1987), 374.

7. Ibid., 383.

8. Ross Douthat, *Bad Religion: How We Became a Nation of Heretics* (New York: Free Press, 2012), 23–25.

9. Thomas Merton, *The Seven Storey Mountain* (New York: Harcourt, Brace and Co., 1948), 171 ff.

10. See Richard Dawkins, *The God Delusion* (New York: Bantam Books, 2006), 15, 76–78.

11. See Terry Eagleton, *Reason, Faith and Revolution: Reflections on the God Debate* (New Haven, CT: Yale University Press, 2009), 110–11.

12. See *Existentialism and Humanism* (Brooklyn: Haskell House, 1977).

13. See Matthew Fox' quotation of a sermon by Eckhart in *Breakthrough: Meister Eckhart's Creation Spirituality in New Translation* (Image, 1980), 180.

14. Max Weber, "Science as Vocation" in *The Vocation Letters*, ed. David Owen and Tracy B. Strong, trans. Rodney Livingstone (Indianapolis: Hackett Publishing, 2004), 13 ff. Weber adapted the phrase from Friedrich Schiller's poem "The Gods of Greece" (1788).

15. Charles Taylor, *A Secular Age* (Cambridge, MA: Belknap Press, 2007).

16. Augustine, *The Confessions of St. Augustine*, trans. John K. Ryan (Garden City, NY: Image Books, 1960), 43.

17. John of the Cross, *The Living Flame of Love*, in *The Collected Works of Saint John of the Cross*, rev. ed., trans. Kieran Kavanaugh and Otilio Rodriguez (Washington, DC: ICS Publications, 1991), 680–81.

Chapter 7

Preaching the Cross of Christ[1]

Barbara E. Reid, OP

It happened about fifteen years ago. I was teaching a course on the Gospel of Mark, and we got to the climactic midpoint in chapter 8, where Jesus asks the disciples, "Who do you say that I am?" followed by Peter's declaration of Jesus as the Messiah, and then Jesus' elaboration on the nature of his messiahship and his coming suffering and death. After Peter's struggle with this, Jesus then says to the crowd with his disciples, "If any want to become my followers, let them deny themselves and take up their cross and follow me" (Mark 8:34, NRSV).

I was waxing eloquent on what this might mean in a context where actual crucifixions on crosses are no longer done, and I confess, I was straying from teaching into preaching (it's hard for Dominicans to draw strict boundaries between those two manners of breaking open the Word!). A student suddenly raised her hand, and, slightly peeved at the interruption, I called on her. She declared, "I hate this text! It is the single most deadly passage in the whole Bible, and if it were up to me, I would rip it out and never proclaim it again!"

I was quite taken aback. I didn't have a clue what she was talking about, but I had the good sense to ask her if she could say more about what she found so disturbing in this text. "Gladly," she said. And then she recounted how, in her work in a shelter for women who were abused by their partners, she had seen it happen over and over, that the thing that most kept Christian women from getting the help they needed was the way they interiorized this gospel text. They considered that any kind of abuse or suffering they endured was their way of carrying the cross with Jesus. Worst of all, she said, was when a woman would finally break the silence about the abuse going on in her home, she would usually confide in her pastor or minister, who, more often than not, would tell her to go home and be subject to her husband and endure this abuse as her way of carrying the cross with Jesus.

I was aghast. I had never heard such a misappropriation of the gospel, and it set me on a path to investigate how we preach the cross and where is the liberating Good News in that, particularly for women.

Shortly after, I began a research project that resulted in my book, *Taking Up the Cross: New Testament Interpretations Through Latina and Feminist Eyes.*[2] I took advantage of a number of invitations to give presentations in México, Bolivia, and Perú, to speak with women in contexts very different from my own, to try to learn how they would understand the cross. One of the questions I asked people in all different parts of the United States, Latin America, Ireland, Australia, and New Zealand was "Why did Jesus die?" In every instance, I got the same simple answer: "To save me from my sins."

As Elizabeth Johnson remarked,[3] Anselm, who developed atonement theology in the eleventh century, should be considered the most successful theologian of all times—his explanation of the cross stuck! I began to investigate all the various metaphors and theological explanations for the death of Jesus in the New Testament, and discovered that while atonement certainly does have a basis there, particularly in Pauline literature, it is far from the only theology of the cross and is certainly not the most prevalent.

What I discovered is that there is a whole host of explanations for the death of Jesus in the New Testament—a rich variety of metaphors, symbols, and analogies that undoubtedly reflects the varied ways in which the early Christians preached Christ crucified. Looking with feminist lenses, some of these theological interpretations can be deadly, and can feed cycles of violence and victimization, especially toward women. Others have a greater liberating potential. I would advance that no metaphor is perfect, and none adequately captures the whole of the mystery of the cross; all have their pitfalls and possibilities. I would like to invite preachers to become more cognizant about the possible deleterious effects of some of the ways we preach about the cross, and to explore others that have not been adequately mined for their liberative potential.

Atonement, Ransom, Justification

The most prevalent way the cross is preached is as atonement for sin. The text that most readily comes to mind is in Romans 3:23-25 (NRSV): "All have sinned and fall short of the glory of God; they are now justified by his grace as a gift, through the redemption that is in Christ Jesus, whom God put forward as a sacrifice of atonement by his blood, effective through faith." One of the first things to notice is that in these three short verses, Paul juxtaposes three different metaphors for the death of Jesus, each of which leads in a slightly different direction. But let us begin with the metaphor of atonement for sin.

The first thing to note is that the word Paul uses in Romans 3:25, *hilastērion*, "atonement," does not mean propitiation of an angry God— such a notion is foreign to the God of the Bible. With the word *hilastērion*, Paul is drawing on cultic language to talk about the death of Jesus in terms of the ritual performed each year on Yom Kippur, in which the mercy seat (*hilastērion*), the top part of the ark of the covenant, was sprinkled with blood. This symbolic act was to effect atonement for the sins of the people (Lev 16:14-16). Paul suggests that just as the blood of temple sacrifices cleansed impurity from the Israelites, so Jesus' sacrifice freed human beings from sin and death. An important thing to note is that Paul is not likening Jesus to the animal that was slaughtered for temple sacrifices. Rather, Jesus is the *hilastērion*, the new mercy seat, that is, the place of contact between humanity and divinity.

In this same text, Paul shifts from a cultic to an economic metaphor, as he speaks of the "redemption," *apolytrōsis*, that is in Christ Jesus (Rom 3:24). This is a word that refers to the buying back of the freedom of a slave or a captive. Jesus' death, then, purchases freedom from sin for humanity. This notion is also found in Mark 10:45 (NRSV) and parallels, where Jesus explains that he came "not to be served but to serve, and to give his life as a ransom (*apolytrōsis*) for many."

Finally, in this same passage of Romans, Paul speaks about justification that comes through the death of Jesus. Now he takes us into the realm of legal language. The biblical notion of justice or justification does not mean everyone getting what they deserve, but rather, everything being in right relation. Paul says it is the death of Jesus that put relations between God and humanity in right order. It is essential to note that Paul says that this is a free gift of God, accomplished through the Christ event, appropriated by believers through faith. Paul juxtaposes metaphors of economic exchange, *apolytrōsis*, "redemption," and sacrifice, which can imply a buying of God's favor, with one that speaks of the free gift of God through Christ.

Scapegoat, Martyr, Silent Lamb

Other New Testament interpretations of the cross are akin to these sacrificial metaphors. There are texts in which Jesus is likened to the scapegoat, onto which the sins of the people were symbolically transferred on Yom Kippur, before it was driven out into the wilderness (Lev 16:10; see Gal 3:13; 2 Cor 5:21; John 11:50). Just as the guilt of the people is transferred to the innocent goat, and the purity of the scapegoat is transmitted to the people, so Christ exchanges status with sinners.

There are also texts in which Jesus is cast as a martyr or model of heroic death. In his letter to the Romans, for example, Paul says, "Indeed, rarely will anyone die for a righteous person—though perhaps for a good person someone might actually dare to die. But God proves his love for us in that while we were still sinners Christ died for us" (Rom 5:7-8, NRSV).

Another related image is that of a silent lamb led to the slaughter. Mark, in particular, portrays Jesus as similar to the Servant in Isaiah who endures beating, buffets, spitting, and humiliation, on whom the guilt of the whole people was laid. Unjustly persecuted, he utters nary a word in protest, standing silent before his accusers (Isa 53:7).

Problematic Aspects

Each of the above metaphors explains Jesus' death as a life sacrificed for others. While there is potential for this interpretation to be freeing, it can also be deadly when it functions to keep people who are abused or oppressed in positions of subservience. In my conversations with women in rural Chiapas, one woman described what was typical of the way most of the women she knows have appropriated the Christian story:

> Jesus taught us how to sacrifice, how to give our lives for others, how to be humble and not self-centered. We sacrifice especially for our children, for our husbands, for our families. When there is not enough food, we give the best portions to our children and husbands. We sacrifice so our children can go to school, selling whatever we can in the market. We do not follow our own desires, but offer up our lives in service for theirs . . . I get up at four o'clock every morning to get water and gather wood and start the fire for breakfast.

I do all the housework, and I work in the fields alongside my husband as well, with my youngest baby strapped to my back. I get no pay for any of my work; we women are completely dependent on what our husbands give us. At the end of the day, I keep tending the children and fix dinner. Afterward, there is more work to prepare for the next day. I don't ever rest or have a day off. Who would carry out my responsibilities? God has made it this way, we have to be humble and sacrifice for others. All the suffering we endure we accept as our way of carrying the cross.[4]

We do not have to travel to Chiapas to hear such a disturbing description. Many women throughout the world understand their lives in this way, and cultures shaped by *machismo* are reinforced by this manner of preaching about the cross. Rather than freeing persons who are weighed down, preaching such a theology of the cross can enmesh persons who are abused in even deeper cycles of violence and victimization. It can lull persons who are victimized into a passive acceptance of every kind of suffering, rather than help them take action to stop abuse where possible. The image of the silent sufferer, who is unjustly persecuted, and who utters not a word of protest, such as the Marcan Jesus before Pilate, emulating the Servant of Isaiah 53:7, is one that can keep an abused person from protesting against the injustices directed at her. An alternate image of Jesus, from the Fourth Gospel, can offer a more liberating possibility. In the scene where Jesus is struck for answering back to the high priest, he does not simply accept the buffeting, but counters: "If I have spoken wrongly, testify to the wrong. But if I have spoken rightly, why do you strike me?" (John 18:23, NRSV).

In what follows, I would like to explore some of the metaphors in the Gospel of John that offer alternatives to that of atoning sacrifice, and which have liberating possibilities. Before doing so, we pause to note several other pitfalls associated with sacrificial imagery and atonement metaphors.

Taking Metaphors Literally

In trying to preach about the paschal mystery, we always move into the realm of metaphorical, symbolic, and analogical speech. There is no way to capture this mystery in language that is literal, and the New Testament writers use a great variety of images and metaphors. None is adequate, and each has its pitfalls and promises. Paul often mixes metaphors, as we saw in Romans 3:23-25, where he juxtaposes atoning sacrifice, redemption, and justification. The metaphors are fluid, as Paul intertwines language from cultic, economic, and legal realms. Yet one of the tendencies in later Christian authors and preachers has been to isolate, rigidify, and literalize the metaphors, especially those of ransom and sacrifice, so that these have come to predominate to the exclusion of others and have sometimes functioned to reduce this most profound of mysteries to a simple formula.[5]

God's Gratuitous Love Obscured

Another difficulty with sacrificial metaphors is that they often put heavier emphasis on human sinfulness than on the gratuitous love of God. God is preached not as one who freely offers salvation out of love for humankind, but as an angry deity who must be appeased for our transgressions. This can have deadly consequences for abused persons who think they deserve to be punished, as well as for those who appropriate to themselves abusive forms of power over others. Moreover, the metaphor of ransom implies that redemption needs to be purchased, obscuring the gratuitous nature of God's saving grace. In addition, some ransom theories are problematic in the way God is depicted as pitted against the devil to gain human freedom, posing a challenge to God's omnipotence.

Unwilling Victims

Another dangerous direction is when unwilling victims are exalted, as when the near-sacrifice of Isaac or the death of Jesus are preached in such a way as to emphasize the obedience of Abraham and Jesus to God. The link between the story of Abraham and Isaac and Jesus' death is forged at the Easter Vigil, where the second reading is Genesis 22:1-18. There is a fundamental difference, however, between the two stories. In the story of Jesus, his free choice is underscored most emphatically (John 10:11, 17-18). In the case of Isaac, he is an unwitting victim, who has no say, much like Jephthah's daughter in Judges 11. Anthropologist Carol Delaney, reflecting on the social implications of religious myth, invites us to ponder what would be the shape of our society if we preached as the supreme model of faith and commitment not a father willing to sacrifice his only beloved son, but one that would do anything in his power to protect the child's life?[6]

Martyr vs. Sacrifice

Another pitfall with sacrificial metaphors is that they can lead to acts of sacrifice intended to redeem another. For example, some women think that they will merit reward for their husbands by accepting suffering and making sacrifices to atone for his sinful behavior. Such an attitude appropriates to human beings what Christ has already accomplished. Another important distinction is that martyrdom is not self-sacrifice for a cause. A martyr, as Joyce Salisbury notes, is one who "accepts death rather than give up their beliefs; they are witnesses," not "people seeking death to force others to change their practices."[7]

Ending Sacrifices and Scapegoating

French anthropologist René Girard has studied the mechanisms of rivalry and social violence that arise when human beings learn to desire what others desire.[8] Societies around the world, he proposes, learned to preserve order by channeling violence onto a scapegoat, whose expulsion brings peace for a time. The cycle repeats again and again, so that there is always need of new victims. Girard believes that sacrificial cult, inherent to most religions, is a ritual means to substitute for scapegoating. For him, the crucifixion of Jesus exposes and opposes the violence inherent in sacrificial thinking and should have ended it once and for all, much as the author of Hebrews states: "Unlike the other high priests, he has no need to offer sacrifices day after day, first for his own sins, and then for those of the people; this he did once for all when he offered himself" (Heb 7:27, NRSV). One can also point to sayings of Jesus that can be understood as challenging sacrificial thinking and acts, such as "I desire mercy, not sacrifice" (Matt 9:13; 12:7 NRSV; see Hosea 6:6).

Salvation and Incarnation

One more problematic aspect is when Jesus' death is preached as a singular act that effects redemption. Such an assertion overlooks the fact that salvation is linked inextricably with the incarnation and Jesus' earthly ministry, not only with his death. In the Gospels of Matthew and Luke, it is in relation to the birth of Jesus that the language of salvation first occurs. In the Gospel of Luke, in the announcement of the angels to the shepherds, the newborn Jesus is called *sōtēr*, "Savior" (2:11, NRSV). In Matthew's gospel, the angel tells Joseph that he is to name Mary's child "Jesus, for he will save (*sōsei*) his people from their sins" (Matt 1:21, NRSV). Matthew then depicts Jesus' whole earthly ministry as salvific, especially in the healing stories, where the verb *sōsein* has a double connotation: "to heal" and "to save" (e.g., Matt 8:25-26; 9:21-22; 14:30-31).[9]

The Gospel of John also links Jesus' saving activity with the Incarnation. Jesus says to Nicodemus, "For God so loved the world that he gave his only Son, so that everyone who believes in him may not perish but may have eternal life. Indeed, God did not send the Son into the world to condemn the world, but in order that the world may be saved (*sōthē*) through him" (John 3:16-17, NRSV; echoed also in 12:47). In all of the Gospels, salvation is associated with Jesus' birth and earthly ministry, not only with his death.

Taking Up the Cross

Returning to the text of Mark 8:34, "If any want to become my followers, let them deny themselves and take up their cross and follow me," there are two important things that preachers would do well to keep in mind. First, in the gospel context, when Jesus speaks to his disciples about taking up the cross, he is talking about a very specific kind of suffering. He is referring to the negative repercussions to which disciples are willing to expose themselves as a direct consequence of following Jesus. He is not speaking about the kind of suffering, such as illness or disease, that can befall anyone. There is nothing inherently Christian in bearing that kind of suffering, although Christians will certainly relate such suffering to that of Christ and derive comfort from that. Nor is Jesus talking about accepting suffering that comes from abuse or injustice. That kind of suffering he always tried to confront and do away with, urging us to do the same.

A second aspect that is extremely important is to recognize that when Jesus speaks to his disciples about taking up the cross, he is talking to people who have freedom of choice. He is not talking to people who have suffering imposed on them. Rather, they have the power to choose whether or not to follow him and thus to expose themselves to the potential negative consequences for doing so. When women and other abused persons have suffering imposed on them, this is not properly "the cross."

As some of the women in Chiapas have recounted, this insight has brought about a dramatic shift in their understanding and praxis. Through reflection on the Bible in groups with other women, many have come to identify with Mary Magdalene and the other Galilean women disciples. They reasoned: If these women could find other ways to care for their traditional duties and leave their homes to preach the Gospel, then why not us? The cross, as they understand it now, is not submitting to verbal and physical abuse, but it is the hardship of walking for hours through the rough countryside to reach the women's meetings, or enduring slander and suspicion when they exercise their newfound ecclesial ministries.

Johannine Metaphors for Self-Surrender to Love

I want to turn our attention now to the Gospel of John, where we find several metaphors that offer alternatives to sacrifice and atonement. These have not been as fully mined for the liberating potential they could have for our preaching. As we explore these, I propose that because of all the pitfalls associated with the language and mentality of sacrifice, we consider using instead the expression of Elisabeth Moltmann-Wendel: "self-surrender to love." As she explains, in contrast to sacrifice, "self-surrender is an act of one's own free will; it is bound up with responsibility and love, and is interested in the preservation of life." [10] This expression emphasizes that an authentic love relationship always includes costly giving of self; but the emphasis is on the love, not on the cost, or the cross to be borne.

Friend Who Lays Down His Life for His Friends

One image that concretizes such a self-surrender to love in the Fourth Gospel is that of a friend who freely lays down his life for his friends out of love (15:13). This builds on what Jesus has said earlier, using the metaphor of a good shepherd, where he asserts that no one takes his life from him; he lays it down of his own accord (10:17-18). The theme of friend who lays down his life for his friends comes to a climactic moment in chapter 11, where Jesus receives the news that his friend Lazarus is ill. Three times (11:3, 5, 35), Jesus' love for Mary, Martha, and Lazarus is emphasized. When Jesus finally decides to go to them, his disciples protest that his opponents there had just tried to stone him (11:8). Thomas' wry remark, "Let us also go, that we may die with him" (11:16, NRSV) is literally true. In this gospel, it is Jesus' raising of his friend Lazarus that is the final straw that leads to his death (11:53).

Foot-washing

Another image that is offered in the Last Supper scene in the Gospel of John is that of foot-washing, where Jesus symbolically acts out his freely offered self-gift by washing the feet of his disciples and instructs them to do the same for one another (13:1-20). The foot-washing is not so much an act of humble service as it is an acted-out parable that interprets his passion.[11] The first verse of chapter 13 connects the foot-washing to the crucifixion. It opens: "Having loved his own who were in the world, he loved them to the end (*eis telos*)." The expression *eis telos* is ambiguous; it can be translated "completely" or "to the end." In the crucifixion scene, Jesus' final words are "it is ended," *tetelestai*, the verbal form of the same Greek word *telos*. The Fourth Evangelist had created a literal link between the foot-washing and the crucifixion, emphasizing the love that stands at the center of this self-surrender of his life for others.

Jesus explains the meaning of his action in the subsequent dialogue. He says he has given the disciples a model (*hypodeigma*) for them to do for one another as he has done for them (13:15). The Greek word *hypodeigma* is also used in 2 Maccabees 6:31 to speak of the death of Eleazar, who desired to leave an "example (*hypodeigma*) of nobility and a memorial of courage" to the young and to the nation by his willingness to go to his death rather than eat pork. Likewise, Jesus' model death (*hypdodeigma*) flows from a life that is devoted to bringing about "life to the full for all" (10:10), courageously confronting whatever inhibits that. Jesus then elaborates that the model he offers is that of servant (13:16; this is akin to Mark 10:45 and parallels in the Synoptic Tradition).

Service, not Servitude

The kind of service that Jesus models is that of friend to friend. As Sandra Schneiders has shown, there are three different models of service.[12] One is that of slave to master, or employee to employer. This kind of service is obligatory, and there is a difference in the status and power of the two. A second model is that of parent to child, or doctor to patient. This kind of service may be more altruistic, but there is still an inequity in status and power, and a certain level of obligation. Schneiders proposes that neither of these models is the type of which Jesus is speaking. Rather, Jesus exemplifies a model of service based on friendship, where any inequities in status are superseded and any act of self-gift evokes the same on the part of the recipient. Such service, as it is extended outward, creates communities of friends willing to go to calamities' depths for one another. Further on in the Final Discourse, Jesus tells his disciples that they are not called servants, but friends of Jesus and of one another (John 15:15).

One caution for preachers is that whenever we are speaking about service, it is very important that those who hear are interpreting from the stance of empowered persons who are able to choose freely to serve. To those who are in a position of servitude, who are bound by others' expectations or unjust systems, a preacher who speaks about service must be very careful not to give divine approbation to unjust situations and systems.

The images we use in our preaching and the interpretations of Scripture that we promote have tremendous consequences, as illustrated by the following true story. This happened in a rural village in Chiapas to a woman whose husband would frequently beat her after becoming drunk. She had become involved with a women's Bible study group, a movement initiated by Don Samuel Ruiz, bishop of San Cristóbal de las Casas (1960–2000) in collaboration with the women religious of the diocese. The women had begun to learn how to read the Scriptures *con ojos, mente, y corazón de mujer*, with the eyes, mind, and heart of a woman. They were learning how to look from another perspective and were asking questions that challenged the patriarchal underpinnings of their faith and the patterns of their daily lives. The woman who told the story had been attending a Bible study meeting, and when she returned home, her husband was drunk and enraged that she was not there to serve him his coffee when he wanted it. He beat her badly, as he had many times before. The next morning, when her friends saw her bruised face and battered body, they decided to act. Realizing that they themselves could suffer repercussions for their actions, they nonetheless knew it was a moment when they had to lay down their lives for their friend. Some thirty women came together to the house to confront the husband. They informed him that if he ever struck his wife again, it would be he who would have the battered face and the bruised body. These women had moved away from emulating the silent suffering Jesus of Mark and had become a community of friends, as imaged in John, who were ready to lay down their lives for their friend. In this particular instance, the result was a happy one, as the husband was so shocked by their intervention that he got the help he needed to stop drinking and cease beating his wife.[13]

Other Johannine Metaphors

The metaphor of friends who serve and who are willing to lay down their lives for one another is only one of many powerful and freeing metaphors in the Fourth Gospel. Others include the uplifting of the bronze serpent (3:15-16), the giving of Jesus' flesh for the life of the world (6:51), the outpouring of water at Tabernacles (7:38-39), and the seed that must die before it can bring forth fruit (12:24). One other that is quite prominent and offers liberative possibilities is that of Jesus' death as a birthing of new life.

Death as Birthing New Life

When we look at the crucifixion scene in the Fourth Gospel, we note that one of the unique features is that immediately after Jesus' death, a soldier pierces his side, from which blood and water flow forth (19:34). As the same liquids that accompany the birthing process, the symbols of blood and water help interpret Jesus' death as the birthing of new life. This scene brings to a climax a theme that weaves throughout the whole gospel. The presence of Jesus' mother at the foot of the cross (19:25-27), a detail unique to the Fourth Gospel, also brings out the symbolism. The one who gave him physical birth is a witness to the new life that is birthed in the community of Jesus' beloved disciples. With the scene at Cana (2:1-11), the only other place where Jesus' mother appears, an *inclusio* is formed that helps to draw out the meaning. There are a number of verbal and thematic links: in both scenes Jesus addresses his mother as "woman" (2:4; 19:26), there is reference to "the hour" (2:4; 19:27), and to belief (2:11; 19:35), and in both water plays an important symbolic role. It is at Cana that Jesus' mother helps to birth Jesus' public ministry, as she recognizes the proper timing of the hour (2:4), just as Jesus knows at the Last Supper, like a woman in labor, that his hour has come (13:1; 16:21).

The theme of birthing is sounded already in the Prologue, where it is said that "all things came into being (*egeneto*) through him (referring to the *logos*, "word"). The primary meaning of the Greek verb *ginomai* is "to come into being through process of birth or natural production, be born, be produced."[14] Thus, it would be possible to render John 1:3 as "all things *were birthed* through him." Further on, vv. 12–13 state, "But to all who received him, who believed in his name, he gave power to become (*genesthai*) children of God, who were born (*egennēthēsan*), not of blood or of the will of the flesh or of the will of man, but of God." The verb, *gennaō*, refers more often to female birthing than to male begetting (as is clearly indicated in John 3:4 and 16:21). The Prologue casts disciple-ship as an acceptance of one's birth as a child of God, and empowerment to engender life in others through faith in the *Logos*.

In Jesus' conversation with Nicodemus in chapter 3, there are seven instances of the verb *gennaō*, "to be born." Jesus tells Nicodemus that "no one can enter the kingdom of God without being born of water and Spirit" (3:5, NRSV). The symbols of water and the spirit link this episode with the crucifixion scene, where the meaning of birth in water and Spirit comes clearer. At Jesus' death, he hands over the Spirit (19:30),[15] as water flows from his pierced side (19:34). Just as in Ezekiel 36:25-27, where the prophet proclaims, "I will sprinkle clean water upon you . . . and a new spirit I will put within you," the symbols of water and spirit signal a rebirth accomplished by divine action.[16]

The symbol of water is central to the next chapter as well, where Jesus offers the woman from Samaria "living water" (4:10), and elaborates, "those who drink of the water I give them will never be thirsty. The water that I will give will become in them a spring of water gushing up to eternal life" (4:14, NRSV). The meaning of "living water" is further de-veloped in the scene during the Feast of Dedication, when Jesus exclaims, "Let anyone who is thirsty come to me, and let the one who believes in me drink. As the scripture has said, 'Out of the believer's heart (*koilia*) shall flow rivers of living water.' Now he said this about the Spirit, which believers in him were to receive; for as yet there was no Spirit, because Jesus was not yet glorified" (7:37-39). In v. 38 the word *koilia*, often trans-lated as "heart,"[17] is actually the word for "womb, uterus,"[18] once again evoking a birthing image, and pointing ahead to the water that flows from the pierced side of Jesus in 19:34.

The referent of the possessive pronoun in 7:38 is ambiguous: it can refer either to the womb of Jesus or to that of the believer. When read in light of 19:34, both referents can be understood to be in view. The life-giving mission birthed by Jesus is carried forward by believers, who are not mere receptacles for living water, but are themselves conduits of it.[19]

The use of the metaphor of birthing is most explicit in the Farewell Discourse where Jesus speaks to his disciples about his impending pas-sion, "Very truly, I tell you, you will weep and mourn, but the world will rejoice; you will have pain, but your pain will turn into joy. When a woman is in labor, she has pain, because her hour has come. But when her child is born, she no longer remembers the anguish because of the joy of having brought a human being into the world. So you have pain now; but I will see you again, and your hearts will rejoice, and no one can take your joy from you" (16:20-22, NRSV). This image evokes that of God, who is described by Isaiah, as laboring to rebirth Israel after the exile: "For a long time I have held my peace, I have kept still and restrained myself; now I will cry out like a woman in labor, I will gasp and pant" (Isa 42:14, NRSV).[20] Presenting Jesus' death as birthpangs, the Fourth Evangelist places the focus on the ensuing joy at the new life that will result; the suffering is not an end in itself, nor is it given atoning significance.

Returning to John 19:34, we can envision the women at the foot of the cross, including Jesus' mother, as midwives who aid in the birthing of the renewed community. Jesus' final declaration, "It is finished" (19:30, NRSV), can be heard as the proclamation of a mother who cries out in joy when the birthpangs are over and her child is born. When the body is taken down from the cross (19:40), it is wrapped in linen cloths, evocative of the image of swaddling a newborn (as in Luke 2:7). And when the risen Christ appears to his disciples and breathes on them, saying "receive the holy Spirit" (20:22), it is like the birth of the first human being, when the Creator breathed into its nostrils the breath of life (Gen 2:7). Finally, the image of the open tomb can symbolize the open womb from which the new life has emerged.

A Long Tradition

It is not only modern feminists who see this birthing imagery in the Gospel of John.[21] As early as the turn of the third century, Clement of Alexandria (153–217) wrote about "the body of Christ, which nourishes by the Word the young brood, which the Lord Himself brought forth in throes of flesh, which the Lord Himself swathed in his precious blood," exclaiming, "O amazing birth!" (*The Instructor* 1.6).[22] Similarly, Ambrose, bishop of Milan (d. 397), refers to Christ as the "Virgin who bare us, Who fed us with her own milk" (*On Virgins* 1:5).[23] Julian of Norwich (mid-fourteenth century) says that Jesus "our savior is our true Mother in whom we are endlessly born and out of whom—we shall come."[24] German Dominican mystic and scholar Meister Eckhart (1260–1328) mused, "What does God do all day long?" His answer was, "God lies on a maternity bed giving birth all day long."

Liberating Possibilities

Preaching about Jesus' death as the portal to new life and of costly self-surrender to love holds many possibilities for ways to engender life in the Christian community and avoid some of the deadly pitfalls inherent in sacrificial language and metaphors. To do so necessitates allowing our imaginations to be freed from some of the constraints of other traditional formulations and of gender stereotypes. Mining some of the overlooked metaphors in the Fourth Gospel, we have fresh images that valorize the female experience and open the way for female disciples to identify more fully with Christ, the Creator, and the Spirit as gender boundaries are blurred and transcended. As all three members of the Trinity are spoken of in birthing terms, a helpful insight is that it is not one single member that is the "female face" of God; the whole of the divine being and divine activity is expressed in female form and action. Preaching from this perspective can lead to a transformed reality. Guatemalan Nobel Prize winner Julia Esquivel articulates what will be the effect when women and men are both equally recognized as the image and likeness of God: there will be "equality in difference, flourishing in a creative, fruitful harmony, in the couple and in the relationships of all peoples and societies."[25]

The metaphor of birthing new life also has its pitfalls. Not all children are conceived by an act of love and not all birthpangs give way to joy. And it is particularly easy for those of us who have never actually given birth to romanticize it. Nonetheless, preaching about the cross as a birth to new life gives value to suffering as part of a natural process, but not as deserved or desirable. Suffering is seen as the consequence of a choice to entrust oneself to love. This metaphor enables us to understand Jesus' self-gift as similar to that of lovers who choose to make painful sacrifices out of love for the other, able to be endured because of that love and because of the new life that will result. Unlike the kinds of economic transactions between God and humanity that are implied in sacrificial and ransom metaphors, the birthing image evokes an exchange of love that is mutual and self-replicating.

A Story of Hope

Most important is that when Christians tell the terrible story of the death of Jesus we do so from a resurrection faith that takes us beyond the terror into new life, hope, and joy—which we taste even now! When our preaching about the execution of Jesus functions to take crucified peoples[26] of today down from their crosses, rather than drive the nails in deeper, then we are living in resurrection faith. As Julia Esquivel says, we live "threatened with Resurrection!" She describes the paradoxes of our Christian life:

> "To dream awake,
> to keep watch asleep,
> to live while dying
> and to already know oneself
> resurrected!"[27]

Endnotes

1. The content of this presentation is taken from my book, *Taking Up the Cross: New Testament Interpretations Through Latina and Feminist Eyes* (Minneapolis: Fortress Press, 2007) and my essay "Birthed from the Side of Jesus (John 19:34)" in *Finding a Woman's Place: Essays in Honor of Carolyn Osiek*, eds. David L. Balch and Jason T. Lamoreaux (Eugene, OR: Pickwick Publications, 2011), 191–214. Used by permission of Wipf and Stock Publishers. www.wipfandstock.com.

2. Fortress Press, 2007.

3. Elizabeth A. Johnson, "Jesus and Salvation," in *CTSA Proceedings*, ed. Paul Crowley (Santa Clara: CTSA, 1994), 49:5.

4. CODIMUJ, *Con Mirada, Mente y Corazón de Mujer* (México, 1999), 17–22.

5. See Stephen Finlan, *Problems with Atonement. The Origins of, and Controversy About, the Atonement Doctrine* (Collegeville, MN: Liturgical Press, 2005), 66, 79.

6. Carol Delaney, *Abraham on Trial. The Social Legacy of Biblical Myth* (Princeton: Princeton University Press, 1998), 5. See also Jon D. Levenson, *The Death of the Beloved Son. Transformation of Child Sacrifice in Judaism and Christianity* (New Haven, CT: Yale University Press, 1993); Barbara Miller, *Tell it on the Mountain. The Daughter of Jephthah in Judges 11* (Collegeville, MN: Liturgical Press, 2005).

7. Joyce E. Salisbury, *The Blood of the Martyrs. Unintended Consequences of Ancient Violence* (New York: Routledge, 2004), 148.

8. See René Girard, *The Scapegoat*, trans. by Yvonne Freccero (Baltimore: Johns Hopkins University Press, 1989); and René Girard, *Sacrifice*, trans. by Matthew Pattillo and David Dawson (East Lansing: Michigan State University Press, 2011). See Reid, *Taking Up the Cross*, 34, for a critique of Girard's theory.

9. See further Reid, *Taking Up the Cross*, 40–42.

10. Elisabeth Moltmann-Wendel, *Rediscovering Friendship. Awakening to the Promise and Power of Women's Friendships* (Minneapolis: Fortress Press, 2000), 43.

11. Sandra M. Schneiders, "The Footwashing (John 13:1-20): An Experiment in Hermeneutics." *CBQ* 43 (1981), 76–92; also in *Written That You May Believe. Encountering Jesus in the Fourth Gospel*. Rev. ed. (New York: Crossroad, 2003).

12. Ibid.

13. CODIMUJ, *Con Mirada, Mente, y Corazón de Mujer,* 134.

14. Frederick W. Danker, ed. *A Greek–English Lexicon of the New Testament and Other Early Christian Literature,* 3rd ed. (Chicago: University of Chicago Press, 2000), 196–99.

15. See Schneiders, *Written That You May Believe,* 179, and James Swetnam, "Bestowal of the Spirit in the Fourth Gospel," *Bib* 74 (1993) 556–76, for reasons why the expression *paredōken to pneuma,* "he handed over the Spirit," (19:30) should be understood as the giving of the Spirit rather than a euphemism for death.

16. Schneiders, *Written That You May Believe,* 121.

17. So NRSV, NJB. The NAB renders it "from within"; KJV as "out of his belly."

18. This is clearly the meaning in John 3:4, where Nicodemus puzzles over how a person can "enter a second time into the mother's womb and be born." So also Luke 1:41, 44; 2:21; 11:27; 23:29. *Koilia* can also mean "belly, stomach" as in Matt 15:17; Mark 7:19; Luke 15:16; 1 Cor 6:13; Rev 10:9. It can also be understood as the seat of inward life, of feelings and desires, thus the rendering of it in English as "heart." See Danker, *Lexicon,* 550.

19. Stephen D. Moore, "Are There Impurities in the Living Water That the Johannine Jesus Dispenses?," in *A Feminist Companion to John. Vol. 1,* ed. Amy-Jill Levine with Marianne Blickenstaff (FCNT 4; New York: Sheffield Academic Press, 2003), 78–97, here 87.

20. See Deut 32:18; Isa 42:14; 49:16; 66:9, 12-13; Pss 22:10-11; 131:2; Job 38:29 for other maternal images of God.

21. The following references and quotations are taken from Josephine Massyngbaerde Ford, *Redeemer, Friend, and Mother. Salvation in Antiquity and in the Gospel of John* (Minneapolis: Fortress Press, 1997), 196–97.

22. For an English translation of the text, see http://www.ccel.org/ccel/schaff/anf02.vi.iii.i.vi.html. Accessed June 6, 2010.

23. For the English translation of the text, see: http://www.ccel.org/ccel/schaff/npnf210.iv.vii.ii.v.html. Accessed June 6, 2010.

24. Julian of Norwich, *Showings* (New York: Paulist, 1978), 292.

25. Julia Esquivel, "Conquered and Violated Women," in *The Power of Naming. A Concilium Reader in Feminist Liberation Theology* (ed. Elisabeth Schüssler Fiorenza; Concilium; Maryknoll: Orbis, 1996), 105–14, here 113.

26. This expression is from Ignacio Ellacuría and Jon Sobrino, "The Crucified People," in *Mysterium Liberationis: Fundamental Concepts of Liberation Theology* (Maryknoll: Orbis, 1993), 580–603.

27. Julia Esquivel, *Threatened with Resurrection. Prayers and Poems from an Exiled Guatemalan* (Elgin, IL: The Brethren Press, 1982), 63.

Chapter 8

The Challenge of *Fulfilled in Your Hearing* to Interpret Life in the Light of the Word

Theresa Rickard, OP

Interpreting life in the light of the word of God is the explicit challenge to preachers in the 1982 U.S. bishops' document, *Fulfilled in Your Hearing: The Homily in the Sunday Assembly*. Responding to our changing pastoral context, the U.S. bishops have published a more recent document, *Preaching the Mystery of Faith: The Sunday Homily* (2012). As noted by the bishops, this document builds on *Fulfilled in Your Hearing* while reflecting anew on the ministry of preaching. *Preaching the Mystery of Faith*, too, encourages preachers to connect the Sunday homily with people's daily lives, stating, "The homily is intended to establish a dialogue between the sacred biblical text and the Christian life of the hearer."

In this essay, I will focus on *Fulfilled in Your Hearing* and its emphasis on inspiring people to connect faith with their daily lives. I will explore preaching as interpreting life through the word of God by reflecting on each of the four sections of the document: the assembly, the preacher, the homily, and the homiletic method. *Fulfilled in Your Hearing* focuses on preaching in the Sunday assembly, the homily, the source and summit of the Catholic preaching experience. However, this document is also a great benefit to laypeople who are authorized to preach in churches and oratories, and, in fact, to all who proclaim God's word in the many and varied ministries of the church. Therefore, when I speak of preaching or the preaching event, I am referring to the homily, which is reserved to the priest and deacon, but also to all the other ways the word of God is proclaimed by religious women and men and by lay preachers in the Christian community.

The vision for the preaching event that finds its impulse in the documents of the Second Vatican Council and thereafter in *Fulfilled in Your Hearing* is that the homily is to be scriptural and liturgical and is to be connected to the lived reality of the congregation. The 1982 document clarifies this by stating that "the preacher does not so much attempt to explain the Scriptures as to interpret the human situation through the Scriptures."

In my work in parish ministry, and most recently at RENEW International, I have experienced a people's great hunger for a word of life in their current circumstances. They are seeking an encounter with the living God. We, as ministers of the word of God, are challenged to help the community discover the biblical God who is presented as taking walks in the Garden of Eden with the first human beings, conversing with the prophets, sending Jesus Christ as God's unique Word among us, and sending forth the Holy Spirit who continues to speak God's word today. Bishop Arthur Serratelli, on the fortieth anniversary of the Second Vatican Council's document on revelation, *Dei Verbum*, wrote, "At the heart of the mystery of the Trinity is relationship, total self-giving: the emptying of that one person into the other. Preaching such a truth becomes more effective when that truth is realized in our lifestyle."[1] This relational God whom we preach wants to be known by us and continues to invite us from silence into conversation, from estrangement into communion, from self-preoccupation into solidarity with our suffering world. Pope Benedict XVI, in *Deus Caritas Est*, reflects on the God who is ever present and always seeking to be in relationship:

> God is visible in a number of ways. In the love-story recounted by the Bible, he comes towards us, he seeks to win our hearts, all the way to the Last Supper, to the piercing of his heart on the Cross, to his appearances after the Resurrection and to the great deeds by which, through the activity of the Apostles, he guided the nascent Church along its path. Nor has the Lord been absent from subsequent Church history: he encounters us ever anew, in men and women who reflect his presence, in his word, in the sacraments, and especially in the Eucharist. (*Deus Caritas Est* 17)

The Assembly

Fulfilled in Your Hearing begins its exploration of preaching in the Sunday assembly with a groundbreaking shift. The document states that the preparation for the Sunday homily has to begin with the "assembly rather than with the preacher or the homily" (FIYH 4). We not only preach out of the context of our communities, but we actually discover God's saving grace in their midst. This makes the role of the community crucial to both preaching and the preaching process.

This shift was influenced by the Vatican II understanding of the church as the people of God and reaffirmation that the Holy Spirit is always active and alive in the gathering of believers. There are two main reasons why the authors of this document on preaching deliberately chose the assembly as their starting point. First, it is essential for preachers to have an accurate understanding of the people they are speaking to so that "good news" can be communicated effectively. Unless a preacher knows what a congregation needs, wants, or is able to hear, the message in the homily may not meet the needs of the people who hear it. Second, contemporary ecclesiology provides us with an even more fundamental reason why the committee chose the assembly as the starting point rather than the preacher or the homily itself. The church assembly is the visible sacrament of the saving unity to which God calls all people. "Established by Christ as a fellowship of life, charity and truth, the church is used by Him as an instrument for the redemption of all, and is sent forth into the whole world as the light of the world and the salt of the earth" (FIYH 4, citing *Lumen Gentium* 9). The people are the church, and the church is the people.

Also, in the section focused on the identity of the church assembly, the Committee on Priestly Life and Ministry highlighted cultural, social, and economic diversity, but they also emphasized that diversity should not blind the homilist to an even greater reality: the unity of the congregation. Members of a church assembly come together because they have been baptized into the one Body of Christ and share, at Eucharist, their common faith in Jesus Christ.

The committee's point about understanding the assembly came early to me. I was working in a parish in the South Bronx, mostly among Latinos. I was teaching a confirmation class, and there before me were about thirty teenagers, most of them slumped in their chairs. You could have been Jesus Christ or Mary, the Mother of God, and they might not have given you a second look. I was speaking about the Trinity and starting to introduce God as a loving Father. One of the kids sat up straight and raised his hand. He said, "Sister, if God is like my father, I don't want anything to do with him." Then they all began to talk about their experiences with their fathers, and it was probably the best theological reflection I ever had with a group of seventh and eighth graders. And then I said to them—it must have been the Holy Spirit—"Who in your life reflects a God who is loving and caring?" And they said almost in unison, "*Mi abuela,*" my grandmother. So we began to explore together God as *Abuela* and how that image could help them understand God better. It was a great revelation that images and experiences that are meaningful for me are not always helpful to the community I am addressing. In order to share God's word more effectively, it is very important to use metaphors and images that come from the concrete community for whom we have the privilege to share God's word. This means a conscious and disciplined effort to immerse ourselves in the community: its culture, language, economic situation, and everyday concerns.

The new emphasis on the assembly as the starting point in the preaching event has called forth a new understanding of the preacher and his or her role. The preacher now becomes first and foremost a "mediator of meaning" instead of an expert who transmits doctrine, piety, or ethics.

The Preacher

Pope Paul VI summed up the renewed role of the preacher in his landmark 1975 document *On Evangelization in the Modern World*: people listen more to witnesses than to teachers, and if they listen to teachers, it is because those teachers are witnesses (*Evangelii Nuntiandi*, 41). This is confirmed by a survey that asked what believers were looking for in their preachers. When the results were in, the answer was clear. The majority wanted a person of faith speaking about faith. Therefore, a preacher is a person of faith speaking to people about faith and life (FIYH 39). The role of the preacher as a person who witnesses to his or her encounter with the living God is particularly meaningful in light of the clarion call by the church to a "new evangelization"—to create a culture of witness, women and men who are joyful witnesses to Christ.

The post–Vatican II preacher has shifted from a person who instructs and admonishes to a witness who inspires and exhorts believers to a deeper faith in Christ, to a richer understanding of the mysteries of our faith, and to daily lives that testify to the Gospel. According to *Fulfilled in Your Hearing*, the preacher is a "mediator of meaning," one who stands in the midst of the liturgical assembly "representing both the community and the Lord," occupying a place between the God revealed in Christ and the community gathered in Christ's name, between the word of God spoken in the past and the word of God being spoken now in the world, especially in the lives of the assembly (FIYH 7). By "making connections between the real lives of people who believe in Jesus but are not always sure what difference faith can make in their lives and the God who calls us into ever deeper communion" with God and with one another (FIYH 8), the preacher fulfills his office of offering a word of meaning to those who hear.

In reflecting on the preacher as mediator of meaning it is important to add that the preacher is not the sole mediator. Communication theory holds that the hearer is also a mediator of meaning. In *Preaching in the Sunday Assembly: A Pastoral Commentary on* Fulfilled in Your Hearing we are reminded:

> This designation [mediator of meaning] could imply that the preacher alone is able to mediate meaning, suggesting the community is relegated to a passive role . . .
>
> The ability of preachers to mediate meaning for a faith community is contingent not only on their being dedicated servants and listeners for how God is speaking through all the means already mentioned (Scripture, Tradition, and the teaching of the magisterium) but also of giving equal attentiveness to listening to how others are also hearing God speak to them. A preacher can only offer—not impose— a word of meaning for the gathered assembly, ideally a message arrived at through collaboration with others, both colleagues in the preaching task and other members of the believing community, especially those participating in the preaching process, as *FIYH* suggested.[2]

Fulfilled in Your Hearing clearly states that in order to make connections between the lives of the people and the Gospel, the preacher has to be a listener before being a speaker. "Listening is not an isolated moment. It is a way of life. It means openness to the Lord's voice not only in the Scriptures but in the events of our daily lives and in the experience of

our brothers and sisters. It is not just *my* listening but *our* listening together for the Lord's word to the community" (FIYH 10). Jeffrey Bullock,
a communication scholar and preacher, uses the image of a "cupped
ear," as opposed to an open mouth, to describe the role of the preacher:

> There is a charcoal drawing framed in rustic wood hanging on the
> wall of a professor's study. It is a large creation, approximately
> eleven inches wide by seventeen inches in height. The charcoal
> image is a little blurry. The image's borders are unclear, and some-
> times even seem to run together. After a time of gazing, however,
> the image becomes more clear. The image is a portrait of a religious
> figure who is probably a rabbi. His beard is long and it flows into
> his robe. He is sitting down, as rabbis do when they teach, but rather
> than an open mouth, the rabbi has one of his hands cupped behind
> his ear. The first move in the rabbi's lesson is a cupped ear rather
> than an open mouth, is to listen rather than to speak.[3]

The preacher then is to put his or her "cupped ear" to the sacred ground
where the community walks and lives out their faith. The preacher
strains to overhear the conversations between God and the community's
fragile human hearts. It is then that the preacher "names the grace" or,
better yet, animates the conversation in such a way that the community
names the grace that the preacher will proclaim from the pulpit.

The preacher mediates God's continuing word to the world, giving
voice to the word in a way in which hearers can "recognize their own
concerns and God's concern for them" (FIYH 8). The Pontifical Biblical
Commission in the 1993 document *Interpretation of the Bible in the Church*
states, "The ministers of the Word have as their principal task, not simply
to impart instruction but also to assist the faithful to understand and
discern what the word is saying to them in their hearts when they hear
and reflect on the Scripture" (III.B.3). However, the preacher's work as
animator and mediator is not complete until that word reaches its fullest
potential: the generating of personal and communal Christian witness
in the world.

The preacher gathers with the community in informal and formal
settings to listen to their experiences of the Word in the context of life,
to animate and mediate an ongoing faith conversation, and to move that
conversation toward Gospel action so that the Word that emerges is truly
dabar yhwh—a Word that is occasion-specific and yearns to do something
in and for the world.

The Homily

The understanding of the preaching event in the context of the Sunday Eucharist, which we now call the "homily," as connecting faith with life has changed dramatically since Vatican II. Whereas previously Sunday preaching was understood to be a "sermon," an exposition of dogmatic teaching and doctrine, the Second Vatican Council spoke specifically of the "homily" in terms of its grounding in Sacred Scripture. *Dei Verbum* reminds us that "all the preaching should be nourished and regulated by Sacred Scripture" (DV 21). The homily is to help people find themselves in the scriptural stories. In addition to the emphasis in *Fulfilled in Your Hearing* on scriptural interpretation in the homily, it is essential to include interpretation of the liturgy itself. In *Preaching in the Sunday Assembly, A Pastoral Commentary on Fulfilled in Your Hearing* this omission is noted and corrected: "It is in the interplay and interpretation of scriptural texts and liturgical texts, actions, and objects, however, that we discover a lens through which to view human existence. This lens is not confined to the perspective provided by the Scriptures but arises out of the interaction between the biblical and liturgical components" (Wallace, 31-32). Also, this does not mean there is not a catechetical facet to homiletic preaching. *Preaching the Mysteries of Faith* explains,

> A good homilist, for example, is able to articulate the mystery of the Incarnation—that the eternal Son of God came to dwell among us as man—in such a manner that his listeners are able to understand more deeply the beauty and truth of this mystery and to see its connections with daily life. . . . And by expanding the congregation's love for the humanity of Jesus, the homilist could also move his fellow Christians to a deeper sense of justice, with a sense of compassion for the most vulnerable and the poor and of the broken humanity of their neighbor. (31–32)

The homily, like the liturgy, is first and foremost an event. As the documents illustrate, the homily is not to be understood as a static teaching moment but a living word that moves hearers to connect the scriptural and liturgical texts with their everyday lives and moves them to Gospel action. The Second Vatican Council's linking of faith and justice encouraged homilies that reflect on both the biblical tradition of justice and the social teachings of the church and that impel people to charitable works and just acts.

The *Constitution on the Sacred Liturgy* is foundational for understanding that the homily not only takes place in the liturgy but also is actually itself a liturgical act and "forms part of the liturgy" (SC 62). The documents of Vatican II recognized the homily as the source and summit of the Liturgy of the Word. The council went even further to include the homily in the other sacraments. The homily now is integral to the encounter with Christ in the sacraments.

Homiletic Method

In order for the homily to touch into the real lives of people, the methods of bringing the homily to birth and into homiletic form needed to be transformed and expanded. The shift in the theological and pastoral understanding of the assembly, preacher, and homily called for new methods of homily preparation and homiletic form. Adoption of an inductive method of narrative preaching that is hearer-centered and experiential has been a welcome change for Catholics who yearn for meaning in their daily lives. *Fulfilled in Your Hearing* calls the preacher to use practical examples, stories, and rich metaphors and images to communicate God's word more effectively. In addition, preachers need to know and assimilate the way today's hearers talk, listen, and learn, especially in a world inundated with new media. The document encourages preachers to communicate the Gospel "in language and images that are familiar to the dwellers of the particular avenue we are traveling" (FIYH 14). The Second Vatican Council confirmed, with respect to preaching, that "the word of God, ought not to be explained in a general and abstract way, but by applying the lasting truth of the Gospel to particular circumstances of life."[4]

The shift from "sermon" to "homily" has inspired new methods of preparation that involve a process of praying with the readings over a period of days. The preacher is urged to prayerfully consider the gospel passage throughout the week, to see the connections between Scripture, liturgy, and life in order to form a spirit-filled message that is contextual and meaningful to a particular gathering of believers. This goal can be achieved by gathering images, examples, and stories for our preaching and by being alert to what we see and hear every day in our ministries, our travels, our recreation, the arts, new and popular media, culture, our reading, our conversations. These links to life are assisted by serious study—that is, by using scriptural and theological resources that expand our understanding of the sacred texts.

Lectio divina, a prayerful reading of the Scriptures, an initial questioning of the text, and a relating of the text to our human experience is an effective practice to assist preachers in both their prayer lives and their preaching. This practice can help us open ourselves to what God is saying to us and our community beyond historical or other critical interpretations.[5]

Technology has had an impact on every aspect of life in the twenty-first century. The preacher must remain open to the use of technology in the preparation and delivery of a homily. The Internet opens up a world of information to enhance homiletic content. Good microphones and sound systems, hearing devices, and sign language can assist people in hearing and understanding the homily. The use of PowerPoint and other forms of media can enhance the delivery of the message.

Fulfilled in Your Hearing points out that preachers need feedback in order to evaluate the effectiveness of their homilies. At RENEW International, we use an online tool called Survey Monkey to gather feedback from participants of our small-community processes. It's easy to use, and people respond to it. You know that if you were asked immediately after a presentation to fill out a written evaluation, you would groan, but if you could respond from your laptop or smart phone, you would be more likely to do it. Any form of evaluation should include the message people heard and ask if it touched into their lives and, if so, how. I know a priest who gives out a card every couple of months and asks that it be returned in the offertory basket: "What was the message you heard?" "How does it connect with your life today?"

The purpose of following a homiletic process, gaining feedback, and immersing ourselves in the Word and the lives of the community is to assist us in more effectively witnessing to our faith in Jesus, the power and compassion of God, in a form that will inspire the assembly to be better hearers and doers of the word of God for the sake of the world.

Conclusion

For the ministry of preaching to be effective—whether in the context of the Sunday assembly, in a church or oratory, in a retreat setting, at the bedside of the dying, or in a small faith community—it needs to possess an event-full character. Most hearers are not engaged by a didactic exposition of the Word but rather by a proclamation that evokes a faith response. People are seeking a word that not only instructs or informs but also inspires and transforms. The task of the word of God is not complete until it moves from touching listening ears to transforming open hearts, finding its purpose in Christian witness in the world.

We are sent from the Liturgy of the Eucharist to the liturgy of the world. The heart of the Eucharist is missiological, reminding us through word and sign that the household of God is not meant to stay in the house. The Gospel we hear and proclaim week after week is God's good news about the redemption of the world, in which we are invited to take part. Every Mass exhorts us to "Go" and be Christ's healing and forgiving presence in our communities. We are gathered and sent to go forth; to go in peace, glorifying the Lord by our transformed lives; to go and announce the Gospel, the good news of Jesus' saving love for the world.

Endnotes

1. Arthur Serratelli, "Reflections on Revelation: *Dei Verbum*'s 40th Anniversary," *Origins* 35:8 (July 7, 2005), 118–121.

2. Donald Heet, Theresa Rickard, and James A. Wallace, "The Preacher," in *Preaching in the Sunday Assembly: A Pastoral Commentary on* Fulfilled in Your Hearing, ed. James A. Wallace (Collegeville, MN: Liturgical Press, 2010), 18–19.

3. Jeffrey Bullock, *Preaching with a Cupped Ear* (New York: Peter Lang, 1999), 1.

4. *Presbyterorum Ordinis: The Decree on the Ministry and Life of Priests,* 4.

5. See Fr. Ed Griswold's article, "*Lectio Divina* and Homily Preparation," in John E. Sassani, *Renewing the Priestly Heart* (RENEW International, 2011).

Chapter 9

"This Intimate Link"—The Ecumenical Contribution of *Fulfilled in Your Hearing*[1]

Bishop Craig A. Satterlee

All preaching is contextual in at least three ways. First, faithfully interpreting Scripture requires that we understand its context. Second, anyone who spends time standing in a pulpit or listening to sermons would agree with Fred Craddock that the preacher "works within an unusual network of trust and intimacy that makes the separation of character from performance impossible" so that "all preaching is to some extent self-disclosure by the preacher."[2] Third, again from Craddock, a sermon "is to be located as much among a particular group of listeners as with a particular speaker."[3] Consequently, we preachers exegete the Scripture's context, pastorally assess the assembly's context, and do our best to self-differentiate so that we are aware of our personal context. Yet, preachers miss an essential ingredient in preaching if we stop there.

In 1982 the National Conference of Catholic Bishops published *Fulfilled in Your Hearing*, a reflection on the meaning of the homily in the Sunday Mass, which reminded the ecumenical church of the sermon's most immediate and accessible context, the context that preacher and assembly share: the liturgy in which the sermon is preached. Though seminal studies of the history of preaching, including that of Yngve Brilioth, identify the liturgical component of preaching as one of three important elements that "establish Jesus' sermon in the synagogue at Nazareth as the most important link in the golden chain which unites the Jewish proclamation and the Christian sermon and which creates a deep continuity in the history of biblical revelation,"[4] many Christian traditions have often overlooked, neglected, or taken the sermon's liturgical context for granted. In many Protestant textbooks on preaching, homiletics classes, and even worship services, the sermon is considered the main event for which everything else in the worship service is but window dressing. It is as if people imagine going to a church some Sunday where, instead of music, prayers, Scripture reading, and singing, the minister enters the worship space, goes directly to the pulpit, and begins preaching. When the sermon is finished, the service is over; there is nothing more.[5] Thus, Lutheran homiletician and liturgical scholar, Melinda Quivik, observes: "*Fulfilled in Your Hearing*'s gift to the ecumenical church is the integral tie it forged between the preaching and the liturgy itself. Too often, our language about preaching suggests that the sermon stands apart from everything else all on its own."[6]

Fulfilled in Your Hearing's ecumenical contribution of, in the language of the document itself, "this intimate link"[7] between preaching and liturgy is evident when we compare the documents concerning preaching of the Roman Catholic Church and the Evangelical Lutheran Church in America (ELCA). FIYH takes as its starting point the Second Vatican Council's *Constitution on the Sacred Liturgy* declaration, "The two parts, which in a certain sense, go to make up the Mass, namely the liturgy of the word and the Eucharistic liturgy, are so closely connected with each other that they form but one single act of worship."[8] In strikingly similar (and, perhaps, borrowed) language, the ELCA's *The Use of the Means of Grace: A Statement on the Practice of Word and Sacrament* asserts that "the two principal parts of the liturgy of Holy Communion, the proclamation of the Word of God and the celebration of the sacramental meal, are so intimately connected as to form one act of worship."[9]

In terms of pastoral practice, the Second Vatican Council asserted that "the homily . . . is to be highly esteemed as part of the liturgy itself; in fact, at those Masses which are celebrated with the assistance of the people on Sundays and feasts of obligation, it should not be omitted except for a serious reason."[10] ELCA Lutherans, who could boldly assert, "Only under extraordinary circumstances would the sermon be omitted from the Sunday and festival service of Holy Communion,"[11] encouraged congregations to hold Word and sacrament together by avoiding either a celebration of the Supper without the preceding reading of the Scriptures, preaching, and intercessory prayers or a celebration of the Supper for a few people who remain after the dismissal of the congregation from a Service of the Word. The Holy Communion is not simply appended to the offices of Morning or Evening Prayer.[12]

Reclaiming Lutheran confessional heritage, *The Use of the Means of Grace* asserts, "According to the *Apology of the Augsburg Confession*, Lutheran congregations celebrate the Holy Communion every Sunday and festival. This confession remains the norm for our practice."[13] This is but one instance of the caricature of Protestant worship revolving around Word and Roman Catholic worship centering on sacrament giving way to an ecumenical understanding of the Sunday worship of the Christian assembly as what the worship book of the United Methodist Church calls a "Service of Word and Table."[14]

As we mark the thirtieth anniversary of *Fulfilled in Your Hearing*, I want simply to name with appreciation some ways this wonderful document calls our attention to the sermon's liturgical context—"this intimate link" between preaching and liturgy, Word and sacrament—and helps the ecumenical church to consider a unique genre of sermon, the liturgical homily. In so doing, FIYH significantly contributes to an ecumenical conversation about preaching the Gospel and the way preaching is taught.

FIYH defines the liturgical homily as "a scriptural interpretation of human existence which enables a community to recognize God's active presence, to respond to that presence in faith through liturgical word and gesture, and beyond the liturgical assembly, through a life lived in conformity with the Gospel."[15] Implications about the role and place of hermeneutics in preaching, the purpose of the sermon or homily, and the way the assembly responds to the sermon all flow from this simple definition. Following the pattern of *Fulfilled in Your Hearing*, I have endeavored to tease out some of those implications using the document's own headings, "The Assembly," "The Preacher," "The Homily," and "Homiletic Method." Obviously, many of the topics, which I am only able to touch on, would themselves make for thoughtful ecumenical conversation.

The Assembly

In liturgical preaching, the liturgy gives the assembly its identity, its raison d'être, and its first opportunity to respond to the good news of the sermon in faith. Many preachers sincerely lament that knowing the people to whom they preach is difficult. Thus, *Fulfilled in Your Hearing* rightly observes, "The Eucharistic assembly that gathers Sunday after Sunday is a rich and complex phenomenon."[16] Preachers therefore spend considerable energy attempting to account for the assembly's richness and address the assembly's complexity in their sermons, because an accurate understanding of the audience is essential to effective communication. Yet, from the perspective of the liturgy, the assembly, while rich and complex, shares a unifying characteristic; the baptismal identity of the Christian assembly overshadows individual identity, authority, and status as the Spirit, through the liturgy, forms a gathering of individuals into an assembly of common identity and purpose.

Melinda Quivik describes the Spirit's work of forming the assembly as biblical. "That the entirety of the worship (responses, prayers, hymns) be based in biblical language was to gather the worshippers into an event whose center is the God-given plumb line of the holy book . . . To engage in worship that is formed with God's word at the heart is to be set within a context whose every fiber means to say the same thing: here in your midst is the Risen One for you."[17] *Fulfilled in Your Hearing* calls the homily "a unifying moment in the celebration of the liturgy, deepening and giving expression to the unity that is already present through the sacrament of baptism."[18] All are united in the Body of Christ. In an important way, each member of the assembly becomes anonymous in favor of all, the larger, encompassing identity within which one finds oneself.[19]

The assembly's baptismal identity determines the purpose of preaching. That the homily is addressed to a congregation of baptized believers who have gathered to worship indicates that the homily's purpose is not to bring about conversion from radical unbelief. The liturgical assembly is not primarily an educational assembly. It is not a rally or demonstration for a cause. Thus, *Fulfilled in Your Hearing* asserts, "the homily is preached in order that a community of believers who have gathered to celebrate the liturgy may do so more deeply and more fully—more faithfully—and thus be formed for Christian witness in the world."[20]

Paul Galbreath, professor of worship and preaching at Union Presbyterian Seminary in Richmond, Virginia, describes liturgical preaching's role as

> encouraging and supporting the assembly's active participation in the imaginative acts of connecting the liturgy with daily life. Rather than providing the congregation with prescriptive solutions or

required beliefs, liturgical preaching, in this sense, fosters an associative rendering of Word and Sacrament with the day-to-day lives of congregation members. This approach to preaching is suggestive in nature in the way that it opens up and offers interpretive options for linking Word, Sacrament, and World.[21]

Jennifer L. Lord, associate professor of homiletics and liturgical studies at Austin Presbyterian Theological Seminary, describes the task of liturgical preaching as helping the assembly "to be grasped by the sacraments, to be explored by them and to inhabit them."[22] For Professor Lord, liturgical preaching frees us to allow the sacraments, by the power of the Holy Spirit, to shape us for all the ways we need to be formed for each other and for the world.

Having united and formed the assembly to receive the sermon, the liturgy provides the assembly with the words, actions, and opportunity to respond to that message in faith. Thus, *Fulfilled in Your Hearing* directs that homilies end with a "Eucharistic attitude"—giving God thanks and praise. "The function of the Eucharistic homily is to enable people to lift up their hearts, to praise and thank the Lord for his presence in their lives."[23] The preacher's task, then, is to offer the community "a word in which they can recognize their own concerns and God's concern for them."[24]

The Preacher

Fulfilled in Your Hearing shapes preachers in four ways: (1) identifying preaching Christ crucified as our homiletic task; (2) naming preaching as the primary duty of pastoral ministers; (3) highlighting the essential role of prayer in the preacher's ministry; and (4) directing that empowering all the baptized to proclaim the Gospel is an essential part of the preacher's task.

First, FIYH says the preacher's task is to enable a community to recognize God's active presence.[25] The way we enable a community to recognize God's active presence in their lives and in the world is to preach Christ crucified. FIYH teaches that the liturgical homily "is characterized by 'proclamation of God's wonderful works in the history of salvation, that is, the mystery of Christ, which is ever made present and active within us, especially in the celebration of the liturgy.' "[26] Lutheran liturgical theologian Gordon W. Lathrop exhorts that *Fulfilled in Your*

Hearing calls the preacher to preach Christ crucified *in this assembly* rather than merely in a systematic, theoretical, or formulaic manner. Dr. Lathrop asserts that the liturgical homily answers the question *cur deus homo* for this assembly by clearly stating the reason for the atonement in the *Christus Victor* tradition and not in the Anselmian or Abelardian way.[27]

That we preach Christ crucified is not to be taken lightly or for granted. As I have written elsewhere:

> So many other issues, topics, agendas, and concerns want to be preached, or perhaps preachers and their hearers want sermons to be about so many things besides Christ crucified. Congregational concerns, social issues, global situations, and life's questions all need to be addressed in preaching, and they should be. Following Jesus' own example as a preacher, we learn that every issue is fair game for preaching; no topic is out of bounds. To say otherwise is to conclude that there are areas of life where Jesus has no place.
>
> The problem with addressing anything and everything from the pulpit comes when the way issues and topics are included and addressed in sermons is not appropriate to Christian preaching. Since we preach Christ crucified, the issue is what Jesus or God has to say. Every issue and topic that gets included in a sermon must be grounded in and related to the biblical story of God's work of reconciliation, particularly the life, death, and resurrection of Jesus Christ. I wholeheartedly agree with venerable preachers like Gardner C. Taylor, who I once heard remark that the gospel has not been preached until the gospel is connected to the issues and concerns of the people hearing the sermon. Some preachers, congregations, issues, and topics demand that the connection between sermon content and gospel proclamation be stronger and more explicit than others. When people cannot miss the relationship between even the most difficult or controversial issue or sensitive topic and the gospel, when the connection is inescapable, when they are convinced that God has something important to say, preachers and congregants may well feel uncomfortable, but most will listen as God speaks to and through them.[28]

Second, as a teacher of preaching, I am grateful that *Fulfilled in Your Hearing* provides needed direction for pastoral ministry.

> "The primary duty of priests is the proclamation of the Gospel to all." These clear, straightforward words of the Second Vatican Council (*Decree on the Life and Ministry of Priests* 4) . . . [make plain that]

the proclamation of the gospel is primary. The other duties of the priest are to be considered properly presbyteral to the degree they support the proclamation of the Gospel.[29]

I suspect many Protestant clergy yearn for such clarity. The demands of ministry, the often-conflicting expectations of parishioners, and their own sense of vocation find many pastors wondering whether they are chiefly administrators, evangelists, counselors, community organizers, theologians, chaplains, missionaries, change agents, or CEOs. FIYH helpfully changes the question from, "How am I supposed to do everything?" to "How does this—whatever *this* is—support the proclamation of the Gospel?"

Third, FIYH reminds preachers that proclaiming Christ crucified in this assembly requires that preachers be listeners before they are speakers, remaining open to the Lord's voice not only in the Scriptures but in the events of our daily lives and the experience of our brothers and sisters.[30] This is where *Fulfilled in Your Hearing* and Roman Catholic preaching have most impacted me personally as I have embraced preaching as my primary spiritual discipline and sermon preparation as prayer. I am not alone. Michael Pasquarello, Granger E. and Anna A. Fisher Professor of Preaching at Asbury Theological Seminary, increasingly emphasizes in his classes that the primary responsibility of the preacher is to be a listener rather than the culturally accommodated role of "communicator." Dr. Pasquarello observes,

> The primary communicator to, in, and through the Christian community is the living God through the presence of the risen Christ and by the power of the Spirit. Prayer is attentiveness and receptivity in the presence of God. The current faddish turn to "topical" preaching does not preach by means of Scripture, but rather skims a "relevant" topic from the surface in order to serve a predetermined agenda, program, or goal. Evangelicals and Mainliners both like this approach. But this leaves no space within the worship of God for the fulfillment of the Word in its speaking and hearing. Luke 4, the inaugural sermon of Jesus, shows just how resistant we are to this kind of vulnerable listening![31]

Attentively listening to the Scripture and the people, FIYH asserts, is perhaps the form of prayer most appropriate to the spirituality of the preacher.[32] Preachers pray over the readings seeking the fire of the Holy Spirit to kindle "the now meaning"[33] in our hearts. We pray that God will open the heart of the assembly, so that God's word falls on receptive ears. We pray for ourselves, that God will guide our preparation, help us maintain our role as what one homiletician has called a kind of "interloper" in the assembly, and grant us grace to differentiate our words from God's, so that we do not preach "what might be expedient, popular, burning in the preacher's heart, the correct answer, or best course of action, but not necessarily a word from God."[34] Preachers pray, asking and expecting the real movement of the Holy Spirit in themselves and in the assembly.[35]

Finally, speaking of the preacher, I would be disingenuous if I did not acknowledge that some of the most profound preaching I have experienced, as well as some of the best insights about preaching I have gleaned, come from Roman Catholic women. Thus, I resonate with the 2010 pastoral commentary on *Fulfilled in Your Hearing*, developed by the Catholic Association of Teachers of Homiletics, which asserts:

> While the Bishops' Committee on Priestly Life and Ministry chose to address FIYH to priests and bishops presiding and preaching at the Sunday Eucharist, the introduction to FIYH acknowledges the role of deacons as ministers of the Word, and also the responsibility of the entire Christian community, by virtue of baptism, for the proclamation of the Word of God.[36]

While not all Christians are called to preach in the context of the Sunday liturgy, the liturgical homily provides the foundational model for all preaching. It would be a grievous loss—for the faithful, but more importantly, for the world—were any baptized Christian to be silenced or disempowered when it comes to proclaiming Christ. Therefore, those who are privileged to preach in the Sunday assembly are responsible for empowering all the baptized to name and claim their "pulpit" and proclaim the Gospel, often in ways and circumstances where those who preach in the Sunday assembly cannot, because Sunday preachers lack the opportunity, authority, or credibility to proclaim the Gospel in many other contexts.

The liturgical homily empowers the "preaching" of the baptized by— and here I am borrowing from Mary Catherine Hilkert, who teaches theology at the University of Notre Dame—"naming grace found in the depths of human experience."[37] The preacher names grace in the homily, teaching and empowering the baptized to name grace in their experience. For this reason, Episcopal priest and author Barbara Brown Taylor calls preaching "a process of transformation for both preacher and congregation alike, as the ordinary details of their everyday lives are transformed into the extraordinary elements of God's ongoing creation."[38] Thus, an essential task of the Sunday sermon is to give birth to the sermons brought into being by the individual members of the congregation, who will continue to proclaim the Gospel as the community disperses to dialogue with and act in the world.

According to Taylor, one way that preachers model proclaiming the Gospel is by tracing their own process of discovery, inviting the assembly to come along and providing them with everything they need to make their own finds. The movement of the sermon leads them past new vantage points on their common experience, so that they look at old landmarks from new perspectives. At each stop, the preacher pauses, pointing in a certain direction without telling the congregation what they should see when they look. It's up to them to discern what the landscape holds. The preacher's job is not to make the trip for the people. The preacher's job is not to block their view. The preacher's job is to take them to the spot where they may best see for themselves. "With any luck," Taylor writes, "where the sermon finally leads both preacher and congregation is into the presence of God, a place that cannot be explained but only experienced. When a sermon like that is over, it isn't over. Everyone involved in it goes away with images, thoughts, and emotions that change and grow as the process of discovery goes on and on and on."[39]

Another way preachers of the liturgical homily empower the preaching of the baptized is by serving as what O. Wesley Allen calls *language teachers* who offer the "vocabulary" of Christian traditions to their congregations to use to shape, define, and create reality, that is, to make meaning of God, self, and the world. According to Professor Allen, who teaches preaching and worship at Lexington Theological Seminary, the real power of the pulpit lies in the extended process of modeling how to use the "vocabulary" of the Christian faith—and here I would emphasize the language, gestures, and actions of the liturgy—so that the traditional "language" of ancient Christian communities truly becomes the "language" of the twenty-first century.[40]

The Homily

Sermons might evangelize, teach, exhort, or testify. FIYH names the liturgical homily as preaching of another kind. While the liturgical homily may well include evangelization, catechesis, and exhortation, "its primary purpose is to be found in the fact that it is, in the words of the Second Vatican Council, 'a part of the liturgy itself' (*Constitution on the Sacred Liturgy* 52)."[41] The homily's relation to the liturgical action of which it is a part determines its very meaning and function. The homily flows from the Scriptures, which undergird the liturgy's prayers and actions, and it enables the congregation to participate in the liturgy as a celebration with faith. In the eucharistic celebration, for example, the homily points to the presence of God in people's lives and then leads a congregation into the Eucharist, providing, as it were, the motive for celebrating the Eucharist in this time and place.[42]

The "intimate link" of the homily to the liturgy of the Eucharist has implications for the way the homily is composed and delivered. FIYH says the homily should flow quite naturally out of the readings and into the liturgical action that follows.[43] Methodist liturgical theologian Geoffrey Wainwright asserts that the constant features and qualitative wholeness of the liturgy also provide preaching with a certain freedom and boldness.[44] Surrounded as it is by the stable elements of Scripture readings, creed, and eucharistic prayer, the unrepeatable sermon can afford a certain boldness of mind and heart as it seeks to bring home the Christian message imaginatively and penetratingly to a particular group of people at this time and in this place. As long as the traditional actions of the liturgy keep the classical expression of the faith before the people, the preacher may attempt new ways of communicating the Gospel demanded by changes in culture.

The freshness of the sermon and the stability of the liturgy also complete each other. For example, while preaching speaks through the ears to the mind and heart, the Gospel proclamation contained in the objects, gestures, and outward signs of the liturgy has great power because truths reach us and can fully develop in us only if they touch the body.

Gordon Lathrop describes this relationship of homily and liturgy, Word and sacrament, in another way. Lathrop rightly observes that speaking about God with just one "word"—one connected to logical discourse, for example—almost inevitably means speaking a distortion because it suggests that God is a consequent idea, not a mysterious presence.[45] For this reason, in the liturgy, side by side with the "proclaimed word" there is also the "visible word" of the table. Without Scripture readings and preaching, the "visible word" of the table may be experienced as a sacred encounter with God in the present time but without any history or any future. Similarly, without the table, the "proclaimed word" may easily become a lecture, a conjecture, a distant history with no "for you" that anchors it in present experience. Lathrop writes, "The table requires the preacher to move toward saying in words what the bread and cup will say. And the sermon calls us to make our celebration around the table larger, 'begging God to bring the time of the great universal feast, giving a name and a history and a future to our eating and drinking.' "[46]

Homiletic Method

In terms of homiletic method, *Fulfilled in Your Hearing* declares that preachers are, above all else, to be prayerful. We are not talking about prayer alongside preparation for preaching, or prayer over and above preparation. Rather, prayer is the very heart and center of preparation, with the goal that the word of God in the Scriptures is "interiorized."[47] FIYH declares, "The homily is not so much *on* the Scriptures as *from* and *through* them."[48] In liturgical preaching, explaining a text or teaching the Bible as an end in itself, is simply insufficient.

Paul Galbreath helpfully distinguishes between biblical scholarship, which seeks to identify the meaning(s) of a particular text, and liturgical preaching, which seeks to use the insights of biblical scholars, but recognizes that scholarship (no matter how careful and well crafted) will not be able to fix a meaning(s) of the text. Instead, liturgical preaching sees the art of proclamation as an opportunity to point the listeners into the mysterious world of the text. To this end, liturgical preaching makes use of the resources of the liturgy in order to open the text in new ways and to present new possibilities.[49] Rather than reading Scripture from the primary perspective of the historical-critical method, preachers develop the skill of recognizing associations between the reading of the text and the place of the sacraments in the life of our communities of faith.[50] FIYH explains,

> Since the purpose of the homily is to enable the gathered congregation to celebrate the liturgy with faith . . . the preacher's purpose will be to turn to these Scriptures to interpret peoples' lives in such a way that they will be able to celebrate Eucharist—or be reconciled with God and one another, or be baptized into the Body of Christ, depending on the particular liturgy that is being celebrated.[51]

Galbreath observes that the widespread acceptance of the Revised Common Lectionary, which is adopted and adapted from the Lectionary for Mass and was developed specifically for services of Word and table, includes many readings that carry sacramental associations. Food images are replete; water images are common throughout the three-year cycle. Galbreath writes,

> Congregations that adopted the lectionary readings (even partially) encountered sacramental images (often subliminally) week after week. In many of these congregations, parishioners listened to texts replete with feeding images while looking across an empty communion table. Similarly, texts full of water and washing images were read in congregations where the baptismal font was empty and/or pushed to the side. In these instances, the power of the Word alone began to prompt both preacher and listener to encounter these texts in new ways. The lectionary prepared the way for congregations to begin a time of sacramental renewal. This period of renewal has been accompanied and supported by the recovery of preaching that engages the sacraments and points steadily to connections between Word and Sacrament.[52]

Reformed liturgical scholar Fritz West notes that the lectionary causes the church to read the Bible differently. In liturgical preaching, Scripture readings are removed from their literary context and placed in the context of the liturgical year and the other pericopes read in worship. The greater context of readings is not the books in which they are found but the Sundays, feasts, and seasons of the liturgical year on which they are read. The immediate context is the worship life of the church where they are related to the other readings, the liturgy of the day, and the assembly at prayer.[53]

Quivik adds, "When the impetus and substance of the sermon comes out of the word appointed for that day through the lectionary, the preaching is born out of the churches' reckoning of time. And because the appointed Scripture readings reflect the churches' witness to Christ Jesus and to the work of the Holy Spirit in the life of the church, the preaching necessarily turns toward the sacramental nature of the gathering, thus fusing preaching and liturgy."[54]

Conclusion

Fulfilled in Your Hearing first articulated what we have come to know as "liturgical preaching," a genre of sermon that shapes our understanding of the key ingredients in preaching—Scripture, assembly, and preacher.

By naming "this intimate link" between sermon and liturgy, FIYH invited an ecumenical conversation that continues to shape both the preaching of the church and the way preaching is taught within the church. For this gift and treasure, the ecumenical church is most grateful.

Endnotes

1. This essay evolved over more than a decade of teaching preaching at the University of Notre Dame and Lutheran School of Theology at Chicago. It originated from my unpublished paper, "How is the Sermon Integral to the Liturgy?" (University of Notre Dame, 1998), various aspects of which are published in Craig A. Satterlee, *Ambrose of Milan's Method of Mystagogical Preaching* (Collegeville, MN: Liturgical Press, 2002), 295–299; idem, *Presiding in the Assembly: A Worship Handbook* (Minneapolis: Augsburg Fortress, 2003), 23–25, 49–51; idem, *When God Speaks through You: How Faith Convictions Shape Preaching and Mission* (Herndon, VA: Alban Institute, 2007), 35–54, 66–68; and idem, "Liturgical Preaching: Introduction," *Liturgy* 25, 4 (October–December, 2010): 1–2.

2. Fred B. Craddock, *Preaching* (Nashville: Abingdon Press, 1985), 23.

3. Ibid., 31.

4. Yngve Brilioth, *A Brief History of Preaching* (Philadelphia: Fortress Press, 1965), 8–9.

5. Satterlee, *When God Speaks through You*, 35.

6. Melinda Quivik, "Re: Fulfilled in Your Hearing," e-mail message to the author, May 30, 2012.

7. United States Catholic Conference, *Fulfilled in Your Hearing: The Homily in the Sunday Assembly* (Washington, DC: Office of Publishing Services, 1982), 1.

8. Second Vatican Council, *Sacrosanctum Concilium: Constitution on the Sacred Liturgy*, 56.

9. Evangelical Lutheran Church in America, *The Use of the Means of Grace: A Statement on the Practice of Word and Sacraments* (Chicago: Evangelical Lutheran Church in America, 1997), 34.

10. *Constitution on the Sacred Liturgy*, 52.

11. *The Use of the Means of Grace*, 9a.

12. Ibid., 34a.

13. Ibid., 35.

14. *The United Methodist Book of Worship* (Nashville: United Methodist Publishing House, 1992), 33–50.

15. *Fulfilled in Your Hearing*, 29.

16. Ibid., 5.

17. Melinda Quivik, "On Liturgical Preaching: The Body of Christ in Time." *Liturgy* 25, 4 (October–December, 2010), 4.

18. *Fulfilled in Your Hearing*, 6–7.

19. William Seth Adams, *Shaped By Images: One Who Presides* (New York: Church Hymnal Corporation, 1995), 29.

20. *Fulfilled in Your Hearing*, 18.

21. Paul Galbreath, "Seeing-As: Liturgical Preaching as a Change of Perspectives," *Liturgy* 25, 4 (October–December, 2010), 43.

22. Jennifer L. Lord, "Preaching to Inhabit the Sacraments," *Liturgy* 25, 4 (October–December, 2010), 48.

23. *Fulfilled in Your Hearing*, 25.

24. Ibid., 8.

25. Ibid., 29.

26. Ibid., 1; quoting *Constitution on the Sacred Liturgy*, 35, 2.

27. Gordon W. Lathrop, "Re: Fulfilled in Your Hearing," e-mail message to the author, May 30, 2012. The term *Christus Victor* refers to an understanding of the atonement that views Christ's death as the means by which the powers of evil, which held humankind under their dominion, were defeated. Anselmian or the satisfaction theory of the atonement teaches that Christ suffered as a substitute on behalf of humankind satisfying the demands of God's honor by his infinite merit. The Abelardian theory or the moral influence view of the atonement explains the effect of Jesus' death as an act of exemplary obedience, which affects the intentions of those who come to know about it.

28. Craig A. Satterlee, *When God Speaks through Worship: Stories Congregations Live By* (Herndon, VA: Alban Institute, 2009), 114–115.

29. *Fulfilled in Your Hearing*, 1.

30. Ibid., 10.

31. Michael Pasquarello, "Re: Fulfilled in Your Hearing," e-mail message to the author, June 6, 2012.

32. *Fulfilled in Your Hearing*, 10.

33. Ibid.

34. Craig A. Satterlee, *When God Speaks through Change: Preaching in Times of Congregational Transition* (Herndon, VA: Alban Institute, 2005), 51.

35. *Fulfilled in Your Hearing*, 10–11.

36. James A. Wallace, ed., *The Sermon in the Sunday Assembly: A Commentary on* Fulfilled in Your Hearing (Collegeville, MN: Liturgical Press, 2010), x.

37. Mary Catherine Hilkert, *Naming Grace: Preaching and the Sacramental Imagination* (New York: Continuum, 2000), 44.

38. Barbara Brown Taylor, *The Preaching Life* (Boston: Cowley, 1993), 85.

39. Ibid.

40. Satterlee, *When God Speaks through You*, 74–75; O. Wesley Allen Jr., *The Homiletic of All Believers: A Conversational Approach to Proclamation and Preaching* (Louisville: Westminster John Knox Press, 2005), 55–56.

41. *Fulfilled in Your Hearing*, 17.

42. Ibid., 23.

43. Ibid.

44. Geoffrey Wainwright, "The Sermon and the Liturgy," *Greek Orthodox Theological Review* 28 (Winter 1983): 346.

45. Gordon Lathrop, "At Least Two Words: The Liturgy as Proclamation," in *The Landscape of Praise: Reading in Liturgical Renewal*, ed. Blair Gilmer Meeks (Valley Forge, PA: Trinity Press International, 1996), 183.

46. Ibid., 184.

47. *Fulfilled in Your Hearing*, 11.

48. Ibid., 20.

49. Galbreath, "Seeing-As," 41.

50. Ibid., 42.

51. *Fulfilled in Your Hearing*, 20–21.

52. Galbreath, 41–42.

53. Fritz West, *Scripture and Memory: The Ecumenical Hermeneutic of the Three-Year Lectionaries* (Collegeville, MN: Liturgical Press, 1997), 30.

54. Quivik, "Re: Fulfilled in Your Hearing."

Chapter 10

Unfulfilled in Our Hearing, or, Why Can't Our Newly Ordained Priest Preach?

Tom Margevičius

My title presumes this is a common sentiment, but I know not everyone shares my lament. Some think today's newly ordained, by and large, are no worse preachers than previous generations—perhaps even better. But often when I tell parishioners, "I taught your new priest," I routinely hear comments such as, "He's good at praying Mass—you taught him well," but rarely do I hear, "He's a good preacher." Let me suggest a few contributing factors why this may be.

The first point concerns the student himself. Not often does someone have the ideal combination of natural gifts—intelligence, charisma, a pleasing voice—and acquired virtues—industriousness, spontaneity, authenticity. If we *do* find such a man, are we not more likely to imagine him as a businessman or entertainer? It's no surprise that we have weak preachers when the men we attract to the seminary are naturally timid, narrow, or just plain boring.

The second concerns the seminary. *Fulfilled in Your Hearing* called for professionally trained homileticians, but frequently homiletics gets the short straw in terms of seminary personnel, or a marginal status in the school curriculum and budget. Sometimes we *teachers* don't teach well and are too lenient when students give a mediocre effort—after all, the church needs more priests. Further, seminary priests ourselves are usually academicians who model cerebral preaching that is often ill-suited for parish life, and students copy preachers they emulate, regardless of what we teach.

Even if we attract the right kind of men and train them well, still we may get mediocre homilies in the parish. A third factor is that our Catholic *ethos* still has a low regard for preaching. Despite advances in scriptural appreciation we persist in the mentality that "Protestants preach; Catholics have Mass." Priests tend to be more anxious about "validly confecting the Eucharist" than about "preaching a valid homily"—we don't even have theological categories for that. Everyone agrees with Pope Benedict's comment that "Given the importance of the Word of God, the quality of homilies needs to be improved,"[1] but there is little consensus on how to remedy that.

Allied to this, American parish life is not structured for homiletic excellence. The old rule of thumb is that a homilist should dedicate one hour of preparation for every minute he or she plans to preach. With all the time demands placed on newly ordained priests, it's rare to find one who can invest seven to ten hours a week preparing for the Sunday homily, to say nothing of daily homilies, funerals, weddings, or school Masses.

Finally, one more factor touches upon *young* priests. We know that those under thirty-five have a different ecclesiology than those over, say, fifty, like me. Whether you label it the John Paul II generation vs. the Vatican II generation, or conservatives vs. liberals, youth think differently from their teachers. The minute the bishop lays hands on their heads, some young priests disregard what they were taught in the seminary and instead preach the way they want. Here might be two reasons for that.

First, youth are idealistic by nature. They see a church needing repair, notice who's in leadership, conclude those leaders must be at fault, and posture themselves in opposition as a matter of principle. As John Foley observed, FIYH favors a Rahnerian theology-from-below. What the last generation called "pastoral accommodation," today's young priests ridicule as "liturgical abuse." They may style themselves "orthodox," but irrespective of theology, *anthropologically* speaking today's young can be as rebellious as 70s hippies. I think several years of immersion in real parish life and some of those rough edges will naturally be smoothed out as the young priests mature in their vocation.

Second—and this is a more deep-seated issue—today's young men grew up in a world different from the 1960s. Back then you lived in the same neighborhood with the same kids you went to school with and saw in church, married someone from your own Catholic ghetto, and raised a family there. Society grounded one's religious identity. Nowadays society is transitory. Even if students' nuclear families remain intact, parents move every few years, and so kids don't get a sense of belonging to a people. In postmodern culture they don't *know who they are* and in that vacuum gravitate toward the stable, the unchanging—the style of Mass and preaching common before Vatican II messed things up.

How do we respond to their dilemma? It helps to acknowledge that even if *they* don't know it, we know many of the young are reacting out of fear. To them the world is *not* the friendly place their parents knew. If they are afraid, we must be gentle. Don't aggravate them: extremism is often borne of threats.

In addition, give them lots of good feedback. Tell them when they preached well, suggest practically how they could improve, and let them know what *you* need to hear. They're good-hearted men, and in the right supportive environment they will respond to the Spirit moving in their hearts and really try to preach so that once again the word of God could be "fulfilled in our hearing."

Endnote

1. Pope Benedict XVI, *Sacramentum Caritatis* 46.

Chapter 11

Preaching Hope in Times of Polarization

Susan McGurgan

Emily Dickinson once wrote:

> Hope is the thing with feathers
> That perches in the soul,
> And sings the tune without the words,
> And never stops at all . . .[1]

The prophet Jeremiah declared, "I know the plans I have for you, says the Lord, plans for your welfare and not for harm, to give you a future with hope" (29:11, NRSV). Paul's letter to the Romans speaks of a hope that "does not disappoint"(5:5, NRSV), and 1 Peter reminds us that our Lord "has given us a new birth into a living hope" (1:3, NRSV).

Our Catholic story is, indeed, a story of hope. This hope is not optimism, or happiness, or warm feelings, or a sacramental version of the Gospel of Prosperity. Rather, it is a gritty hope, born in a crushing death and the echoing silence of an empty tomb. It is a radical hope that can look upon such a death and say, "This is not the final word."

Hope. Our history is filled with it. Our sacred texts proclaim it. Our liturgy celebrates it. Our sacraments make it present to us. Our people are starving for it. So, why is it that Sunday after Sunday we hear so little of this hope preached from the pulpit?

We come to church, bruised and limping—beaten up by the economy, by a loss of dreams, by illness or betrayal, by tension and polarization in the political arena, by tension and polarization in the church itself. We know firsthand that marriages fail; that children turn away from their childhood faith; that pews are increasingly empty; that friends can betray you; that companies are seldom loyal to the workers who pour out their lives for the bottom line; that health is precarious and precious. As Christians, these wounds mark us, but they need not define us. We long for evidence that Christ is present and working in our lives, sustaining us. We thirst for a drink of water from a preacher who knows where to find the deep wells.

Rev. James Forbes, senior minister emeritus of the Riverside Church in Manhattan, once said, "When you preach, something about what you are saying ought to be taking place. If you preach about healing, hearts ought to be softening. If you preach about justice, there ought to be bread appearing on tables. If you are preaching hope, people should begin to see a new reality."[2]

But what happens? A parishioner comes to Mass, desperate for a word of hope after his daughter is killed in a car accident. What he hears is a reading of the cardinal's annual appeal letter along with detailed instructions about filling out the form. *How do you preach hope, when you are drowning in Mission Sunday, Stewardship Sunday, Appeals Sunday, and Coat Drive Sunday?*

"People don't know the faith anymore, so you'll just have to teach during the homily. Cafeteria Catholics are ruining the church, so preach the catechism each week and tell them what to do!" *How do you preach hope, when some days, all you can hear is the clamor for issues-based preaching and the demand for marching orders?*

"Modern culture is a cesspool. Society is corrupt, and we need to stand apart from the taint of this world in order to become holy." *How do you preach hope, if you believe the world is drowning in evil and people are essentially damned? How do you preach hope if you believe that God is failing us today?*

If preaching emerges from spaces that are cluttered, desolate, fearful or angry, there can be very little room left over for hope. In this landscape, preaching becomes little more than a political ad, an exhortation to orthodoxy or even a scorched-earth campaign. In this landscape, the wager behind the Catholic sacramental imagination—the wager that God's fingerprints can be found everywhere in the human experience, becomes one that few gamblers would place and few bookies would accept.[3] When preaching emerges from these spaces, the listener is often left frustrated and empty, having been offered words more suited to a jury summation, a financial report, or a catechism class than a sacred conversation.

If you are not preaching hope, then you are not preaching the Gospel. Many Christians seem to believe that we have entered an era so broken and so dark that we have moved to a place beyond hope. To counteract such attitudes in his own era, Blessed John XXIII said, "Distrustful souls see only darkness burdening the face of the earth. We prefer instead to reaffirm all our confidence in our savior who has not abandoned the world which he redeemed."[4]

We long for assurance that our Savior has not abandoned us; for evidence that Christ is here with us, sustaining us in the midst of suffering and evil. We need to hear that there is no place so lonely, so desolate, so foul that Christ has not been there first, and is there now, waiting to lead us out. Although no one can cause or control hope, as preachers, you can evoke it. To do this, you must be deliberate in crafting homilies that allow space for redemption and grace.[5] A preacher may never be able to solve the problem of suffering and evil, but a preacher can stand in the midst of that pain and proclaim a message of Christian hope. In the end, that is all we need—to hear fresh words of hope from the mouth of one who truly believes.

The following suggestions are offered as starting points for reflection. It may be helpful to begin by considering your own theology of preaching. Why do you preach? What is essential to Catholic preaching? What do you hope to accomplish? What are your dreams for your community? Crafting a simple *Preaching Mission Statement* will help you articulate and refine these thoughts. This mission statement consists of a simple sentence or two articulating your core beliefs about Catholic preaching and your vision for the role preaching can play in your community. A written mission statement holds you accountable and encourages you to preach out of that vision regardless of the circumstances. A personal preaching "manifesto" provides a framework for catechetical, doctrinal, and special events preaching, and challenges you to preach from your core beliefs and gifts.

1. *Choose your words carefully.* Words are the tools of preaching, and like all tools, they have both power and purpose. They can wound or heal, alienate or invite, bind or loose. Words from a creative God can explode galaxies into life. But words are not equal, and when it comes

to preaching, just any old word won't do. Sunday after Sunday, listeners enter church, eager for powerful words of hope and possibility; hungry for healing words of peace and reconciliation; in need of challenging words of truth and liberation. But we often leave frustrated and empty, having been offered words more appropriate to a lecture, an impromptu chat or private musings than a sacred conversation.

Words don't just reflect possibilities, they create them. Preaching hope requires an understanding of both the power of words and the emotional aspects of communication. The language of hope is dialogic, oral, evocative, concrete, and vivid. The language of hope is depth language. It should appeal to our senses and our core beliefs.[6]

2. *Covenant with your community to keep the dismissive attitudes of partisan divisiveness and the polarizing words of the political landscape out of your worship and liturgy.* This doesn't mean we avoid difficult conversations. On the contrary, difficult conversations seem destined to accompany the cross. It does mean, however, that we understand the power of words and engage in those conversations differently. Liturgical preaching leads to the Eucharist, so the language of liturgical preaching should be always the language of the table: words of hospitality, relationship, abundance, invitation, nourishment, and reconciliation. This is language in which meaning overflows. It puts us in touch with what we cannot say but understand at some deeper level. It is language that allows "a deeper mystery, the offer of grace, to become more concretely present and available in human life."[7]

3. *Commit yourself to clarity in preaching.* Clarity is not just a structural nicety or a way to make your point more logically. Clarity is not simply about grammar, sentence structure, or ease of understanding, although those elements are important for effective preaching. Rather, clarity is deeply theological. Clarity in preaching makes a theological statement about the accessibility of God and the availability of hope and grace. Convoluted or obscure preaching implies a God who is too distant and too complex for us to approach. Clarity in preaching reminds us that God is closer than we dare to imagine, more immanent than we know.

4. *Concretize the Gospel message of hope.* Preachers tend to speak concretely when naming the bad news and abstractly when discussing the Good News. Sin, suffering, pain, and death are examined in excruciating detail while the Good News of love, forgiveness, and healing are described in lofty and abstract terms. In order to offer listeners genuine

hope, your examples of grace, joy, reconciliation, mercy, and redemption should be concrete, vivid, and real—as real as the bad news people experience daily. Abstract or obscure language creates a significant distance between the listener and the preacher and between the listener and God. Abstract language can lead to abstract hope—and ultimately an abstract faith.

5. *Find hope in the act of preaching and in the ministry of other preachers.* Preaching hope involves more than the words spoken or the attitude projected from the pulpit. It means seeing the hard work of the preaching process, from preparation to delivery, as transformational for both you and the listener. Count yourself among those blessed by your message, and see your preparation time as prayer. Celebrate the opportunities you have to evangelize.

6. *Spend time in the world of art, music, and poetry—even if that world seems strange and new.* Art can convey truths that textbooks cannot. Images, music, and poetry can transport us from where we stand now to unexpected contexts and new and vibrant worlds. Like visual prophets, images remind us that the way things look today is not the way things have to be. Art can shock us from our complacency, move us in ways that words cannot, teach us truths that lie just beyond our own skin.

7. *Embrace the beauty and goodness of the created world and the society in which your parishioners live.* The world of hockey rinks, football fields, backyard cookouts, business, school, and family life is a world of both splendor and heartache. It is beautiful and broken and ours. It is the place we have been given to live out our earthly vocations to work, marriage, family, and community. Accept the wager that God's grace can be found everywhere in the human experience, and help us name those experiences as holy.

8. *Finally, no matter what life has given you to bear, do not step into the pulpit to preach your own pain, your own fear, or your own despair.* Preaching is not a therapy session or a place to work out a crisis of faith. The task of shepherding can be a lonely one, and preachers must find an effective system of support and nourishment outside of their community. When you preach, never forget that some of us have come to this place at great cost. You may never know or understand the price we have paid to be present. Preach an assurance of grace, for the people listening deserve nothing less. Remember, you are called to preach hope, even as you are standing on the bones of the past.[8]

Endnotes

1. Emily Dickinson, "Hope Is the Thing with Feathers," *The Manuscript Book of Emily Dickenson: A Facsimile Edition*, #254, R. W. Franklin, Editor, Belknap Press, 1981.

2. Rev. James Forbes, Academy of Homiletics keynote address, 2005.

3. For a discussion of the sacramental imagination and preaching, see Mary Catherine Hilkert, *Naming Grace: Preaching and the Sacramental Imagination* (New York: Continuum, 1997), 30–44.

4. December 1961.

5. See Henry H. Mitchell, *Celebration & Experience in Preaching* (Nashville: Abingdon Press, 1990), and Frank A. Thomas, *They Like to Never Quit Praisin' God: The Role of Celebration in Preaching* (Cleveland: Pilgrim Press, 1997), for a discussion of the theology, dynamics, and design of celebrative, hope-filled preaching.

6. For a discussion of depth language, see Karl Rahner, "Priest and Poet," in *Theological Investigations*, vol. 3: *Theology of the Spiritual Life*, trans. Karl-H. Kruger and Boniface Kruger (New York: Crossroad, 1982), 294–317.

7. Hilkert, *Naming Grace*, 33.

8. John Rucyahana, *The Bishop of Rwanda: Finding Forgiveness Amidst a Pile of Bones* (Nashville: Thomas Nelson, 2008). John Rucyahana, a Tutsi refugee, was a leader in the Anglican Church of Uganda during the genocide of his people in Rwanda. He moved back in 1977 with his family to lead the largest and most devastated diocese there, helping people to name the horror and build repentance and forgiveness. He speaks of standing on the bones of the past and claiming the hope God promises for the future.

Chapter 12

African American Contributions to Our American Catholic Preaching Challenge

Maurice J. Nutt, CSsR

When the black preacher is moving the hearts and souls of a black congregation through powerful preaching, a loud shout of "tell the story, preacher" may be heard from some satisfied soul sitting in the pew.[1] One of the most interesting and faith-filled stories within the Catholic Church in America is that told by African American Catholics. It is a story that tells of a people who were both faith-filled and faithful to a God who never fails. It is a story of persistence and perseverance under discouraging circumstances. It is a story of a people who held tight to God's unchanging hands when the dark clouds of racism clouded their way. With great self-determination and steadfast activism, African Americans carved a place for themselves within the Roman Catholic Church in America. Once known as a mission church and a mission people, the African American Catholics of today are a people committed to the work of spreading the Good News of the Gospel among themselves and others.

African American Catholics experience a double invisibility. In the black world, they are marginalized because of their religious identity as Catholics; in the Catholic world, they are marginalized because of their racial and cultural identity. Nevertheless, African American Catholics have not allowed their perceived double invisibility to deter their mission of evangelization.

In their pastoral letter *What We Have Seen and Heard*, addressed to the Catholics of the United States, ten African American bishops made the bold statement that African American Catholics have "come of age."[2] African American Catholics had matured to adulthood and were no longer the helpless missionary children of the predominantly white Catholic Church of America. While the tone of the pastoral letter was respectful and appreciative of the many gifts that had been shared with African American Catholics, the African American Catholic bishops nonetheless affirmed that they, too, as African Americans, had gifts to share with the universal Catholic Church. The African American Catholic bishops wrote that "evangelization means not only preaching but witnessing; not only conversion but renewal; not only community but the building up of the community; not only hearing the Word but sharing it."[3]

There remains today a great vitality among African American Catholics to spread the word of God among themselves and others. African Americans are a biblical people. The word of God has been a tremendous source of support and consolation through the anguish and afflictions that they have had to endure. Many times it has been "a word from the Lord" that has sustained them throughout their struggle with the evils of racism. However, in most cases the word of God is not effectively preached to many African American Catholics. Every Sunday, many African American Catholics endure homilies that are neither filled with the Holy Spirit nor relevant to their situation or life circumstances. The homilies are not based on the Scripture readings and do not inspire the people to be a witness to the goodness of Jesus. It is truly a mystery how African American Catholics continue to return to the liturgies that give them neither life nor the hope of eternal life. Some African Americans contend that Mass has always been fairly boring. Others maintain that their love for the Eucharist calls them back to the Catholic Church every Sunday. Some also acknowledge that their faith is so strong that even if the priest doesn't have the Word, the word of God is still deep within them.

For the most part preaching in our Catholic churches is notoriously uninspired. African Americans throughout this country almost unanimously will attest to this fact. Those who feel called to minister to African American congregations must see it as their duty to develop the art of effective, spirit-filled preaching. Black preaching is a black folk art, but this does not mean that whites cannot be trained in certain techniques of this black liturgical art. Some white pastors have acquired the ability to preach in the black genre without doing a disservice to the integrity of their white identities. Conversely, many white preachers use their identity as an unacceptable excuse for mediocrity. Preaching in the black genre implies preaching with an eloquence that exegetes both the scriptural text and the congregation. The Good News must be addressed to this particular people, and the hermeneutical application of it must be made to their own situation.

Challenges

The Catholic Church in urban neighborhoods throughout the United States is faced with a serious challenge. Many urban neighborhoods are plagued by deterioration and decay. Where once stood thriving communities with stable neighborhood residences, corner grocery stores, and other economic endeavors, now remain abandoned buildings, vacant lots, and the ruins of former successful businesses. In some neighborhoods the large, beautiful Catholic church buildings remain, signs of a once-flourishing immigrant Catholic community. The once-strong immigrant neighborhoods (German, Irish, Polish, and Italian) are now inhabited, in many cases, by a struggling and depressed African American community. In some instances, the ornate edifices dedicated to God and once populated by the Roman Catholic faithful have been sold to growing Protestant and nondenominational congregations in desperate need of extra space. Familiar Catholic names, such as "St. Mark's," "Most Holy Name of Jesus," and "St. Ann Shrine" have been replaced by new names reflective of new congregations, names such as "Emmaus Way Missionary Baptist Church," "New Jerusalem Cathedral Church of God in Christ," and "Transformation Christian Church." These once-densely populated former Roman Catholic churches are now standing-room-only churches. The word of God is powerfully preached, the music ministry moves the congregation to make a joyful noise unto the Lord, the doors of the church are opened, and a call to discipleship is extended; the congregants have the Good News about Jesus Christ to take with them to share all week long; and the word of God leads them to service within and outside their church.

In most cases the Catholic churches in African American neighborhoods throughout this nation have remained. However, there are significantly fewer parishioners. Dioceses and archdioceses have closed or merged many of their parishes in urban communities. Lack of parishioners and lack of funds have topped the list of reasons for the increased mergers. Pastors have somberly noted that all of the Catholics have moved to the suburbs. Yet there remain in our urban communities a vast number of African Americans who are unchurched or lapsed Catholics or inactive baptized believers. For too long there has been the perception that any semblance of blackness must be left on the front steps of Catholic churches and that admittance means assimilating to the dominant Eurocentric expressions of Roman Catholic liturgy and worship. There have been few methods and/or models of inculturated evangelization of African Americans to the Catholic Church. In short, there is a great harvest of souls among African Americans that the Catholic Church must find ways of effectively evangelizing.

Preaching plays an important role in the evangelization of African Americans:

> We blacks are people of the Word. We are by culture, by history, preaching orientated. We come from a preaching tradition. Preaching sustained and nurtured us during the days of slavery. Preaching gave us hope "in days when hope unborn had died." Preaching enables us to keep in keeping on. Preaching enables us to be truly opened to receive Eucharist, the bread of life. So one of the greatest gifts, we, as black people, can give to the Church today is preaching. For in authentic black preaching the spirit is renewed.[4]

The Holy Spirit calls us all to the work of evangelization. It is important that those who have received the Gospel of Jesus Christ spread the Good News. Like Paul, Christians must be compelled to confess, "Preaching the gospel is not the subject of a boast; I am under compulsion and have no choice. I am ruined if I do not preach it!" (1 Cor 9:16).

Evangelization is both a call and response. It is the call of Jesus reverberating down the centuries: "Go into the whole world and proclaim the good news to all creation" (Mark 16:15). The response is, "Conduct yourselves, then, in a way worthy of the gospel of Christ" (Phil 1:27). Evangelization means not only preaching but witnessing, not only conversion but renewal, not only entry into the community but the building up of the community, not only hearing the Word but sharing it.

The Good News of the Gospel not only transforms those who hear it, but it must also transform those who preach it. "The person who has been evangelized," Pope Paul VI wrote, "goes on to evangelize others" (*Evangelii Nuntiandi* 24). However, evangelization is not done in a vacuum; it is performed within a particular context. Pope Paul VI, in writing on the subject of evangelization in the modern world, states:

> The obvious importance of the content of evangelization must not overshadow the importance of the ways and means. This question of "how to evangelize" is permanently relevant, because the methods of evangelizing vary according to the different circumstances of time, place and culture, and because they thereby present a certain challenge to our capacity for discovery and adaptation. On us particularly, the pastors of the Church, rests the responsibility for reshaping with boldness and wisdom, but in complete fidelity to the content of evangelization, the means that are most suitable and effective for communicating the Gospel message to the men and women of our times.[5]

The *National Black Catholic Pastoral Plan* promulgated by the National Black Catholic Congress in 1987, while stating that its primary purpose was to discuss issues relating to the evangelization of African Americans on the local level (within dioceses and parishes), never adequately addressed the need for a model of inculturated evangelization of African Americans to Catholicism. The *National Black Catholic Pastoral Plan* merely encourages the development of evangelization programs that are rooted in the black spiritual experience. I submit that the preaching of the word of God in a style that speaks to the heart and soul of the African American community is vital and must precede any programs of evangelization. In the great commission, Jesus did not instruct us to "go ye therefore" and set up programs, policies, and procedures. He instructed us to go preach!

Understanding the Black Preaching Style

Call and Response

Evans Crawford, professor of homiletics at Howard University's School of Divinity, offers this concise example of the call and response technique in his book, *The Hum: Call and Response in African American Preaching*:

> Wyatt T. Walker, a noted pastor and preacher, tells of a revivalist preacher who established a pattern of call and response using the parable of the prodigal son. Under the title *The Wonderful Father*, he

set the scene of a returning son and a waiting father at the edge of the porch in a chair. A week passed, "but the father kept on waiting." Two weeks passed, "but the father kept on waiting." Three weeks passed, "but the father kept on waiting." Once the refrain was established, the congregation picked it up and repeated it every time the preacher did. That's call and response.[6]

Black preaching is not a one-sided event in which the preacher preaches and the congregation sits quietly listening. A key characteristic of the black preaching style is that it evokes a total response to the proclaimed word of God. The black style, which includes the pattern of call and response, is deeply embedded in African American culture. Such responses require a participating audience. Mitchell argues, "If the black preaching tradition is unique, then that uniqueness depends in part upon the uniqueness of the black congregation which talks back to the preacher as a normal part of the pattern of worship."[7]

It should be noted here that whereas *Fulfilled in Your Hearing* recommends a joyous response to preaching that points to God's goodness in our lives, the response is by and large an internal feeling of gratitude. However, black preaching evokes a total response that goes beyond an internal feeling to an overt, emotional response. Black preaching appeals to both the head and the heart, the intellect and the emotions. Critics have made a grave mistake considering black preaching to be merely a thoughtless, emotional process. It is true that black worshipers want to be stirred; they want to have an emotional experience. But they also want to be stretched, enlightened, renewed, or helped. "They want the cream of the black pulpit; they want the kind of preaching that is highly relevant in content and charismatic delivery. When such content and imaginative delivery grips a congregation, the ensuing dialogue between preacher and people is the epitome of creative worship."[8]

During the preaching, responses given may be overtly or covertly emotional, verbal, or nonverbal. Perhaps the most obvious and widespread manifestation of the freedom of religious expression is the custom of responding to the preaching with "Amen!" or other emotional verbal expressions (i.e., "Preach it; that's right; yes, Lord; sure you're right"). Mitchell posits that the spectrum of responses to good preaching is almost endless. He states, "The black worshiper does not acknowledge the Word delivered by the preacher at the end of the service; he talks back during the preaching."[9]

Traditionally, the verbal emotional responses elicited by black preaching are a way of letting preachers know that they are on the right track and that what they say rings true to the Spirit's presence in their midst. For James Cone, "An *Amen* involves the people in the proclamation and commits them to the divine truth they hear proclaimed. It means that the people recognize that what is said is not just the preacher's ideas but God's claim, which God lays upon the people."[10]

Furthermore, when a person hears Bible truth preached within his or her own cognitive grasp and clearly to one's contemporary needs, it is verily impossible *not* to make an audible response. Audible responses are not only an overt sign of agreement with what the preacher is saying, but, further, they are an urging, a coaxing, an encouragement to the preacher to help him or her sustain the ministry of proclaiming God's holy word.

Another emotional response to black preaching is the nonverbal response. In essence its function is the same as the overt response, namely, to show agreement and to visibly confirm the proclamation of the preacher. The nonverbal response may simply take the expression of a person nodding his or her head in agreement, the congregation clapping their hands, or a catharsis of tears of joy or sorrow from the congregation.

While the nodding of heads and the hand clapping are fairly self-explanatory, mystique surrounds the response of tears. When someone cries helplessly in response to an experience of powerful proclamation, African Americans usually say that person was truly *touched* by the word of God. To be *touched* by the Word means that something was heard that spoke to the life situation of that individual. Something said may have convicted a person into realizing that they *had better make a change in their life and get on the path of righteousness.* Perhaps something said in the sermon or homily gave a person hope and the ability to realize that they are special and loved by God. Maybe something is said that gives a person an added lift as he or she strives to walk his or her Christian journey. African American elders also equipped with words of wisdom describe this catharsis of tears, for whatever reason, as being *God's way of trying to tell you something.* They would say, "He preached that sermon just for you this morning."

Storytelling

Unquestionably, storytelling is a hallmark of black preaching. The preacher must tell the story using a method that is an end in itself, even through he or she may intersperse anecdotes to sustain the obvious relevance of the action in the story. Throughout the story, a good storyteller must be so motivated as to give the impression that he or she had seen it happen. Likewise, the storyteller must also play all the roles and make the story live. The storyteller must communicate the story as to cause the congregation to feel as if they, too, are at the scene of the action.

While storytelling actively engages the emotions, it should not be understood as being merely entertainment. Preachers, like the writer of a play, have messages to convey. Mitchell states, "No matter how charming the story or how captivated the audience, the preacher must take care of business and lead the hearer to do something about the challenge of the Word of God."[11] The story in black preaching is told to pull the congregation into the preaching event. It serves to help individuals identify with the proclamation, to see themselves in the Word and to be challenged by the Word. Storytelling is a practical reminder or a first-time challenge to put into practice the message of the Gospel.

The black storytelling style also interprets the biblical story in the black idiom and transforms the biblical story into the black biblical story. *Telling the story* is the essence of black preaching. Cone argues that storytelling from a black perspective means "proclaiming with appropriate rhythm and passion the connection between the Bible and the history of black people. The preacher must be able to tell God's story so that the people will experience its liberating presence in their midst."[12] Quite often in the black community, someone is heard asking whether the reverend told the story. It is so important that black people hear the old, old, biblical story told in a way that speaks to them in their life and living.

Intonation

Intonation, which involves the use of a chantlike musical tone, is a very common characteristic in black preaching.[13] According to Mitchell, intonation vividly expresses black identity. It is rooted in the African custom of sung public address. Besides serving as an identity signal in black preaching, intonation also serves to enhance the sermon climax.[14]

Today the intonation technique is not often used by many preachers, black or otherwise. Perhaps the reason is because one needs to know how to sing, how to carry a note and pitch and to do it well. Intonation is reaching a climactic point where the preacher becomes so caught up in the revelation of the Good News of the Word that he or she moves from preaching the Word to chanting or singing the message. However, more and more African American churches no longer require intonation for a religiously climactic experience. In fact, many preachers use climactic material rather than moving into a chant. Sometimes preachers will use old, well-worn climax clichés. Preachers using material-based climactic endings tend to incorporate solid content from their message while maintaining power and momentum in their preaching.

Repetition

According to Mitchell, "Repetition simply refers to the restatement of texts, aphorisms and other significant words and phrases for emphasis, memory, impact and effect."[15] Repetition is not only present within the call and response rhetorical elements but within the general course of the sermon as well. Mitchell observes that repetition is seen by the black church mainly as an indication of the worthiness of the dialogue and its context. It is believed that such repetitive material may be retained by the hearer well after the sermon has ended because of the vividness of its impact.

Increasingly preachers using the black preaching style have adopted this technique by inspiring the congregation to interact among themselves. For instance, a preacher may instruct the congregation to turn to a neighbor and say, "The Lord is blessing you right now." The congregation does as instructed by repeating after the preacher. Inevitably, the preacher continues the repetitive process by instructing the congregation to turn to the neighbor on either side and say, "And I know that I am truly blessed!" This technique engages the congregation in a more meaningful way. The listeners become preachers of the Word to those around them within the congregation. In essence this is in-house preparation for their commission to go forth and preach to all the nations.

To illustrate how this particular technique of the black preaching style is used in the context of an African American Catholic homily, I turn to Rev. John T. Judie, an African American priest from Louisville, Kentucky. The following excerpt is transcribed from Judie's homily entitled "Turning and Re-turning to God":[16]

> Our first step to being renewed is our turning and returning to the God who made us. And the starting point of everything we do in life needs to be turning to God in prayer. If there's anything at all that we as followers of Jesus; as church-going folk need to do, it's

to know how to bow our heads, bend our knees and turn to the Father in prayer. You see, Jesus was a praying man. He was:

– a teacher and a preacher but, most of all, he was a praying man!

– a walking man and a talking man but, most of all, he was a praying man!

– a confronting man and a forgiving man but, most of all, he was a praying man!

It is very clear that the repetition technique in Judie's homily is both memorable and most effective. A congregation hearing this homily will definitely leave the liturgy knowing that Jesus was a "praying man."

Rhythm and Rhyme

Rhythm refers to the pacing and movement of the preached sermon. This includes intonation, volume, and pitch. The sermon or homily develops a certain pattern that invites the congregation to "pick up the beat" and move with the preacher. Mitchell, in general, underplays this element of the black style. He concludes, "While rhythm is vitally important in black music, it is, to say the least, unimportant in black preaching."[17] However, I adamantly disagree with Mitchell's assertion that rhythm is not particularly important. Rhythm enhances the movement of one's preaching. The congregation is kept attentive to the preaching when there are variances in the rate, pitch, and intonations of the preacher's voice.

Rhyme refers to the matching of words with similar sounds to enable the congregation to remember important points of the preached Word. It also serves to hold the congregation's attention and to entertain. If good preaching were like cooking a good meal, I would compare the rhyme technique of black preaching to that needed spice that makes the dish taste just right. Rhyme is the spice of black preaching that gives the message vigor and life. Rhyme grabs the attention and permits the congregation to laugh, smile, and most importantly to remember what was said. For instance, here are a few phrases used by Catholic preachers who use rhyme most effectively: "The saints and the ain'ts"; "Sashay if you may, but you won't get in that way"; "The Lord gives us healin' for the dealin'"; "When God starts to bless, the devil starts to mess"; and "I'm too blessed to be stressed!"

Song (Musicality)

Finally, I address the element of song in the black preaching style. The use of singing is a distinguishing mark of good black preaching. It can be used by the preacher either working up to a climactic point where he or she begins to sing the message (like intonation) or by the preacher singing an appropriate spiritual or gospel song relevant to the message within the context of the preaching.

Song is a very important ingredient in African American worship. Most black people believe that the Spirit does not descend without a song. Song opens the hearts of the people for the coming of God's Spirit. Cone says, "That is why most church services are opened with a song and why most preachers would not attempt to preach without having the congregation sing a *special* song in order to prepare the people for God's word. Song not only prepares the people for the Spirit but also intensifies the power of the Spirit's presence with the people."[18]

Many European American priests preaching in African American Catholic parishes have noted that this technique of introducing a song either at the beginning or at the end of their homily does not only open the people to the Word but also makes the preacher feel free and relaxed to preach God's word. For many white preachers preaching in African American Catholic settings, the gift of song (if they can sing) is possibly the easiest of the black preaching techniques to incorporate in their preaching.

African Americans have formulated a genuine preaching style to *tell the story* among themselves and others. Today, as seen in the growing number of "mega churches" throughout our nation, many non-African Americans are preaching in the black idiom. Why? Because the preacher's powerful preaching seemingly satisfies the soul.

Essential Elements of Black Catholic Preaching: The Holy Spirit, Celebration, and Liberation

Before exploring an African American Catholic theology or understanding of preaching, one must first ask if there is an "official" Catholic theology of preaching. Dominican theologian Mary Catherine Hilkert maintains that with the liturgical renewal of the 1950s and 1960s and the Second Vatican Council, the Catholic Church officially reclaimed a theology of revelation centered on the word of God. Hilkert asserts, "The

Dogmatic Constitution on Revelation, Dei Verbum, urged a return to the word of God as the source of renewal for the entire church. While the Catholic Church has consistently moved toward a stronger emphasis on preaching and its importance, we still have no fully developed theology of preaching."[19]

Therefore, Catholics look to their theology of revelation prescribed by *Dei Verbum* to glean insights into a possible Catholic theology of proclamation. *Dei Verbum* describes an understanding of grace and a sacramental theology of revelation as "the mystery of God's self-communication in love which occurs in and through creation and human history: a mystery recognized and named in salvation history and culminating in Jesus Christ" (*Dei Verbum* 6).

Any Christian theology of preaching must center on Jesus Christ as Word of God. According to Hilkert, an appropriate starting point of any Catholic theology of preaching is the incarnation; the mystery of God's fullest word has been spoken in history, in a human being, in human experience. Rather than beginning with the power of God's word as something totally other and beyond our experience, Hilkert proposes we begin with the revelation of God, which is to be discovered in the midst of—and depths of—what is human. She asks the question: "Can we reflect on the mystery of preaching as the naming of grace in human experience?"[20] Implicit to this quotation is the additional question as to whether we can announce God's path of liberation from the midst of the disgrace of our experience. As we move toward articulating characteristics of an African American Catholic theology of preaching, African Americans answer these questions with a resounding, "Yes, we must!"

The Holy Spirit and Preaching

Holy Spirit–filled preaching is a requisite for many African American Catholics. In fact, the person who preaches the Gospel makes a statement about the Holy Spirit just by entering the pulpit. Even before the first word is uttered, presuppositions and definitions from across the centuries speak volumes about the Spirit-led event to be experienced by the preacher and the congregation. According to Rev. Dr. James Forbes, "The preaching event itself—without reference to specific texts and themes—is a living, breathing, flesh-and-blood expression of the theology of the Holy Spirit."[21] In formulating an operative theology of proclamation, Forbes maintains:

> The preaching event is an aspect of the broader work of the Spirit
> to nurture, empower, and guide the church in order that it may serve
> the kingdom of God in the power of the Spirit. It is a process in which
> the divine-human communication is activated and focused on the
> word of God and is led by a member of the community of faith [the
> preacher] who has been called, anointed, and appointed by the Holy
> Spirit to be agent of divine communication. That person's authority
> is grounded in the self-revealing will of God as articulated and elabo-
> rated in the biblical witness. In addition, the preacher's authority is
> confirmed or ordained by the community of faith in response to the
> continuing counsel of the Holy Spirit.[22]

If preachers intend to preach the Gospel of Jesus Christ, who calls them
to serve the kingdom in our time, they need all the power available to
them. We live in a culture that has lost contact with the living spirit of
Jesus. We need preaching that is more than delightful rhetoric. At the
other end of the spectrum, mere ranting, raving, and excitement from
some spirited preacher will also not suffice. The people of God need and
want some sense of the Spirit accompanied by power sufficient to comfort and sustain them in the struggle of their Christian journeys.

Pope Paul VI, in his exhortation *Evangelii Nuntiandi: On Evangelization
in the Modern World*, emphasizes the important role of the Holy Spirit in
Catholic preaching by maintaining that the Holy Spirit impels each individual, as evangelizer, to fervently proclaim the Gospel. The Pontiff
in his teaching was thoroughly convinced that without the Holy Spirit
powerfully present in our preaching and Christian witness, Catholic
evangelization would be ineffective: "Without the Holy Spirit the most
convincing dialectic has no power over the heart of man."[23]

Additionally, *Fulfilled in Your Hearing* encourages Catholic preachers
under the inspiration of the Holy Spirit to preach so as to lead the faithful
to praise God. This document contends that preachers must first recognize the active presence of God in their own lives, as broken and shat-
tered as they may be, and out of that brokenness affirm and witness to
the congregation that it is still good to praise him and even give him
thanks. There is a clear mandate from the Roman Catholic Church that
urges Catholic preachers to be Spirit-filled preachers. Unfortunately, in
many cases, many Catholic preachers have not received the urgency of
this message. Therefore, it is a fallacy that the Catholic Church does not
promote Holy Spirit–filled preaching. It suffices to say that many preachers refuse to receive the church's message and thus the anointing.

Within the context of black preaching, the preacher expects to be anointed by the power of the Holy Spirit before there is any attempt to preach the Word. The preacher cannot preach without the Holy Spirit. Regardless of one's ability, strength, or study habits, the sermon or homily is ultimately a product of the power of the Holy Spirit, which enables the preacher to utter "what thus says the Lord." James Cone indicates that there can be no preaching unless the preacher is called by the Holy Spirit: "In order to separate the preached Word from ordinary human discourse and thereby connect it with prophecy, the black church emphasizes the role of the Spirit in preaching. No one is an authentic preacher in the black church tradition until he or she is called by the Spirit."[24] Cone is on target. Preaching in the black preaching tradition is indeed dependent upon the Holy Spirit. The challenge for preachers in the African American Catholic community is to free themselves to be used by the Holy Spirit and to cease trying to quench the Spirit. An African American Catholic theology of preaching requires Spirit-filled proclamation—a requirement that is certainly nonnegotiable.

Preaching as Celebration

In African American preaching, the preacher always presents a revelation. This revelation is always communicated with inspiration and celebration. It is a matter of glorifying God and involving the hearers.

The preacher is not just an impartial reporter of what happens between God and God's people in human history as recorded in Scripture. The preacher is one who has also experienced what those in the stories experienced, and therefore the preacher is both recorder and witness of the story being related. The biblical story is the preacher's story, and it becomes the congregation's story as well. When deliverance, healing, hope, or miracles come to the biblical story, the same goodness is experienced by the preacher and congregation alike. The chorus of the old hymn "Blessed Assurance" serves as a good example of this: "This is my story. This is my song. Praising my Savior all the day long. . . ."

In gratefulness for these manifold blessings, African Americans tend to shout; they celebrate with the abiding conviction, "If I don't praise him, the rock's gonna cry out." (This is the chorus from the song "If I don't praise the Lord.") Celebration is an integral, authentic, and wholesome aspect of worship in African American preaching and worship. The point of celebration comes when the biblical story becomes the preacher's and the people's story. The preacher and the people are in a celebrative mode because the testimonies of the participants in the story also become their testimonies. In other words, there is a "blessed assurance" that what God did for the biblical characters of old, God is doing for them right now.

Celebration is a word commonly used by Roman Catholics in reference to the celebration of the Eucharist. Roman Catholics refer to the priest presiding at the eucharistic celebration as the celebrant. In many instances, however, the experience of Mass in many Catholic parishes has been anything but a celebration. Lifeless preaching has contributed to this valid criticism. Yet the aim of celebrating Eucharist is to remember and celebrate the salvation that Jesus offers through his paschal mystery. *Fulfilled in Your Hearing* contends that the "challenge to preachers is to reflect on human life with the aid of the Word of God and to show by their preaching, as by their lives, that in every place and at every time it is indeed right to praise and thank the Lord."[25]

African American sermons or homilies do not only end in celebration, but the whole preaching event itself is a celebration. So the meaning of celebration as climax must be reexamined. This meaning is often too limited. According to Mitchell, "We in the African American tradition have cultural roots which demand that the sermon end in celebration."[26] It is true that climax might be that concluding portion of the sermon in which phrases and sentences are presented in ascending order of rhetorical forcefulness. However, this might or might not be the point of highest celebration of the preacher and audience.

I posit that the conclusion is not the only point of celebration in "good" traditional black preaching. If celebration means ecstatic talking and hearing and involvement in the story, then in most black sermons the celebration is interspersed throughout, with greater intensity toward the end. Olin P. Moyd states, "When the preacher engages in narration and storytelling with imagination and with celebration at several places throughout the proclamation, the preacher and the audience are drawn into an identification with the biblical characters in the story, and the historical event becomes an existential event. Thus, celebration is the natural response."[27]

If the sermon or homily is celebration, there is a substance in the proclamation that elicits celebration, and that substance is the *kerygma*, the Good News. An African American Catholic theology of preaching affirms celebration within the preaching event. African American sermons reflect black people's lived experience of the Word. Through both black sermons and black preaching, the faithful are theologically informed; they are inspired; and they are empowered to "run on just a little while longer," knowing that by God's grace everything will be all right: this is something to celebrate.

Preaching for Liberation

For liberation theologians, God intends to liberate the world from oppression. African American homiletics professor Carolyn Ann Knight defines oppression as "a form of sin in which a person or community exploits other persons or communities. Oppression is frequently systemic, that it results from patterns of thought, feeling, and behavior that are transpersonal."[28] The oppressive tendency is so deeply embedded in some social structures that oppressors do not even know that they are oppressors! Among the most common and deeply entrenched systems of oppression are racism, sexism, poverty, classism, ageism, handicappism, homophobia, and ecological abuse. Religion, too, can be used to oppress. African Americans are victims not only of racism; they are victims of all of the aforementioned oppressions.

Liberation preachers, including those who preach in African American Catholic parishes, believe that God operates through the processes of history to free humankind and nature from oppression. Knight posits that "God aims for all people and all elements of the natural world to have their own integrity, secure living conditions, freedom, opportunities to relate with all created entities in love and justice. The best liberation preachers are aware that oppressors are oppressed by their oppressive ideas, feelings and actions."[29] Those preaching for liberation alert both oppressed and oppressor to God's present activity in using individuals and groups to move toward a world in which all live together in love, justice, dignity, and shared material resources.

Pope Paul VI expressed similar sentiments in regard to preaching and living the truth that truly liberates. He states, "The Gospel entrusted to us is also the word of truth. A truth that liberates and which alone gives peace of heart is what people are looking for when we proclaim the Good News to them."[30] In the same vein as Pope Paul VI, Pope John Paul II urges us to "defend with force the dignity and the rights of every [person] against the oppressions and vexations of the powerful. Set oneself to true reconciliation among [humanity] and Christians."[31]

The U.S. bishops assert in *Fulfilled in Your Hearing* that faith leads to an active response and a transformation of one's life: "That response can take many forms. Sometimes it will be appropriate to call people to repentance for the way they have helped to spread the destructive powers of sin in the world. At other times the preacher will invite the congregation to devote themselves to some specific action as a way of sharing in the redemptive and creative word of God." [32] Unfortunately, in most American Catholic parishes, preaching on social issues, especially racism, is either weak or nonexistent. Even the statement in *Fulfilled in Your Hearing* concerning the need for Catholic preachers to address societal ills seems patronizing at best. In the context of liberation preaching as it is best promoted by our Protestant brothers and sisters, there is never a directive such as "sometimes it will be appropriate to call people to repentance for the way they helped to spread the destructive powers of sin in the world." I strongly believe that injustices in the world must *always* and at *all times* be condemned by the Christian preacher whether Catholic or Protestant.

In addition to the emotion so important to African American preaching style, preachers in African American settings have a moral and theological responsibility to develop a sound hermeneutical approach to the Gospel. This demand, while not exclusive to the African American community, is an expectation from the people because of their constant struggle with racial, economic, and political oppression. The preacher is compelled to say something that addresses the needs of the people, directing the message to their head and heart. This holistic message will teach blacks how to live as Christians and how to relate their religion to freedom practices.

Those who sit in the pews need to hear a word of power and spirit—a word of liberation. With the help of the preacher, blacks are able to celebrate in spite of the reality of oppression and injustice because they believe that God is faithful and just. Preaching without celebration is de facto a denial of the Good News in any culture. The preacher celebrates and encourages others to celebrate; however, the preaching ministry must also include liberation. Without liberation, there can be no authentic celebration.

Conclusion

Any attempt to formulate an African American Catholic theology of preaching or to understand the African American contributions to our American Catholic preaching challenge must take into consideration at least three salient directives. First, an African American Catholic theology of preaching is null and void without the anointing of the Holy Spirit. Only under the influence of the Holy Spirit can a preacher boldly speak a prophetic message of consolation and challenge to God's people. Second, an African American Catholic theology of preaching is one of celebration. The preacher in African American Catholic settings must identify—become one with God's word and God's people—and announce and experience the Good News of God's ongoing deliverance. Finally, an African American Catholic theology of preaching is de facto liberation preaching. Preachers in African American Catholic settings are charged with helping the community envision the practical implications of liberation and encouraging the people to join God's liberating initiatives. Homilies must encourage oppressors to repent, to turn away from complicity in oppression and to turn toward God's liberating work in history. Preachers must uplift the oppressed with God's message of hope and the assurance that "trouble don't last always."

Endnotes

1. While it is most common to use the term "African American" in making reference to the children of the African Diaspora, for the purpose of this work "black" and "African American" will be used interchangeably.

2. *What We Have Seen and Heard: A Pastoral Letter on Evangelization from the Black Bishops of the United States* (Cincinnati: St. Anthony Messenger Press, 1984), 2.

3. Ibid.

4. Glen Jeanmarie, "Black Catholic Worship: Celebrating Roots and Wings," in *Portrait in Black: Black Catholic Theological Symposium*, ed. Thaddeus J. Posey (Washington, DC: National Black Catholic Clergy Caucus, 1978), 85.

5. *Evangelii Nuntiandi*, 40.

6. Evans E. Crawford, *The Hum: Call and Response in African American Preaching* (Nashville: Abingdon Press, 1995), 56.

7. Henry H. Mitchell, *Black Preaching* (New York: Harper & Row, 1970), 95.

8. Ibid., 98.

9. Ibid., 44.

10. James H. Cone, *Speaking the Truth: Ecumenism, Liberation and Black Theology* (Grand Rapids, MI: Eerdmans, 1986), 24–25.

11. Mitchell, *Black Preaching*, 133.

12. Cone, *Speaking the Truth*, 24.

13. Mitchell, *Black Preaching*, 165.

14. Ibid.

15. Henry H. Mitchell, *Black Preaching: The Recovery of a Powerful Art* (Nashville: Abingdon Press, 1990), 93.

16. On Luke 11:1-13; date unknown.

17. Mitchell, *Black Preaching*, 167.

18. Cone, *Speaking the Truth*, 25.

19. Mary Catherine Hilkert, "Naming Grace: A Theology of Proclamation," *Worship* 60 (1986): 440.

20. Ibid., 448.

21. James Forbes, *The Holy Spirit and Preaching* (Nashville: Abingdon Press, 1989), 19.

22. Ibid., 20.

23. *Evangelii Nuntiandi*, 75.

24. Cone, *Speaking the Truth*, 23.

25. *Fulfilled in Your Hearing*, 28.

26. Henry H. Mitchell, *Celebration and Experience in Preaching* (Nashville: Abingdon Press, 1990), 12.

27. Olin P. Moyd, *The Sacred Art: Preaching and Theology in the African American Tradition* (Valley Forge, PA: Judson Press, 1995), 109.

28. Carolyn Ann Knight, "Preaching from the Perspective of Liberation Theology," in *Patterns of Preaching*, ed. Ronald J. Allen (St. Louis: Chalice Press, 1998), 223.

29. Ibid.

30. *Evangelii Nuntiandi*, 78.

31. John Paul II, *Fear Not: Thoughts on Living in Today's World*, ed. Alexandria Hatcher (Kansas City, MO: Andrews McMeel Publishing, 1999), 73.

32. *Fulfilled in Your Hearing*, 19.

Chapter 13

Becoming a Cross-cultural Preacher

Kenneth G. Davis, OFM Conv

Doña Blanca is the president of the Guadalupe Society, a daily communicant, and pillar of Immaculate Conception Parish. However, faithful Doña Blanca is unsatisfied. She also regularly attends the Assemblies of God services every Sunday after Mass because, as she claims, "I need to feed my soul with Scripture."

Now the Scriptures are preached in her parish, but her pastor's homilies are translations of the same ones he gives in English, which he reads haltingly in Spanish. A good, hardworking priest past retirement age, he's doing his best to serve a parish whose population has shifted dramatically in the past generation until it is now half Hispanic.

This chapter offers help to just such pastors. However, its aim is modest. There is an obvious and growing need for intercultural competency in many U.S. Catholic parishes because in them a plurality of cultures now interacts in ways unprecedented and unplanned. Although arguably everyone (or at least leadership) would be well served by developing knowledge, attitudes, and skills about how cultures interact, the intention of this chapter is to address only a small but significant part of that development, namely, liturgical preaching by non-Hispanic priests within a Hispanic context. First, it will summarize demographic changes in the church over the last generation and suggest some of the challenges those changes present to preachers. Second, it will analyze the rhetorical method of César Chávez as a possible homiletic method for those preachers and, based on that method, propose a description of cross-cultural preaching.

Demographic Changes

The Center for Applied Research in the Apostolate (CARA) reported that in the year 2000, 22 percent of parishes regularly celebrated Mass in a language other than English. Today, closer to 29 percent do so. And almost 81 percent of these non-English Masses are Spanish, an increase from 76 percent in 2000. On average, the proportion of parishioners who are non-Hispanic white has decreased as Catholics of other races and ethnicities make up a larger part of registered parishioners.

As this chapter goes to print, Boston College is about to conclude its two-year National Study of Catholic Parishes with Hispanic Ministry. It already estimates that nearly 25 percent (approximately 4200) of all U.S. Catholic parishes have developed some form of Hispanic ministry.

However, such statistics are even more persuasive when studying youth and young adult Catholics. In 2012, Catholic Online quoted U.S. census figures indicating that when examining only the "under age 5 population," nearly 25 percent of all U.S. counties are already half Hispanic. These same census figures were analyzed by Instituto Fe y Vida (Stockton, California) to research specifically Catholic youth and young adults, resulting in the tables on the following page.

Thus, several independent demographers agree that the U.S. Catholic liturgical assembly on average is more culturally and linguistically diverse than ever. All projections indicate that this trend will continue. Although with the recent economic downturn, fewer Mexicans are entering the country, and this downturn has had less effect on immigrants from other Spanish-speaking countries. Moreover, as Instituto Fe y Vida demonstrates, even if all immigration ended, the fact remains that the majority of all Catholics of childbearing age in the United States are already Hispanic.

Immigrant Hispanic Catholics have more children on average than non-Hispanic Catholics. Although second- and third-generation Hispanics tend to be less Catholic than immigrants, the trajectory toward a majority Hispanic Catholic U.S. church seems inevitable. A logical consequence of that conclusion is the hypothesis that by the time today's first-year seminarian is pastor, he will likely preach in a second language and/or to a liturgical assembly distinct from his own home culture.

U.S. Catholics in 2011 by Age Cohort	% Hispanic
Catholics under age 10	55
Catholics ages 10 to 19	53
Catholics ages 20 to 29	52
Overall Catholics	41
Catholics over age 30	32

Source: Instituto Fe y Vida 2012

Catholics in the U.S. by Age and Race/Ethnicity on December 1, 2011

Race/ethnicity	Age Group		
	0 to 13	14 to 17	18 to 30
White, non-Hispanic	37.5%	40.2%	39.3%
Hispanic, 1st Gen.	3.7%	9.9%	24.2%
Hispanic, 2nd Gen.	31.2%	25.0%	17.3%
Hispanic, 3rd+ Gen.	20.1%	16.8%	10.6%
Black/African American	3.4%	3.8%	3.7%
Asian/Pacific Islander	2.6%	2.9%	3.5%
Native American & Other	1.5%	1.5%	1.3%

Source: Instituto Fe y Vida 2012

Challenges Those Changes Present to Preachers

As this chapter is written, the U.S. church celebrates the thirtieth anniversary of the bishops' document on preaching, *Fulfilled in Your Hearing*. Since at that time vastly less attention was given to Catholic Hispanics, there was little response to that document from Hispanic scholars. Thankfully, both of those situations have changed; that is, researchers who study the U.S. church are more likely to include Hispanics in their surveys, and more Catholic Hispanics are themselves scholars able and willing to critique such studies.

An example is the recent "Fifth National Survey of American Catholics," and Hosffman Ospino's observations of it.[1] Although the survey asked questions of Hispanics and in Spanish, that did not mean that questions and concerns of Hispanics themselves were surveyed. Thus, although Hispanics were included in the poll of U.S. Catholics, the questions and concerns of Hispanics themselves were not studied. Rather, when surveyed, Catholic Hispanics are often only asked about the questions and concerns of other Catholics under the apparent presumption that such questions and concerns are normative for all Catholics because they are the universal experience of some (i.e., non-Hispanic) Catholics. Such a presumption is frequently based on the fallacy that the only significant difference among Catholics is language—a difference surmounted by simply translating survey instruments.

As such unhelpful presumptions often also underlie preaching as well as polling, it is instructive to compare Ospino's observations concerning the "Fifth National Survey of American Catholics" with the much earlier document *Fulfilled in Your Hearing*. The direct quotes below are from *Fulfilled in Your Hearing*; the arrow points that follow are comments by Ospino compared to that document; a summary of the comparison ensues.

"The preacher acts as a mediator, making connections between the real lives of people. . . ." (FIYH, 8)

- ▶ Each generation and each culture brings different concerns/questions.
- ▶ Concerns of mainstream Catholicism are not always those of Hispanics.

" . . . they know and identify with the people to whom they are speaking." (FIYH, 9)

- ▶ Hispanic Catholics should be included in such knowledge.

"The homily will be effective . . . only if individuals in that community recognize there a word that responds to the implicit or explicit questions of their lives." (FIYH, 22)

- ▶ Formulation of questions should be mindful of language, culture, history.

"Priests will have to decide what form of preaching is most suitable for a particular congregation at a particular time." (FIYH, 26)

- ▶ Consider ideological positioning of mainstream Catholics vs. ecclesial survival of Hispanics.

▸ Strive for inclusive leadership in a culturally diverse church.

▸ Involve Hispanic scholars in understanding Hispanics.

▸ Partner with Hispanic organizations and faith communities.

▸ Differentiate by regions, age/generation, country of origin.

Without attempting to speak for Ospino, his comments applied to *Fulfilled in Your Hearing* can lead to the conclusion that whomever asks the questions frames the story! Politicians and other rhetors understand this dictum. Ospino states directly that if the concerns of Hispanics are not included in the formulation of survey instruments, methodology, and piloting leading to studies of Catholics, then the conclusions of those studies will necessarily not be representive of Hispanic concerns.[2] However, whomever asks the questions frames the story is a truism applied to preaching as well. Thus his comments apply indirectly but instructively to preachers, too. If the preacher does not make connections with the lives of *all* the "real people" by expanding his knowledge of *all* the people with whom he is speaking to influence his homily, then those whose questions and concerns are left out (e.g., Hispanics) will not recognize (even in Spanish) in his preaching a word that "responds to the implicit or explicit questions of their lives." Hence, knowing and making connections with all the people of the parish, including those distinct in culture and speech, is necessary if a preacher is to "decide what form of preaching is most suitable for a particular congregation at a particular time."

Like all humans, preachers often hold unreflected attitudes about their own and other cultures or lack knowledge about other cultures, which leads to an insufficiently developed skill set of rhetorical methods appropriate for culturally diverse circumstances. Such lack of knowledge may lead to expressions of ignorance; unexamined attitudes may also lead to real or perceived bias; and an inappopriate rhetorical skill set based on the assumption that the values and beliefs universal to the preacher's experience are necessarily normative for those who do not share his cultural experience means he may not connect with his assembly's questions and concerns. If it is true that whomever asks the questions frames the story, then good communication across cultures requires the communicator (preacher) to progress beyond his own cultural framework in order to listen and respond to the questions and concerns that culturally distinct communities pose to the Gospels. This often requires new knowledge, reflective attitudes, and flexible skills that help the preacher progress beyond his home culture in order to listen to the questions and concerns of diverse communities so that he can connect to their particular experience.

However, such presumptions are belied by those few surveys that actually ask Hispanics about what is important to them, such as the Pew Research Center's 2007 "Changing Faiths: Latinos and the Transformation of American Religion." Although there are significant differences among Hispanics based on data such as assimilation and country of origin, two characteristics common among many Catholic Hispanics that also distinguish them from non-Hispanic Catholics appear to be: (1) spirit-filled religious expressions such as praying in tongues, miraculous healings, and prophetic utterances; (2) ethnic-oriented worship displayed by the raising of hands, clapping, shouting, or jumping. Finally, Hispanic Catholics are more likely than non-Hispanic Catholics to believe that Jesus will return during their lifetime. Although this conclusion may reflect Spanish-speaking Catholics more than other Hispanics, it is nonetheless significant for surveying Hispanics about their own concerns.[3]

If, as section one concluded, non-Hispanic priests will be preaching to liturgical assemblies increasingly Hispanic, and if, as the Pew study demonstrates, those Hispanics bring distinctive concerns to the Gospel, bishops, seminary rectors, and others may ask: How well are priests typically prepared to self-reflect on their home cultures' (necessarily) limited communicative perspective? How well prepared are they to use this self-reflection to progress beyond that communicative framework in order to listen humbly and respond appropriately to the questions of culturally distinct communities?

To answer these questions one must turn to the current edition of the *Program for Priestly Formation* (PPF). Fortunately, for this more recent church document there is a more direct commentary, namely, Timothy Matovina's *Latino Catholicism: Transformation in America's Largest Church.*[4] Once again, the direct quote below is from the PPF, the arrow points that follow are comments by Matovina compared to that document, and a summary of this comparison ensues.

PPF 215 states: "seminarians should also learn the practical skills needed to communicate the Gospel as proclaimed by the Church in an effective and appropriate manner. . . . Where appropriate, seminarians should be able to demonstrate a capacity for bilingual preaching."

▸ Fewer than half of the forty-six major seminaries in the U.S. offer Hispanic immersion or Hispanic study programs.

▸ Those that do are usually optional rather than required.

▸ Seminaries have few or no personnel who are Hispanic or have expertise in Hispanic ministry.

▸ Most priests are also left to decide if/how to preach in Spanish or with Hispanics.

▸ Few continuing education programs exist for clergy who preach with Hispanics.

Without speaking for Matovina, it would appear that thirty years after *Fulfilled in Your Hearing*, few seminaries require their seminarians to prepare themselves for the future that demographers are predicting. Half of the major seminaries seem ill-equipped to provide such training even if a seminarian requested it. And clergy who volunteer or are asked to learn to preach well within the context of the U.S. Hispanic church have few educational options.[5]

An objective comparison between the challenges demographic changes present to preachers and the preparation that seminarians or priests receive to meet those challenges would have to conclude that both before or after ordination the average priest is too often insufficiently prepared to faithfully preserve, expound, and spread the speech of God[6] from one language/culture (their own) to another (the assembly) if such preaching necessarily requires attention to speech that "is most suitable for a particular congregation at a particular time (*Fulfilled in Your Hearing*, 26)."[7] Such is the case frequently and increasingly in the U.S. church but perhaps most often when the preacher is not Hispanic and the assembly is.

The Rhetorical Method of César Chávez

The proper preparation of preachers for U.S. parishes that have become increasingly diverse in ways unprecedented and unplanned is a multi-faceted task. First, it might include knowledge of Spanish, which is the area where there is the most support for seminarians and priests.[8] Second, it may include greater knowledge of the socioeconomic differences between communities, which was a theme of *Preaching the Teaching:*

Hispanics, Homiletics, and Catholic Social Justice Doctrine.[9] Third, it might address attitudinal challenges to cross-cultural communication, which was a topic of *Preaching and Culture in Latino Congregation.*[10] Fourth, it could include the role of the preacher mentioned in "Preaching to Hispanics in the United States"[11] and *Hispanic Ministry and the Future of the Catholic Church.*[12]

Although each of those related areas still needs development, an appropriate homiletic method specific to U.S. Hispanic Catholics has yet to be proposed. Hence, it is the intent of this chapter to address the fact that until now most models or methods used for preaching in the Catholic Church have been created for and by white, non-Hispanic, monolingual English speakers.[13] And while they work well in the environment for which they were created, since they were not created for Hispanics or by Hispanics, we have no reason to assume that they work equally well outside the environment that created them. This may explain why Hispanic Protestants have created their own preaching methods, e.g., *Manual de Homilética Hispana.*[14]

Imported homiletic methods/models from Spain and Latin America used in the United States are questionable for the same reason; that is, the particular ecclesial context for which they were created is very different from that of U.S. Hispanic Catholics: hence the need to propose and debate a homiletic method for the U.S. Hispanic Catholic context. A logical proposition is Chávez's rhetorical method because he was a U.S. Hispanic, a Catholic, and a successful orator. Although not the only possible method nor necessarily the best one, a discussion about the oratorical approach of this bilingual Catholic Hispanic invites the needed debate on what method(s) would be most appropriate for preaching to U.S. Hispanic assemblies.[15]

Before presenting an analysis of Chávez's typical method, three caveats are required. First, this analysis only studies his public discourse and not his private life or conversations. Second, although intimately related to his public discourse, the analysis will not study his public prayer, fasting, or use of popular religious symbols. Finally, it is precisely in his public discourse rather than in the details of his union organizing that scholars emphasize his Catholic identity.

César Chávez (1927–1993) was a bilingual Mexican American farm worker and Navy veteran. Baptized Catholic, his faith was rekindled by the Cursillo movement, and he studied Catholic social doctrine along with the organizing principles of the Community Service Organization.

Around 1962, he cofounded the United Farm Workers Union and served it successfully until his death. In life he was the best-known Catholic Hispanic orator in the country. His successful rhetorical method may be analyzed by form, content, style, and purpose.

One might describe Chávez's rhetorical form as "Don." In Spanish, "Don" (or "Doña" for women) is an affectionate and honorific title. It combines the honor of a title ("Señor") with the affection of a first name to express both respect without pomp and warmth without pity. "Don" connotes the respect Chávez showed his audience and his ability to identify with their questions and concerns in ways always empathetic but never condescending. This rhetorical form was distinctive.[16] Contemporary Mexican orators were typically more bombastic and other Mexican American speakers at the time even violent. Chávez, however, dressed like a farm worker, used a tone and body language that was conversational, and employed many personal pronouns to form a discourse that was assertive but not aggressive.[17]

This was the perfect form for the content of his speeches, which combined narrative with analysis. Chávez claimed the right to narrate his and his people's own lived experience, which he buttressed with logical reasoning and abundant facts. He then addressed the questions and concerns of his people's own experience by analyzing their narrative through church teaching and collective "American" values. He employed examples and anecdotes familiar to his audience, which included a trenchant criticism of the labor system. However, he took care to refute that system without loss of reputation because he virtually never engaged in personal invective.[18] In this way, the content of his speech fit the form but could be stylistically adapted.

Chávez's style was consistent but contextual. He was consistently brief and clear. Speaking on average fifteen minutes, he used copious rhetorical signposts, employed obvious transitions and accessible vocabulary. Perhaps his most distinctive stylistic technique was the *anaphora* ("consecutive sentences beginning with identical or almost identical words and phrases"). He employed this technique often as an emphatic summary to an argument, sometimes with antithetical balance or rhetorical questions.[19] Although he developed a consistent style of speaking, he was keenly aware of the context of his speeches. Hence, while in Spanish he would often use familiar proverbs, directly invoke religion, and appeal to cooperative self-help, in English he would raise larger moral questions and appeal for broader-based support (e.g., boycotts).[20]

During his long career, Chávez spoke to the illiterate and the sophisticate at once cognizant of the context and consistent in his distinctive style. Consistent in style, he was insistent in purpose.

The purpose of Chávez's public discourse was not to garner applause but to further the cause—and the cause was justice. "Justice" is the most frequent word in his public discourse. The form of his discourse modeled the respect and empathy necessary for justice; the content of his discourse claimed the right to discredit the injustice of his adversaries' policies without any invective branding them personal enemies; the style of his discourse adapted to particular contexts while remaining consistently distinctive; and this was all integrated into a single method whose purpose was not to overwhelm with his personality but to appeal to shared morality. Form, content, and style all served the purpose: the justice of the cause rather than personal applause.[21]

What are some homiletic possibilities for Chávez's rhetorical method? One may not slavishly imitate any orator nor can a non-Latino preacher mimic Chávez. But non-Latinos may study him as they study other great orators in order to create more flexible skills that will allow them to honor the experience of those whose cultural roots are distinct from the preacher's own.

Possible Cross-cultural Homiletic Method

Because Catholics have devoted so little attention to cross-cultural preaching, it is difficult to assess Chávez's method since there is no agreed standard with which to judge.[22] One assessment, however, is proposed by Rogers and de Souza.[23] Although not focused exclusively on Catholics, it uses interviews and literature review to propose the most useful ways concerning "how preachers, especially non-Hispanic ones, might rethink and adjust sermons for a better fit when preaching to U.S. Hispanic Americans." Again, direct quotes below are from Rogers and de Souza; the bullet points provide comparisons with this analysis of Chávez's method, and a summary of that comparison ensues.

"Preaching should consciously reinforce . . . relationships."

- The form "Don" reinforces relationships by expressing identification with the audience based on respect and empathy.

". . . preaching must . . . be done in a way that allows all hearers to see themselves in it."

- The content of Chávez's discourse narrates his shared experience and analyzes it from the perspective of the hearer.

". . . a language of images—not propositions."
"Using simple sentences, repeating them if necessary, and never showing off . . ."

- Chávez's style employed anecdotes, examples, proverbs, and religious metaphors to adapt to various audiences while remaining consistently accessible to each.

- His speeches were brief, clear, and used the repetitive technique of anaphora.

". . . decision-making toward a life committed to creating freedom, solidarity, justice, and love."

- Chávez's form, content, and style all served the purpose of justice and appealed to listeners for a commitment to that purpose.

Based on this comparison, one may conclude that Chávez's rhetorical method is not inconsistent with cross-cultural preaching although it would require adaptation. For instance, while Chávez could and did identify with (largely Hispanic) farm workers, a preacher who is not Hispanic can never completely identify with his assembly. He can, however, treat them as "Don." This would be an attitude of respect and empathy that influences the form of his speech. Second, such empathy would lead to homiletic content that poses to the Gospel knowledge of the questions and concerns of the people he holds in his heart as he prepares his preaching and with whom he consults both before and after the homily. Third, he can become so skillful in his particular assembly's proverbs, popular religion, contemporary and historical cultural icons, to be sufficiently fluent that his congregation not only understands his grammar and pronunciation but hears in the style of his preaching the familiar echo of their home culture. Fourth, if the purpose of the homily is to faithfully preserve, expound, and spread the speech of God (and not just one peculiar cultural incarnation of that speech) in a way most suitable for his particular congregation, then it is the work of the whole church, although the priest is the steward of this ministry. Finally, some evidence suggests that Hispanic assemblies welcome longer homilies that apply church teaching to the practicalities of their lives.

Conclusion: A Description of Cross-cultural Preaching

Good liturgical preaching in a culturally diverse parish is aided by: (1) an attitude of empathy by the preacher for assemblies culturally or linguistically distinct from him that forms his homily such that the assembly experiences that empathy; (2) knowledge gained from the confidence of the assembly generated by that empathy as well as through consultation with parishioners and experts inform the content of the homily in a way that poses the assembly's questions and concerns to the liturgical texts; (3) a style that evokes the assembly's cultural memories in a way so skillful that the style serves rather than distracts from (4) the purpose of faithfully preserving, expounding, and spreading the speech of God received through one culture (the preacher's) to a different culture (the assembly's) in such a way that Christ the Word is encountered by both cultures as a single, shared "great co-mission."

It is human nature to emphasize that with which we empathize. Empathy with the assembly is the attitude that moves the preacher to recognize how his own limitations conceal the ways of God others reveal. Such recognition helps the preacher to learn to reframe homily preparation in a way that invites the assembly to participate through the preacher's new knowledge and/or consultation with the assembly. This empathy leading to new knowledge fires the persistence to acquire the rhetorical skills diversity requires. The just purpose of the cross-cultural homily, therefore, is not unlike the New Evangelization, that is, a co-mission for the whole church of which the preacher is the steward to proclaim Christ the Word to all cultures.

A steward serves Scripture in a way that feeds Doña Blanca's soul since he knows what to emphasize because he understands how to empathize. Liturgical preaching nourishes when, like Eucharist, it is broken in empathetic love and communicated through the language and culture of the recipient because she or he is cherished as is. Chávez's rhetorical method as a U.S. Hispanic, a Catholic, and a successful orator is one worthy of study by non-Hispanic preachers who require knowledge, attitudes, and skills to meet their empathetic desire to steward that Bread of Life.

Endnotes

1. "Hispanics Changing the Character of American Catholicism: A Response," Symposium *American Catholics: Persisting and Change*, based on the Fifth National Survey of American Catholics, Boston College, Boston, MA, November 2, 2011.

2. Ospino makes the accurate observation that non-Hispanics are served by consulting Hispanic scholars. For an example of how today's technology makes it easier to research questions and concerns specific to Hispanics, see *America 2012*, a research study published by Conill.

3. See http://www.pewhispanic.org/2007/04/25/changing-faiths-latinos-and -the-transformation-of-american-religion/.

4. Princeton, NJ: Princeton University Press, 2012.

5. Among the questions and concerns of Hispanics Matovina documents are community organizing efforts in parishes and apostolic movements beyond parishes. For his analysis of priestly formation, see pages 155–157.

6. *Catechism of the Catholic Church* (Washington, DC: United States Catholic Conference, 1994), 81.

7. Allan Figueroa Deck, SJ, seems to concur: "The central challenge facing priests and all pastoral agents today [is] the integration of intercultural competencies into formation programs," *Seminary Journal* 16, 3 (Winter 2010): 35.

8. Here again, however, there appears to be a discrepancy between the ministry of future priests and their preparation. Sr. Katarina Schuth, OSF, PhD, reported to the Second Biennial Joint Conference on Inter-Cultural Competency (June 10–13, 2012, in Philadelphia, PA) that although twenty-three seminaries offered immersion programs unrelated to Spanish acquisition (e.g., to the British Isles), only thirteen sponsored Spanish immersion programs.

9. Kenneth G. Davis and Leopoldo Pérez, eds. (Scranton, PA: University of Scranton Press, 2005).

10. Kenneth G. Davis and Jorge L. Presmanes, eds. (Chicago: Liturgy Training Publications, 2000).

11. Privately published (Saint Meinrad, IN: Saint Meinrad School of Theology, 2009).

12. CD/DVD by Kenneth G. Davis (Now You Know Media, 2011).

13. The best known include Walter J. Burghardt, David Buttrick, Fred Craddock, Eugene L. Lowry, James A. Wallace, and Ken Untener.

14. CLIE, 2008.

15. For instance, the study by Roberto Suro, et al., "Changing Faiths: Latinos and the Transformation of American Religion" (Pew Hispanic Center, 2007; http://www .pewhispanic.org/files/reports/75.pdf) suggests a charismatic method of preaching. Another significant conclusion from this study is that Hispanic Catholics are more likely to interpret the Bible literally than non-Hispanic Catholics. They also indicate greater support for preaching that addresses issues such as immigration reform, discrimination, war, the death penalty, and poverty. Whether or not the preacher is himself Latino is of relatively less importance.

16. Winthrop Yinger, *Cesar Chavez: The Rhetoric of Nonviolence* (Pompano Beach, FL: Exposition Press of Florida, 1975). Yinger does not use the term "Don," but actually a more Catholic scholastic one borrowed from Kenneth Burke, namely, "consubstantial."

17. John C. Hammerback and Richard J. Jensen. "The Rhetorical Worlds of César Chávez and Reies Tijerina," *The Western Journal of Speech Communication* 44 (1980), 166–176.

18. John C. Hammerback and Richard J. Jensen. "'A Revolution of Heart and Mind': Cesar Chavez's Rhetorical Crusade," *Journal of the West* 27, 2 (1988): 69–74.

19. John C. Hammerback and Richard J. Jensen, *The Rhetorical Career of César Chávez* (College Station, TX: Texas A&M University Press, 2003).

20. John C. Hammerback and Richard J. Jensen, "Cesar Estrada Chavez," in *American Orators of the Twentieth Century*, eds. Bernard K. Duffy and Halford R. Ryan (Westport, CT: Greenwood Press, 1987).

21. Jose A Gutierrez, John C. Hammerback, and Richard J. Jensen, *A War of Words: Chicano Protest in the 1960s and 1970s* (New York: Praeger, 1985).

22. Capuchin Richard Hart is among the few exceptions: see his articles in *Pastoral Life* (January 2003) and *The Priest* (September 2010).

23. Thomas G. Rogers and Mauro B. de Souza, "Preaching Cross-Culturally to Spanish-Speaking U.S. Hispanic Americans," *Homiletic* 28, 1 (Summer 2003): 1–10.

Chapter 14

Preaching Among the Poor:
A Panel of Holy Cross Priests

Joseph Corpora, CSC; Bill Wack, CSC;
and Ronald Raab, CSC

Joseph Corpora, CSC

I had the great privilege of serving as pastor of St. John Vianney Parish in Goodyear, Arizona, for twelve years (1990–2002). At that time, it certainly was one of the ten poorest parishes in the Diocese of Phoenix. Following that I had another great privilege of serving as pastor of Holy Redeemer Parish in Portland, Oregon, for seven years (2002–2009). Holy Redeemer was not as poor as St. John Vianney, but because of the growing Mexican community at Holy Redeemer, it was becoming poorer. And now that I am no longer a pastor, I spend Christmas week and Holy Week at a parish in a very poor village called Tequepexpan, which is located in the Diocese of Tepic in the state of Nayarit, Mexico. These are my experiences of preaching to the poor and being shaped by this preaching.

There are a couple of thoughts that I would like to share with you as I reflect on years of preaching to the economically poor. In most ways, it is easier to preach to the economically poor. In a few ways, it is more difficult.

1. *The poor do not feel any entitlement to God's grace or God's love or God's mercy . . . or to anything, for that matter.* They never expect it or think that these things are theirs by right. For them God's mercy is a gift. They are surprised by God's grace and so grateful for God's mercy. They are able to find God's grace in many situations that others might not be able to. They are able to see the Providence of God in all sorts of situations that others might not be able to detect Providence. They have never imagined that they could earn God's mercy or God's grace, and because of this they are delighted to receive it. So preaching about the kingdom of God as God's free gift to us is easy for the poor to accept.

Perhaps the fastest-growing cancer in our world today is entitlement. Entitlement kills the spirit of gratitude. And it creeps up on you without you hardly noticing.

Here's an example from my own life. In my job I travel way too much, so much so that I am a platinum flyer on Delta Airlines. This means that I get upgraded to first class a lot, perhaps 70 percent of the time. And when I don't get upgraded, I get mad . . . as though I should be upgraded by right. This is entitlement. It's bad. I should be super grateful when I get upgraded, and I am. But I have no right to expect it. I am beginning to feel entitled to it.

The poor are not like this at all. They are grateful.

2. *The poor are able to say much more quickly and from the heart* "lo que quiere Dios," *or* "a ver lo que dice Dios," *i.e.,* "whatever God wants" *or* "let's see what God says." They are resigned to his will in ways that I find it difficult to do. It is easier to preach that God will always take care of us because they have known this to be true in many situations and at many times and in many ways.

3. *The poor really believe that the Gospel is Good News.* They believe that God is going to save them. They believe that God is at work at all times, in all places, in all situations, saving them. They don't need to figure out and understand all the particulars. They just know that God is going to save them, that God is indeed saving them even when they have no sense of it or do not feel it at all. So many things don't make sense to them, but they trust in God.

4. *Not only do they know that God will save them, the poor want to be saved.* They know that they need to be saved. They know that they cannot do it alone. The homilist doesn't have to convince them to be saved. They

are less self-reliant, less self-important, and less self-assertive. And so they want to be saved. It's easy to preach that God will save because they want to be saved.

5. *The poor have tough lives.* They lack so many privileges that the world can give. They struggle. They work physically hard. They work long hours. They work weekends. Though they believe that God is going to save them, they often have a hard time believing that God truly loves them and cares about them. And sometimes they have a tough time really believing that God will forgive them. Somehow they have internalized that perhaps their poverty is related to some sin. We know that this is not true, but sometimes they have a tough time believing that. I had to preach regularly and often and strongly of God's infinite and gracious and unconditional love, of God's relentless forgiveness. Often they found this hard to accept. In this way, preaching to the poor was more difficult.

6. *The poor love Christ crucified.* They identify with him. They love him on the cross. They know him on the cross. They love being with him on the cross. They are one with him on the cross. He's for them. They know what it is to be on the cross. They know that he suffered on the cross for them. Sometimes you have to remind them that he has been raised from the dead and now lives. Well, honestly, they do know this, but they love Christ crucified.

The poor have taught me why, for the most part, the people of God have celebrated more intensely Good Friday than Easter Sunday. It's not that they don't believe in Easter. It's just that Good Friday allows them to identify with the suffering and dying Jesus. And in identifying with the suffering and dying Jesus they can find strength to endure their own sufferings. They can find strength to endure their own weaknesses and failings and their own inability to improve. The suffering and dying Jesus makes them depend on God so much.

The death of Jesus on the cross is a symbol of the suffering that comes from living life in all its messiness. I must confess that I find more hope and understanding and strength in this helpless God on the cross than in the all-powerful and almighty God. Because I feel so helpless in the face of my sins and my struggles and my weaknesses and my failings, I can identify with the helpless Jesus on the cross. The poor taught me this.

The poor don't prefer the dying Christ to the resurrected Christ. Well, maybe they do. But they can identify more with the helpless one. They know that it's both dying and rising. But it is in Jesus on the cross that they renew their hope that death does not have the final word. In that cross their faith is ultimately strengthened. That's where they live: Christ crucified.

Bill Wack, CSC

Let me start by saying that it is a tremendous honor to be included on this panel, especially with my fellow Holy Cross priests here who are wonderful homilists and presiders.

I remember a homily given by Fr. Ron Raab, CSC (one of the panelists here). Actually, I don't remember the content of the homily, only that he began by standing in the middle of the church and saying, "I really don't know how to begin this homily, so I'm going to start in the middle!" Well, I don't know any better way to begin my little presentation except by starting at the end. So what I say to you, in summary, is: "Be yourself, and do not make assumptions when you are preaching to or with or among the poor." This is important not just for ministry in general but in preaching in particular. I find that I need to keep returning to these truths again and again.

When I was in the seminary, I spent a summer at Andre House, a house of hospitality in Phoenix, founded in the tradition of the Catholic Worker Movement. It dawned on me halfway through my time there that I would be renewing my vows of poverty, celibacy, and obedience that summer among that community. I had hoped to do it in a quiet little private ceremony with the priest and another witness, or maybe even with the staff of Andre House in the midst of a Mass. The director, however, thought that it would be fitting if we could invite the whole community: volunteers, staff, our guests from the streets and the shelters, and our neighbors.

When I realized that this would happen I felt ashamed and embarrassed, thinking how I was going to make a profession of poverty among people who were *really* poor (not just spiritually poor or living simply by choice, as I was doing). And so I was dreading that day when I should have been looking forward to it. I wanted to get it over with quickly. When the time came I got up there and started off with the profession: "I, William Albert Wack, of the Congregation of Holy Cross. . . ." Then for the vows I said, "I make to God for one year the vows of celibacy, obedience, and poverty." I garbled the last word because I didn't want anyone to stand up and say, "Poverty? You don't *know* what poverty is about! I'll show you poverty!" After the Mass, however, we gathered for a celebratory meal and several of the guests came up to me to offer their congratulations. One man spoke for the others and said, "That was awesome. I could never do that. I could never take vows like you just did." He wasn't put off by my desire to profess the evangelical counsels; he was inspired by it.

Another story also comes from my work at Andre House. We celebrated a Mass every morning when I was there. It was a simple celebration in which we gathered around a card table that served as the altar, and everyone was invited: the guests, the volunteers, and the regular staff. One day I was preaching about the story of Lazarus and the rich man (Luke 16:19-31). I went on and on about "you who are poor" (referring to our guests present), saying that they are like Lazarus now, but they will experience the glory of eternal life in heaven when they die. And I was quick to condemn people who, like the rich man, stepped over them every day and ignored them in their need. I thought that I had really "opened the Scriptures" for our guests because it was clear that they would identify with Lazarus.

After Mass, however, one of our guests came to me and said, "Chaplain, you missed the whole point of that story! You see, it's not a story about Lazarus; it's all about the rich man. And we are like the rich man, ignoring our brothers and sisters around us. It's a warning to *us*, chaplain." Once again, I assumed that I knew what they needed or wanted to hear, but they were waiting to be challenged to live the Gospel instead.

One more story, and this is not about preaching to the poor, but it is relevant to our topic today. Presently, I work at St. Ignatius Martyr Parish in Austin, Texas, and we have a mixed community of Hispanics, Anglos, people from other cultures and lands, and a sizeable deaf community (because of our proximity to the Texas School for the Deaf, located just down the road). One of our Masses every week is interpreted for the deaf and hard of hearing. One week I proclaimed the Gospel passage in which Jesus challenged his hearers to "Listen!" Three times Jesus tells them to pay attention: "Those who have ears, hear my voice." I didn't want to look at either the interpreter or the community of deaf people gathered in front of me. After the Mass, I said to the interpreter, "Wow, that must have been difficult. How did you interpret the part about Jesus challenging us to listen?" Without skipping a beat, she said, "That wasn't difficult at all. Jesus isn't talking about hearing audibly; he wants us to hear with our hearts. So instead of signing 'hear' by touching my ear, I made the sign over my heart." I was truly humbled by her understanding of Jesus' words and of her desire to help others to hear it that way as well.

In ministry and in preaching we cannot assume that we know what the other person needs to hear. Our task is to be faithful to the truth and let them wrestle with it in order to determine what God is saying to them at that particular time. Yes, we must try to learn as much as we can about the needs and cultures of those whom we serve, but that doesn't mean that we should try to tailor our homilies to what we *think* they need to hear based on a previous assumption. On the contrary, we who would preach and minister to others have to listen to them and be open to what God might be teaching us through them and their experiences.

I said that we shouldn't make assumptions. A positive way to put it would be, "Get to know the people to whom you are sent to minister." Being present to our congregations and communities is an invaluable help to our ministry. Another lesson for me—and many of the presentations at this conference have mentioned this—is that we who preach must be people who *listen*. It's ironic that at a conference dedicated to preaching the Word we are devoting so much time to listening! This was what Jesus was all about. He didn't just talk to the people; he was *with* them. He lived with them, walked with them, ate with them, celebrated with them, cried with them, died with them. A great deal of his ministry was accomplished without even saying a word. We would all do well to listen with our hearts and to share in the life of the poor and those we serve. This isn't just part of our ministry or good for our preaching; it is the *foundation* of all that we do in Jesus' name.

Ronald Raab, CSC

In 2002 Fr. Bob Loughery, CSC, invited me to come to what was then the Downtown Chapel in Portland, Oregon, an urban parish community that serves people who are homeless, mentally ill, and addicted. I remember the night Bob picked me up from the airport. He brought me to the parish, to a building that does not look like a church. He opened the door, and I brought my bags into the lobby. I stopped, paused, and looked at him. He looked at me and said, "You'll get used to the smell." So I'm in my eleventh year there and, believe me, I've gotten used to the smell of urine and feces and sweat and wet backpacks and blankets and clothing and all the things that make up the ministry there among people in urban poverty. I came there broken myself, and these ten and a half years have been an experience for me of deep and profound healing. Some of those things I'd like to share with you.

First, I would like to encourage all of us to never use the phrase "the poor." This phrase puts people and the issues of their lives in abstraction. It separates people from the experiences of their lives. If you are going to speak about "the poor," please use phrases such as "people surviving generational poverty," "people struggling with long-term illnesses and addictions" or "people surviving mental illness." Do you see the distinction? We are not separate from them. We recognize their human dignity. This is very important as we begin any kind of discussion about "the poor."

One of my ministries at St. Andre Bessette Church is a thirteen-hour immersion experience into the issues of poverty called the Personal Poverty Retreat. One Friday a month we gather people from around the archdiocese to spend some time exploring what poverty means. We recognize our own poverty. We are not all economically poor, but on this side of the grave we all need something in our lives. We all need to be yanked out of our own selfishness, our own inability to do things for ourselves. We need to explore the ways in which we all need God, and that is also poverty.

Preaching among people who are surviving such forms of poverty reveals to me that first and foremost preaching is about intimacy. Preaching is about the revelation of relationship, and without the relationship nothing is going to happen. In our small community there are no large structures or committees that separate the preacher from those who are experiencing such issues. You stand naked in front of people, and they know very well if you believe what you say or not.

One thing I want to say is that I have come to believe in Christ Jesus. After twenty-nine years of priesthood and many years of ministry in different places, believe you me, I have come to a greater depth and reliance on the power of God than I ever have in my entire life.

A gentleman comes to us every few months traveling about an hour to the parish. He is a professor, and he suffers horribly from mental illness and depression. He just happens to be an atheist. He attends the parish because he knows that the word of God is going to be proclaimed with honesty. He said that he cannot find any other church in his neighborhood or city or town or anything between his home and ours where the word of God is proclaimed and the preaching has anything to do with honesty. He tells me that when he hears the word of God among people who smell and who are wet and wander around the church because of their mental illness, something happens from the inside out. He says there is a glimpse, there is a moment when healing happens in his soul. He tells me every time I see him that there is no medication that has ever done that for him. There is no psychiatrist that has ever done that for him. The real presence of Christ Jesus in the Word is healing him. I have never ever heard it described with such profoundness.

I also hear from people who will never be healed. A woman in our community was severely abused as a child and will never be healed. As I stand in the center aisle in that particular community to preach the word of God, she is always on my left. I have to in some way recognize that she needs to be lifted up a little bit, but she will never completely understand that she is loved by God. It's never going happen. Only being in relationship recognizes this kind of powerlessness with people. She teaches me further, deeper, in a more profound way, a new reliance on the power and Spirit of God within my own life, like nothing ever has. I am a "Triple-Domer," a three-time graduate from the University of Notre Dame, but nothing has taught me more about how to believe in God than our people in poverty.

Another issue concerning preaching among people in poverty is that we have to recognize that the entire church is soaked in alcohol and the issues of codependency. That's very important for the preacher because no matter how much we try, we are not going to change people. We have to recognize our boundaries as preachers. This has something to do with not only their addictions and our relationship with them but also our own wanting to change things that cannot be changed and our own codependency. We must be aware of all the things that are stirred up within the church around the issues of alcohol.

Another thing that I have learned about preaching there is that we are very good at welcoming people into our hospitality center. We connect with about fifteen colleges, universities, seminaries, and nursing schools. We are very good at offering hospitality on a daily basis. Hospitality is a Gospel value made very real in our particular place, and yet I have to do the same with preaching. Our ministry among the poor outside of the Eucharist teaches me about how to be hospitable with the words that I am using as a preacher. This connection is vital. We must preach resisting violence, dishonesty, and blame. We must not blame people for being poor. If there is one thing that I have learned in ten and a half years at the parish it is that we as a society, as a church, and as a culture blame people for their poverty. If you read the newspapers, you will read many examples of people putting other people down. If we recognize our own personal poverty, that realization levels the ground. We are all the same if we all need God. The ways in which we put others down form us as we hear the word of God.

Loneliness is the great killer in our neighborhood. Preaching is a moment, a glimpse, and an inspiration of communion. We can do an incredible amount of good if we recognize this loneliness and if we recognize the loneliness of our own hearts.

No matter our ministry or our preaching, we cannot fix people as much as we try. Honesty goes a very long way as a preacher. We must not give up connecting the Eucharist to service and to justice. I've been writing and saying that and proclaiming that for thirty years with a jaw that doesn't work very well when I speak. I hope that I can continue to say that as long as my jaw holds out.

We must recognize that the love of God is manifest among people who need God. I want to call you into a much deeper and more reverent experience of the holy. You need to ask yourself if you really believe this stuff or not. I am telling you if you preach among people who have less than you, know very well that people know with all their hearts, strength, and minds whether or not you believe in what you are saying.

We must create a church that is of the poor and not a church that is only for the poor. What a difference this makes in preaching. Preaching becomes an intimate act of relationship. This intimate act of preaching is a mystery that must be surrendered to God.

I want to close with one last story. A gentleman, a pillar of our parish, has been coming to the parish for thirty years. He is a year older than I am, so when he found out that I am a year younger, he started calling me "Ronnie the Kid." You can imagine how people detest Christmas. We celebrate with our guests every year on Christmas Eve day. On this particular day we had two hundred people. We then have the noon Mass afterward. My friend always sits in the back, but during the first reading he got up from his seat and moved just a few feet from the ambo. I proclaimed the Gospel, and as I kissed the Gospel book and put the book back down on the ambo, he yelled out at me, "Ronnie the Kid, I'm not going to have diarrhea, am I?" I said, "No, you will be fine." There was a three-second pause, then he said, "Ronnie the Kid, I'm not going to have diarrhea, am I?" I responded, "No, you will be fine." Another three-second pause, then he said, "Ronnie the Kid, is everything going to be all right?" At that moment I had all that I could muster within my own faith and life, with everything that has been and everything that will be, to say to him with all my might as a preacher, as a minister, and as a priest, "Yes, everything will be all right."

It seems to me that question is ultimately the question for all of us who are searching desperately for belief and desperately to learn how to preach among people who need God. Perhaps you can begin your homily preparation with this question, "Is everything going to be all right?"

Chapter 15

New Directions in the Funeral and Wedding Homily: The Preacher as the Minister of Hospitality of the Kingdom of God

Guerric DeBona, OSB

In her chapter entitled "Ashes to Ashes, Dust to Diamonds: How to Turn Your Loved One into Jewelry and Why," Lisa Takeuchi Cullen details for us a lively tour of the new American way of death. Deceased actor Don Atkinson was cremated and turned into a diamond, courtesy of his adoring wife and a company called LifeGem, which, as of 2006, makes over a hundred such human diamonds a month. Cullen's book, *Remember Me,*[1] accounts for a variety of these techno-friendly forget-me-nots in contemporary funeral practices in an attempt to celebrate life. From rendering the deceased fashionably biodegradable to comfortably air-tight in a fabulously expensive casket, the eclectic and eccentric funeral practices in American culture have for many years been a mirror of the age of individualism and late capitalism. Diamonds are, after all, forever. This extravagant behavior, somewhat reminiscent of the tragic-comic moments about the funeral industry portrayed in Evelyn Waugh's *The Loved One* (1948), should not surprise us: we daily make our rounds in a country whose backbone of individualism and nonconformity has maintained itself in a more or less fixed capacity since its foundation. As Ralph Waldo Emerson famously wrote in "Self-Reliance": "Trust thyself: every heart vibrates to that iron string . . . Whoso would be a man, must be a nonconformist. He who would gather immortal palms must not be hindered by the name of goodness, but must explore if it be goodness. Nothing is at last sacred but the integrity of your own mind. Absolve you to yourself, and you shall have the suffrage of the world."[2]

Emerson's essay hints strikingly at what has faced the religious community in America over the years. More specifically related to the present topic, in my view, is that our way of encountering death (shall we say more directly: disposing of one another?) has long ceased to ritualize how societies and communities grieve but has become a postmodern fragmentation of personal desires and mawkish sentiments, gushing eulogies and, in some cases, outlandish and expensive spectacles—in a word, a morbid cafeteria catering to self-reliant tastes. The same mentality prevails, obviously with a somewhat different outcome, to weddings, in which a traditional ritual celebrating community has become a series of competitive and exotic theatrical events held on Waikiki or Mount Fuji, far from the community that raised the couple. The religious faith tradition of many different beliefs may well ask: Is this how a community celebrates its communal gratitude for the life of a deceased loved one? Or, again, how a community ritualizes the rite of passage from single life into the union of two selves?

The struggle present in crafting the homily is magnified in the larger cultural context. Preachers come with the word of God and a rich liturgical tradition grounded in historical memory to speak to a world that has lost the collective memory, which is the backbone of Scripture and tradition. To put that another way is to remind ourselves of Jean-François Lyotard's celebrated expression: the metanarrative in human history has been delegitimized, only to be replaced by personal micronarratives.[3] And for the Judeo-Christian tradition, this means the collective amnesia of salvation history and a collapse into the narcissistic personal and idiosyncratic eruptions of the compulsive, private self. How is the Catholic preacher at funerals and weddings to become what *Fulfilled in Your Hearing* calls "a mediator of meaning?" How do we preach Christ crucified if we have very few common foundational symbols or gestures that speak of grieving or loss, unity and regeneration?

Along these lines, I am suggesting that those who preach might do well to investigate chapter 53 in the *Rule of Saint Benedict*, "On the

Reception of Guests," which showcases hospitality as a foundational and cross-cultural symbol. I emphasize the word "foundational" because I believe that hospitality forms a necessary anthropological and theological response to a fragmented world. In a sense, I am introducing, or better yet, echoing a sociological category discussed by Redemptorist James Wallace in his fine book, *Preaching to the Hungers of the Heart*,[4] where he suggests that there are essential hungers to find meaning, to belong, and to find wholeness that preaching answers in a fundamental way. I want to claim that in an alienated society, bereft of what many would call "home," we seek shelter under God's protective care in the hospitality of the Kingdom. Preaching is the mustard seed sown in the field of the Lord that happens to be the twenty-first century. It is there in that muddy earth that the birds of the air come and build their nests of every kind, a visible sign of the Kingdom. By exploring the role of radical Christian welcome in the scriptural funeral and wedding texts, we might consider what I am calling the "Preacher as Minister of Hospitality in the Kingdom of God."

Preaching Funerals

In the April 9, 2012, issue of *Newsweek*, Andrew Sullivan recommends that we jettison the jejune world of church and its politics and reduce life to the essential Jesus, modeled on someone like St. Francis. Sullivan, who is a thoughtful cultural critic and, in many ways, raises some intelligent issues in his article, might better ponder the role of the faith community in the life of Jesus and Francis. That humanity, taken, blessed, broken, and given, is an integral part of the world of Christ is without question. "Go into all the world and proclaim the good news to the whole creation" (Mark 16:15, NRSV). How is it possible to separate Jesus from the community he came to redeem? Does Sullivan imagine that there is there a free-floating hologram of the Savior to which religious subjects are supposed to attach themselves? That the human, frail, and flawed community also discloses God's presence even in its sin is the mystery of grace, a fine point that Sullivan seems to have excised from his Bible, together with his mentor Thomas Jefferson, who evidently practiced a cut-and-paste Gospel as well. We are a community wounded by sin and alienation; it needs reconciliation, healing, and forgiveness, and so the Incarnate God himself brought individual cures to lepers and the blind; but with that restoration came a transformation of the community into wholeness. That communal healing means reconciliation and forgiveness must be present from the family to the larger church, if Christ is to be witnessed in the world. At the same time, if there is a new atheism on the rise, as rightly Sullivan points out, the response of the Christian community ought not be division and polarization and the flight from community, but the ground zero of living together as one body: forgiving seventy-seven times—that is to say, endlessly. Like Thomas the Apostle, we are called to explore the wounds of Christ in a fractured community, not shorn of politics and refusing to "wear man's smudge and share man's smell,"[5] but find in these traces of bloody violence God's mercy, compassion and, I hasten to add, the hospitality of the Kingdom.

Chapter 53 of the *Rule of St. Benedict* famously begins: "All guests who present themselves are to be welcomed as Christ, for he himself will say: I was a stranger and you welcomed me."[6] This reception of *omnes super venientes hospites* as a christological epiphany is rightly considered nothing less than radical hospitality, a welcome of love not only to pilgrims but to anyone who presents him/herself at the fragile doors of the monastic enclosure. Indeed, Benedict will lay special emphasis on receiving the poor since it is in them that Christ is especially visible. "All humility should be shown in addressing a guest on arrival or departure. By a bow of the head or by a complete prostration of the body, Christ is to be adored because he is indeed welcomed in them." The disclosure of Christ in the stranger as guest appears even more peculiar in the eyes of contemporary America, which has all too quickly walled itself up with the isolation of gated communities and luxury automobiles fit only for one.

Fittingly enough, for Benedict the guest is attended to with the welcome of the word of God and an accompanying ritual. "After the guests have been received, they should be invited to pray; then the superior or an appointed brother will sit with them. The divine law is read to the guest for his instruction, and after that every kindness is shown to him." The abbot himself will pour water on the hands of the guests and with the entire community wash their feet. Perhaps passages in Scriptures were read to the guests, which themselves showcase how important hospitality has been to the Judeo-Christian community, such as Abraham receiving the three visitors in Genesis; or Jesus' encounter with the woman who washes his feet with her tears and dries them with her hair in Luke 7:36-50; or the early church devoting themselves to breaking bread together in their homes in Acts 2. Taken together, these acts of hospitality, which lavishly adore Christ in the guest, are proclamations of God's presence and grace in the world. Hospitality is the silent language that speaks of God living and active among his people. In Benedict's time, a period of upheaval and fracture may be something like our own, the sign of the kingdom was revealed in the act of love shown to a stranger and a pilgrim. I would like to now suggest that these signs of hospitality are still present among us in the celebration of our liturgical rites in the church, and those signs are mediated by preaching during funerals and weddings.

In his consideration of preaching within the sacramental rites of the church, Fr. Wallace reminds us that *Fulfilled in Your Hearing* says that effective preaching springs from an awareness of the experiences that touch the lives of the community. Wallace goes on to point out that "the preacher must be conscious of the daily experiences of the community that can lead to its recognizing the presence of the living God, or, perhaps more common in our age, to questioning whether God is really active and present at all in our world today. Only then is it possible to mediate meaning by bringing together the Christian revelation, especially as it is articulated in the biblical texts read during the liturgy, and the events of the world we live in."[7] For Wallace, Christian preaching inside the sacramental rites answers a foundational hunger present in all people: the hunger for meaning. Along these lines, I am suggesting that the sacramental language of hospitality speaks for the hunger for home and presence, a way to discover meaning. For pilgrims and strangers who come to the church door waiting to find meaning in grieving the loss of a loved one, the preacher as minister of the kingdom will help those gathered, as Mary Catherine Hilkert puts it, "to name grace."[8]

Consider, if you will, the ritual action of hospitality already present in the *Order of Christian Funerals*. Since the church is the place where the community of faith gathers, the Rite puts a special emphasis on the reception of the body, which "has great significance" (72). "In the act of receiving the body, the members of the community acknowledge the deceased as one of their own, one who was welcomed in baptism and who held a place in the assembly." These are signs of radical hospitality, welcoming the deceased, without regard to social status or standing, into the antechamber of the kingdom. With the exception of the rites of initiation, the funeral liturgy is the only time in which the presider formally answers the door, so to speak, by greeting those gathered at the entrance of the church. The broad symbol of the church welcoming back the departed is clear enough but so is the welcome extended to all of those gathered. As a guest of honor, the deceased is washed again with the symbols of baptism and clothed again with a white garment. These are the signs of hospitality that the church offers those who have come from the dark night of bereavement and are hungry for hospitality—a divine welcome that is beginning to be disclosed in the lavish generosity of ritual. The presider as host welcomes the guest, along with his or her family and friends, back into the church with its baptismal font, ambo, and table where the guests will be consoled by Scripture and fed. In the end, the guest of honor will be put to rest to await the morning of the resurrection.

The funeral liturgy itself and the Scriptures hold the key for the preacher to unlock the treasure of God's hospitality in the sacramental rites. The opening prayer (outside the Easter season) focuses on the God "in whom sinners find mercy and the saints find joy . . . admit him/her to the joyful company of your saints and raise him/her on the last day to rejoice in your presence forever." A mirror of God's hospitality, here is the voice of the church knocking on God's front door asking for a place of welcome for a brother or sister to join the others who have gone before. At the prayer of commendation, the presider asks that God receive the loved one personally: "Into your hands, Father of mercies, we commend our brother or sister in the sure and certain hope that, together with all who have died in Christ, he or she will rise with him on the last day." These are prayers that hope for an admittance into God's presence at the last: "May the angels lead you into paradise; may the martyrs come to welcome you and take you to the holy city, the new and eternal Jerusalem." The funeral liturgy is a consoling presence of God's hospitality.

When it comes to the Scriptures, the church has recommended several texts, of course, that might be deployed for preaching funerals. Ideally, the family and friends will be able to partner with the preacher in order to discern which texts begin to speak to them at this time of grief. I will confine myself here to the Gospels and suggest five strategies that might be used to uncover the metanarrative of God's graciousness as revealed in the Word.

1. *Account for the overall place of hospitality as a plot device in the passage.* Luke's account of the raising of the dead man at Nain, Mark's representation of the raising of Jairus' daughter, and John's passage on the resurrection of Lazarus all restore the dead to community, family, and home. What are the implications?

2. *Are there problems or knots in the text that need to be acknowledged that may appear to suggest that God's welcome is far from us?* John's account of the raising of Lazarus shows us that Jesus waited before he returned to visit his sick friend, who eventually died. Some people wonder about this delay. Does Jesus' hesitation suggest an abandonment of divine hospitality? Then again, what provokes Martha's faith response when Jesus does appear? Can this mystery be explored and allowed to unfold for a grieving congregation?

3. *What about the transformation of the characters in the story?* Martha chides Jesus for not being around when her brother died. How has she changed by the end of the story? In a way, Jesus is first welcomed by Martha in her home and near the tomb of her brother. But now Jesus is the new host, welcoming Martha and Lazarus into the threshold of eternal life by a transforming sign. How do we imagine that the disciples changed when Jesus told them about the grain falling to the ground and dying in order to yield much fruit? These changes imply that the characters had to make room in their own homes for God to do something new. What about welcoming God in the presence of the mystery of death? In confronting this text, perhaps the preacher will need to be among the first to make room for the Lord.

4. *Observe carefully what the metaphors and symbols are doing in the passages, especially in regard to hospitality and welcome.* Jesus portrays himself in John 14:1-6 as one who prepares a place for his disciples in his Father's house, which, he says, has many dwelling places. The language of the church speaks of death as a journey home. In September 2005, the Catholic and world presses widely reported that the final words of John Paul II (spoken in Polish) before he died were, "Let me go to the House of the Father."[9] Here again, the picture of the heavenly home is visualized as a place of welcome, an enormous comfort and source of faith that the Creator will not forsake the creation at the last hour. Similarly, in John 6:51-58, Jesus reckons himself as a meal for the guests who will live forever; he is the "living bread that came down from heaven." Can the preacher unpack these symbols as signs of the kingdom present among us?

5. *What is the text asking the assembly to do in regard to Christian welcome?* The texts recommended for funerals for adults include accounts of the crucifixion. What do we make of this from the perspective of the assembly? The preacher will need to move the congregation to understand this seminal moment as God's gift to his people, the ultimate act of hospitality

in which the incarnation of the living God shared our home and died like us. That moment of seeming defeat, however, becomes an opportunity for faith: the resurrection transforms this dark death into new life. That is the reason we preach Christ crucified: a new door has been opened that was seemingly shut from sin. That is the gracious invitation that awaits the beloved. All of us become guests welcomed as pilgrims at a monastery door, washed with the blood of the Lamb and fed at his table.

Preaching Weddings

When it comes to weddings, we all have our anecdotal information about the less than fervent state of the sacramental bond as well as the fragmentation of community that this loss implies. As much as the contemporary church may despair about the drop in traditional marriage ceremonies, this sociological shift has been occurring for decades with no sign of change or letting up. When researcher Daniel Yankolovich asked women in the 1950s to respond to why they would get married, one woman replied, "Why do you walk with two feet instead of one?" But by the 1960s Elizabeth Douvan found "that marriage and parenthood are rarely viewed as necessary, and people who do not choose these roles are no longer considered social deviants."[10] A recent census taken in American households finds that over the last decade there has been an increase of 40 percent of those who have chosen to cohabitate and not get married in any way, shape, or form.

I hasten to add that this analysis on the state of marriage is a complex issue. There is probably some strong economic evidence for this movement away from a permanent union between couples, having to do with financial issues, together with the shedding of social stigmas attached to those who live together but are unwed. The bottom line may just be a question of relevance: an astonishingly large proportion of people are finding marriage simply irrelevant. As more and more children are being raised in single-parent families, the trend to stay unmarried will probably continue to grow. What is the relevance of pronouncing public vows, still less ones that are imbued with an aura of religiosity? Paradoxically, a good portion of the population seems to obsess over royal and celebrity weddings, but they themselves return to either a single dwelling or cohabitation. Maybe that says something, maybe not. We might chalk up the sociological trend of the decline of marriage to episodic thinking or the psychological caution instilled in a culture with increasing divorce rates, yet these are undoubtedly forces with which the church must reckon in its pastoral approach to marriage. But whatever the multiple factors that are contributing to the public celebration of two people exchanging lifelong vows together, we can agree that the ritual of marriage and its preaching are not speaking at their full potential to our culture in ways that they could, especially regarding God's love and hospitality. Although there may be those who find marriage irrelevant, the people of God still yearn for a sign of divine hospitality in order to find meaning in the world and to offer themselves as a home for one another.

Can the church and its preachers provide a language of hospitality for the coming together of two disparate selves, a movement from alienation to community when they might as well leave the "union" simply to living together, sharing a table, a bed, and maybe a few kids? This is the challenge not only of preaching but, indeed, of the vital sacramental life of the church. The preacher deepens the consciousness of the congregation into the very meaning of the sacrament of marriage unfolding before them, disclosing the sign not unlike Christ himself revealed in the wedding at Cana in John 2 when the Lord becomes the new host at the banquet, transforming old water for ritual purity into the new wine of the kingdom. The preacher's task at weddings will be to reveal that same new wine of God's hospitality hidden in the sacramental exchange of vows, where the future husband and wife become a new home, a new dwelling place for one another: a guest who is welcomed at the threshold of the kingdom. In so doing, this couple becomes a symbol of God's presence abiding in the world, making new what was old. The *Rite of Marriage* ultimately discloses the possibility of divine charity embedded in sacramental language. The faithful who witness the vows are themselves catechized by symbol to begin anew, welcoming one another into one another's presence as strangers and guests.

As with the *Order of Funerals*, monastic hospitality provides something of a window into the celebration and preaching of Christian marriage. The procedure for receiving guests in the early monastic communities was quite intimate. As I indicated earlier, Benedict calls on the whole community to act as servant to the guest who comes as Christ himself. No longer strangers, the abbot washes the hands of the newcomer, and the whole community together with its pastoral shepherd washes the feet of the pilgrim.

We can easily see the connection between this hospitality of service and the theological and sacramental meaning of marriage. If you will permit me a metaphor to briefly guide this discussion, I would like to suggest that the preacher/presider at weddings is akin to a host who guides a guest through a new home. Since the presider officiates on behalf of and in the name of the church, he bids the couple and their guests welcome. The metaphor of a guide becomes especially appropriate when we consider the parallels between the guests entering the cloister walk and doorways of a monastery and the entrance into their own home: both become the threshold of welcome at the entrance of which the preacher stands. The door of this home imagined by the preacher for the couple might open up onto a lavish foyer/living space; this forms the preparation for marriage. Here we can find an abundance of appointments, as it were, theological expressions, catechesis, and self-understandings. The preacher is at a distinct advantage in discussing the preparation for the sacrament of marriage since its living quarters is a place of dialogue with the rich historical and catechetical tradition of the church. The couple can be encouraged to receive this tradition as one would be welcomed as a guest into a large home, full of historical treasures. In this living space, a place of preparation and understanding, the preacher might access the liturgical texts that will be used for the wedding liturgy, opening them up like a family album, filled with tradition; some of these texts will provide a rich source of reflection from which the couple will be able to choose. What do these prayers say about the theology of marriage and how the couple makes sense of that mystery? What about taking the nuptial blessing and parsing out the various phrases for understanding God's blessing on their union? "Lord, grant that as they begin to live this sacrament they may share with each other the gifts of your love and become one in heart and mind as witnesses to your presence in their marriage. Help them to create a home together . . ." (66). The preacher could accentuate the creation of a home with the bond of love: that hospitality and making a home is the fruitful playground of friendship and love. Additionally, there may be a team of further conversation partners who share this room with the preacher and those preparing for marriage: other couples who have welcomed them on a pre-Cana weekend, for instance. This is the living space in which a couple also continues to be in dialogue with the preacher with their own understanding of who they are and are becoming as baptized Christians, including their struggles and challenges along the way.

When the journey into the interior of the home continues, the kitchen is laid out for the preparation of the Word, as it were, made ready to be consumed. This is certainly a crucial point for the preacher to both hear and reveal to the couple. Why have they chosen these particular readings? How do they speak to them about the marriage they have seen unfolding in their previous discussions? Collective understanding of the readings can potentially form the spine of the homily for the preacher, who can treat this encounter with the couple as a collaborative hermeneutic; it may be a modified version of what John McClure has called "round table preaching."[11] Needless to say, how the couple understands the readings and God's activity in their lives is vitally significant in deepening their own awareness of the sacrament as well as those who will witness this rite. Additionally, some reflection on the Eucharist is appropriate here, if this particular wedding will occur in the context of Mass. How does the couple see the various presidential prayers in the context of their union together? What does sharing the Body and Blood of the Lord for the first time as husband and wife mean to them? How do they see the eucharistic life of the church unfolding in their married life?

When the preacher leads the couple to the last room, the bridal chamber, it is here that hospitality is fully unfolded: husband and wife become self-gift for one another, a new home to dwell in. The exchange of vows is the centerpiece for this room since it is a final commitment until death. As Christ becomes the bridegroom for his church by offering himself as a complete self-gift, so too does this couple become wedded into the same surrender of the individual ego into one. This moment is nothing less but consent freely given with a steadfast hope and trust in the goodness of God and the support of the church. This very vulnerability of love bespeaks of our role as creatures who trust in God's mercy to carry out what was begun in us from the moment of our birth. If the church's welcome into the house of love culminates in this last room, its priority of place suggests that the physical intimacy for the couple is fully integrated into a kind of theology of hospitality: the full surrender of the self is literally an exchange between two persons of goodwill offering their futures to one another. This is their own gift of hospitality, a symbol of Christ's love for the church, which might serve as a sign for the larger culture, wounded by violence and division but which longs for a symbol of unity and peace.

This whole process of welcoming from throughout this house of hospitality will undoubtedly put demands on the preacher since listening to the couple, pondering the Scripture texts, together with exegeting the assembly, are crucial features to be attended to in the unfolding of the marriage. Getting to know the couple will obviously be important, and a simple "generic" homily will not be sufficient. The assembly of family and friends will quickly absorb how hospitality has been extended to the couple and to the congregation itself as partners in this act of self-giving love. It is impossible to exaggerate the demonstrative character of the church offering hospitality to the couple who are themselves offering up their lives in mutual self-giving in the community of love.

As we might expect, the liturgy and the scriptural readings recommended for the wedding homily can be mined with the couple for various insights. The preacher might again bear in mind how hospitality runs through these texts and use them as guideposts in crafting the preaching event. Indeed, the *Rite for Marriage* encourages lavish symbols of welcome, as the presider awaits the bridal party to join him at the sanctuary. This union suggests the coming together of separate selves under the welcome of the church that officiates at the mutual hospitality of husband and wife about to unfold. In some sense, the sanctuary of the church is already symbolizing a home, a foundation where the exchange of vows between the couple are made, in the consent where the new husband and wife will "take" each other to themselves, even as a host takes in a new guest into the home. The rings speak of the vows that have made a covenant of love, sealing the hospitality of two people for each other for a lifetime; they are also gifts of mutual hospitality extended to one another. As they move out into the world of others, the couple welcomes strangers as well as friends, their own children as well as those whom society has not nurtured and defended.

As with texts recommended for the funeral liturgy, the readings that can be explored for weddings are numerous, but I will limit myself here once again to the Gospel texts because of spatial considerations:

1. *Note the way the passage deals narratively with relationships, and ask the text what it has to say about hospitality.* The wedding at Cana obviously represents a seminal moment in Jesus' hospitality, as I have already suggested. We can really sense the need on the part of the couple who become the beneficiaries of God's graciousness. As we know from the narrator, this little episode in John's gospel is the first sign in Jesus' ministry. How does the Lord's presence at this wedding further reveal the sign of God's presence among his people? If the couple chose this passage, why were they drawn to it?

2. *Are there problems or knots in the text that need to be acknowledged that may appear to suggest that God welcomes only some into the kingdom?* There

are many encouraging texts that might be used for the celebration of a wedding, but the Gospel text especially might appear difficult to understand for those in the congregation who are unchurched or distant from the church. The preacher will need to work diligently to evangelize without casting aspersions on those who do not live their lives as "salt of the earth," or who have been divorced. Can hospitality form a virtue, a sign of God's kingdom, without shaming the congregation?

3. *What about the transformation of the characters in the story, and how have they been altered by hospitality?* I have often wondered what ever happened to the Pharisee-lawyer who came up to him one sunny day and asked the Lord which of the commandments of the law is the greatest. I suspect that he probably did a lot of thinking about priorities, and so he was undoubtedly different after his encounter with Jesus. The same transformation might be said about the crowd who were listening to the Sermon on the Mount in Matthew 5. We never meet the couple from Cana, but the new wine of the kingdom discloses a transformation through divine hospitality and generosity. If that is the case, then the couple and the assembly also await transformation with the hearing of the Gospel. That change will involve opening our own doors for conversion.

4. *Observe carefully what the metaphors and symbols are doing in the passages, especially how these suggest sacramental signs.* After the Beatitudes, Jesus offers the crowds a further challenge: to be salt of the earth and light of the world. He recommends in Matthew 7 that those who put his words into practice will be like a wise man who built his house on rock. That sturdy house is certainly a fitting metaphor for a couple about to build their own home together. The preacher might help those about to be married understand how they go about preparing a home together with God's help. This particular Gospel image of the house allows the preacher to put on the role of a host and take the couple on a tour of their home. What kind of rooms will they find, and are they prepared for the visit? How will they both contribute to the building of such a dwelling unselfishly? What does this welcome say about the goods of marriage?

5. *What is the text asking the assembly to do?* The texts used for the marriage liturgy are not only for the couple but for all. What are the invitations that the Scriptures extend to all those present, bidding them to welcome the Word? For those who are married, it may be an opportunity to renew their own covenant of love. For those who are not in a sacramental bond, it may a chance to see how living out a public and religious sign might

be a transformative moment for the world, to which they might give effective witness. The love of the couple has been demonstrated in this sacramental sign in the same way that Jesus shows his love for his disciples and the church. The process of marriage, as well as its preparation, will invite this new couple to open their doors to God's grace; this is the hospitality required for all of us in baptism, as we see Christ in the stranger, the pilgrim in our midst and at our table. Finally, how is the congregation challenged to support this newly married couple in welcome over the years?

Conclusion

I have been speaking here about the language of hospitality, God's generous gift of self-communication in Christ in the paschal mystery. I believe that mining the language of hospitality in Word and sacrament in preaching funerals and weddings discloses a deep, cross-cultural, multigenerational language that will speak to a contemporary culture hungry for welcome. That hospitality, quite visible in the *Rule of St. Benedict* as a sign of God's unfailing love to pilgrims and guests, remains an ever-present sign of the kingdom in the presence of the people of God. It provides, in the end, a crucial common language of meaning and hope for the future. Celebrating and preaching weddings and funerals gives the preacher the opportunity to evangelize with the well of human kindness and divine welcome in the midst of what seems like a cultural diaspora of violence and antipathy. Additionally, this sacramental preaching can provide what is new in the so-called New Evangelization. The preacher's fundamental function as mediator of meaning is also the mediator of memory—God's memory. It is sacrament that provides the language for restoring memory of God's works to the people living in an episodic, fragmented diaspora. As Fr. Wallace reminds us, "as language event, the preaching is one of the integral components of the rite, crucial in bridging the gap between the Liturgy of the Word and the Liturgy of the Sacrament, between anamnesis and mimesis, between remembering what God has done in the paschal mystery of Christ and what we are presently engaged in doing as an act of realizing the presence of salvation in our midst."[12] Finally, the community is invited to share in this work of remembering God's graciousness present in their very midst as the Word is fulfilled in their hearing.

Endnotes

1. HarperBusiness, 2007.

2. From *Essays: First Series*, originally published in 1841.

3. See Jean-François Lyotard, *The Postmodern Condition: A Report on Knowledge*, trans. Georff Bennington and Brian Massumi (Minneapolis, MN: University of Minnesota Press, 1984), 31–41.

4. Collegeville, MN: Liturgical Press, 2002.

5. Gerard Manley Hopkins, "God's Grandeur," in *Gerard Manley Hopkins: The Major Works*, ed. Catherine Phillips, Oxford World Classics (New York: Oxford University Press, 1989), 128.

6. *RB 1980: The Rule of St. Benedict in English and Latin*, ed. Timothy Fry (Collegeville, MN: Liturgical Press, 1980), 255.

7. James Wallace, *Preaching to the Hungers of the Heart: Preaching on the Feasts and within the Rites* (Collegeville, MN: Liturgical Press, 2002), 70.

8. "The preacher speaks the word of God in naming the community's experience in faith of the unexpected grace in ordinary human history." See Mary Catherine Hilkert, *Naming Grace: Preaching and the Sacramental Imagination* (New York: Continuum, 1998), 36.

9. See www.nbcnews.com/id/9377134/.

10. Robert N. Bellah, et al., *Individualism and Commitment in American Life: Readings on the Themes of Habits of the Heart* (New York: Harper and Row, 1988), 103–4.

11. See John S. McClure, *The Roundtable Pulpit: Where Leadership and Preaching Meet* (Nashville: Abingdon, 1995).

12. Wallace, 78.

Chapter 16

Preaching and Children

Ann Garrido

Among the many populations that preachers attempt to reach, young children are perhaps the most challenging. They wiggle in their seats, root through their mothers' purses, and drop the hymnals in the middle of prayerful pauses. They burp during all-school Masses and collectively find it *very* funny (that is, when they haven't already decided the homily would be the best time to visit the restroom). The Lectionary does not make the task any easier with tales of David lusting after Bathsheba, God telling Abraham to sacrifice his son, and Jesus behaving badly in the temple. In the Roman Catholic tradition, the challenge of connecting Scripture to the everyday lives of children can be particularly difficult. The majority of our Sunday preachers are committed celibates with little daily exposure to children. Growing administrative demands and increased regulations around appropriate contact with children keep these little people and their ways an uncomfortable mystery. Perhaps this is why, in the case of children, the church makes a rare official exception around who can preach. "With the consent of the pastor or rector of the church," reads the *Directory for Masses with Children*, "one of the adults may speak to the children after the gospel, especially if the priest finds it difficult to adapt himself to the mentality of children."[1]

At the same time, many preachers recognize that the early years of childhood are a profoundly important period in terms of faith formation, and they value the presence of little ones in the pews. These preachers want to prepare a meaningful message for children but are unsure how. In this essay, I want to introduce a growing body of insight about children culled by a movement called Catechesis of the Good Shepherd (CGS) and consider how CGS might serve as a resource for preachers with a passion for reaching the next generation.[2]

The Catechesis of the Good Shepherd is an international movement originally founded in Rome in the mid-1950s by two Italian women. The first, Sofia Cavalletti, was a Hebrew Scripture scholar active in the academic life with little interest in children. At the insistence of a friend who was dissatisfied with the sacramental preparation options for her seven-year-old son, Cavalletti began to work with the boy and was quickly intrigued by the fresh questions he brought to study. She sought out a child development expert, Gianna Gobbi, who had trained with famed educator Maria Montessori. Cavalletti and Gobbi formed a dynamic partnership that lasted for over fifty years before Gobbi passed away in 2002 and Cavalletti in 2011. The two repeatedly asked, "Who is the child before me? What are this person's needs? Questions?" And then, "What resources do we have from our scriptural and liturgical tradition to help the child to wrestle with those questions?"[3] In essence, the two regularly engaged the same kind of process preachers engage in homiletic preparation.

Cavalletti and Gobbi created an experimental space called an "atrium" in which they could listen to children's questions and reflect with them on the faith using hands-on materials related to Scripture and liturgy. Modeled after Montessori's "Children's Houses," the children could work repeatedly with the materials that most drew them. Over half a century in partnership with other catechists using a similar method, the pair gleaned much information about how children integrate faith by observing which materials they returned to again and again. Here I want to emphasize five key observations about children from Catechesis of the Good Shepherd that may at first glance appear remedial but merit continued attention as they constitute a solid foundation for preaching with the young.

The Religious Depth of the Child

First, CGS notes that even young children are not "blank slates." Whereas many religious education programs begin with the assumption that children have no previous knowledge of God before being instructed, CGS presumes that children do have a relationship with the divine but often have a hard time expressing the depth of their encounter. They seek language and images that can help them to conceptualize and articulate their experience. In CGS, conversations often begin with phrases such as "You already know . . ." or "Many times you have wondered about . . ." In response, the children most often nod. They appreciate the fact that their experience is being acknowledged and respected.

Preachers can benefit from a similar approach. Adult congregations can tell when the preacher speaks to them as if they were ignorant or incapable of understanding profound things. They bristle at "being treated like children." But it turns out that even children do not like "being treated like children." When approached more like one might approach an adult, with respect for the hearer's knowledge and life experience, the child listens with greater concentration. And when the preacher is able to offer language to help express a shared experience, the child responds enthusiastically.

I remember one six-year-old who experienced great joy when praying but was unsure what to say to God. I said that sometimes, in the history of our faith, when persons wanted to express their joy to God, they used the word "alleluia." "Alleluia" became this child's favorite prayer. During Lent, when we had "buried the Alleluia" in our local CGS atrium, she exclaimed, "I just can't stand it anymore: Alleluia! Alleluia! Alleluia!" She had found a word that truly connected to her profound experience of the divine. The episode mirrored what occurs in every good preaching: a congregation delights in the language of faith helping to illumine the religious potential embedded in their everyday lives.

The Essentiality of the Child

One of the great gifts of children to the larger world is the gift of essentiality. Children are able to winnow through large amounts of linguistic chaff and only allow the nourishing words to pass through. They are interested in the big truths that adults sometimes try to ignore—the proverbial "elephants in the room." They are not prone to listen for long if they judge the speaker to be waxing on about things they consider unessential, but when the speaker touches upon something they do consider essential, they can actually demonstrate quite profound and lengthy concentration. Their bodies will become calm and often they will sigh.

What do children consider essential? A surprising insight of CGS is that children possess a deep hunger to be oriented to reality. In essence, they want to know how the world ticks and how they can function successfully within it. More than fantasy, they are fascinated by "real" things—pots and pans, cell phones, computers, tools—the things they see adults use in their daily lives. At one level, orientation to reality includes showing children how things work and how to use them. But the quest for reality goes deeper than everyday survival. It extends into the realm of the metaphysical: What is it that keeps the world turning? What makes humans tick? How was the world created? In many ways, religion is the most fascinating subject to the child because it deals with what is "most real" in the universe and hence most essential.

Preachers, then, have a natural advantage in conversing with children because their subject matter, if framed rightly, is of great interest to little ones. Yet, in the words of Cavalletti, "We must give children rich food and not too much of it." Preachers will want to stick to only the "rich food" or the most essential truths of the faith—the incarnation, the kingdom of God, the paschal mystery, baptism, Eucharist—and leave the curiosities of history and doctrine until a later period in life. At the same time, they must not offer "too much of it." Preachers must choose their words on these topics wisely, making sure that they understand what they want to communicate first. As Cavalletti once noted, the less a catechist knows about something the more she will be tempted to say. Only when we ourselves have meditated deeply on these essential truths will we be able to say anything comprehensible to children. Children's homilies need to be short, limited to *one* key point stated in as few words as possible. Any stories used should be real (vs. imaginary) and in service of that one key point.

The Wonder of the Child

"Orientation to reality" done truthfully is no simple matter. As adults, we can feel confident and comfortable teaching our children how to sweep a floor or peel vegetables, but the zeal with which children embrace the quest for reality goes beyond such straightforward tasks. As noted above, a fulsome orientation to reality involves delving into the really big realities that not even the wisest of gurus has entirely grasped. Cavalletti noted that the questions of children about reality tended to fall in three main categories revolving around:

- The mystery of relationship: Who are you? Who am I in relation to you? What does it mean to be in relationship with each other? What are the "rules" of this relationship? How do we celebrate the relationship we share?

- The mystery of life and death: What is life? Where was I before I was born? What is death? What has happened to my grandmother who has died? Will I die?

- The mystery of time: What is time? Is time "going somewhere" or is it cyclical? What was before the beginning of the world? Does the world have an end?

Cavalletti notes that if the child (and, we might add, "adult" as well) is to live a satisfying, psychologically sound life, he or she must make peace in some way with these mysteries. The mysteries, of course, are not "solvable." But the work of any religious tradition is to share its wisdom regarding these core mysteries and a community with which to ponder them. These are the questions to which faith attempts to speak.

Successful children's preachers keep these core human questions in mind when preparing to preach and create explicit links between the questions and the word of God. For example: "Many times now in our lives, we have heard about someone dying, and we might wonder, 'Why do people have to die?' In fact, Jesus' friends often wondered the same thing, and Jesus knew this was a very big question for them. And so he shared this parable. . . ." Or, "Sometimes when I look up at the stars at night, I wonder about how far away they are and how many years it would take a rocket to travel there, and then I am amazed. Is it true that God is so big that God is beyond even the farthest star? Who really is God? In our reading today, we find out that long ago people were already pondering these questions, and this is what they had to say. . . ." Preaching initiated in such a manner allows children to know that their questions are normal and important, and that Scripture is the first place we turn as Christians for wisdom on such matters.

However, it is also key to remember that it is not the job of the preacher to "answer" children's deepest questions or to "explain" them away. Questions of justice and the afterlife and the destination of the universe are true mysteries: they are to be lived into, not solved. The best model we can offer children is that of a witness who also ponders these questions but does so in a faith community—a witness who acknowledges that others have wondered about these questions also and bonded themselves to one another in their questioning so as not to go it alone into such deep waters. We want to impress upon children that the church is a place where they will always find co-wonderers for life's biggest questions their whole life long and a treasury of resources for the quest. Preachers should feel free to acknowledge before children that they are still pondering these questions themselves and don't have them all wrapped up, but that they consider the children to be full partners in pondering: "When I heard the very frightening news about a shooting at a school, I, too, wondered, 'Why does God allow these things to happen?' You know what? I don't know. But today, like every day, we sit with the Scriptures, and we know that God has a word to speak to us that can help us when we are frightened and sad. I want you to help me to try to figure out what God is trying to tell us today. I have some ideas, but I bet you will have some ideas, too. . . ."

The "Absorbent Mind" of the Child

Based on the research of Maria Montessori about how children learn, CGS draws attention to the fact that children do not acquire new information and skills via explicit instruction so much as by "osmosis." The younger the child, the more this is true. Before the age of five, for example, the typical child learns an average of nine words per day simply by living in a speech-filled world, not because anyone sat down with flash cards and intentionally taught new words. Beyond language, children absorb culture, worldviews, and patterns of behavior. I remember when my own son was two, I found him walking through our apartment with the Bible held high over his head singing "Alleluia." Had I ever pointed out to him which book in our house was the Bible or how to treat it? No, but obviously he was absorbing his church experience. Of course, at the same age, he took my hair dryer and ran through the hallway using it as a gun. Would he ever have seen such behavior in our house? At this age, not even on the television. And yet he had absorbed something from the wider culture.

Preachers will find it helpful to remember that it is not just what they say that children will remember; indeed, it is likely that what the preacher says will be the least memorable part of the preaching event. While the preacher speaks, children will be absorbing. They will be absorbing the preacher's words but also his dress, posture, the larger worship environment, and even the preacher's character. Preachers will want to consider: How can I minimize anything in me or the environment that would distract from the Word? Often this means becoming simpler—in speech, in vestment, in appearance—removing unessential visuals.

A touching story from the original CGS atrium in Rome recalls a fiftieth anniversary event in which the first children Cavalletti and Gobbi served returned to visit the space. Now in their fifties and sixties, these former atrium participants noted what they remembered from their early childhood. One man, who had spent nine years in the atrium as a child, said to Cavalletti, "I am very sorry, Sofia. I remember the way the light came through this window. I remember working with this material. I remember thinking for a long time about this parable. But I don't remember you at all. I apologize." She hugged the man and said, "You have given me the greatest gift of all." It is the hope of every preacher that the Word is what will be absorbed rather than the preacher, and that whatever of the preacher *is* absorbed is entirely consonant with that Word.

The Smallness of the Child

Finally, it is so obvious that it seems silly to note, but children are small. They live in a world in which everything around them is built for bodies larger than their size. They have to step on a stool to reach the sink, jump to get into bed, stand on tippy toes to look out a window. But whereas the larger world equates smallness with weakness, children know that this is not the case. In fact, over and over again, they point out that there is a mightiness in the smallest of things, that small things have great power inside them. Indeed, children are often drawn by small things. They notice small features in a room that no one else pays attention to. In stories, they note the small characters seemingly peripheral to the plot. When reading the story of the prodigal son with a group of preschoolers, Cavalletti recalls they were very concerned with the question, "But what happened to the pigs when the son decided to go back home? Who would feed them?" The experience of smallness and perceived insignificance becomes a lens through which children understand all of reality, including Scripture.

One of the great gifts, therefore, that children offer the church is the insight that God, too, seems to have a special eye for the small—that, indeed, God operates out of a preferential option for the small. Children highlight that all the way throughout Scripture the great and mighty God consistently chooses the smallest and "weakest" as collaborators in salvation history rather than the powerful. Of all the people with whom God could have entered into covenant, God chose the insignificant nation of Israel. In all of Israel where God might choose to take on flesh, God chose the tiny town of Bethlehem. Of all the ways in which God might have come, it was as a baby born to a young woman from the backwater village of Nazareth. It is in weakness, the apostle Paul summarizes, that God is strong (2 Cor 12:9-10).

Those who preach to children can find it very helpful to spend time regularly reading the Scriptures *with* children in advance to see what aspects of the reading appear most important to them and what characters leap off the page for them. Slowly the preacher can develop a habit of reading "with the eyes of the small" and employ this hermeneutic as part of the preaching preparation process.

One note of caution: many adults, when speaking about small things, especially small things related to children, tend to use diminutive language. For example, when telling a story to children, they will speak of "the itsy bitsy baby Jesus" or "the fluffy little sheep." In referring to children's insights, they will use language like "Isn't that cute?" or "Oh, how sweet." Such language, while intended to be affirming, diminishes the significance of the story and the seriousness of children's contributions. It contradicts the child's core insight that in the small there is strength and power.

Elsewhere, I have noted that the thread of "smallness" so permeates the way that children think about Christianity that their approach to faith might best be described as "mustard seed theology."[4] Jesus' parable about the almost invisible seed, the size of a fleck of ground pepper, which grows into a bush so large that birds can build nests in its branches, captures the heart of the Good News from a child's point of view. Preachers who are able to grasp and articulate a mustard seed perspective will not only find an easy resonance with a congregation full of children, but they will also frequently discover they are meeting the needs of an adult population as well.

The truth is, as the great theologian Karl Rahner once noted, each of us carries within us an eternal child.[5] And although we develop new capacities and layers of understanding through maturity, at the core, each of us still possesses a profound religious potential; a hunger for the essentials, deep questions that make us wonder, an absorbent mind, and the sense of being small in a universe much bigger than us. When as preachers we are able to touch the child in our congregation, we are unwittingly speaking to what is most truly human, and the Word becomes a feast for all.

Endnotes

1. Congregation for Divine Worship, *Directory for Masses with Children* (November 1, 1973), 24.

2. The author, associate professor of Homiletics at Aquinas Institute of Theology in Saint Louis, MO, is also a formation leader for the National Association of Catechesis of the Good Shepherd. For more information on CGS, see www.CGSusa.org.

3. For a fuller description of Cavalletti's and Gobbi's methodological approach, see Sofia Cavalletti, *The Religious Potential of the Child* (Chicago: Liturgy Training Publications, 1992) and Gianna Gobbi, *Listening to God with Children* (Loveland, OH: Treehaus Publications, 1998).

4. Ann M. Garrido, *Mustard Seed Preaching* (Chicago: Liturgy Training Publications, 2004).

5. Karl Rahner, "Ideas for a Theology of Childhood," *Theological Investigations*, vol. 8, trans. David Bourke (New York: Herder, 1971).

Chapter 17

The Challenges Ahead for Catholic Preaching in the Twenty-first Century

Archbishop Robert J. Carlson

According to the Second Vatican Council's *Decree on the Ministry and Life of Priests* (*Presbyterorum Ordinis*), the primary duty of priests and bishops is to proclaim the Gospel of God to all.[1] Of course, *all* the baptized are called to proclaim the Gospel![2] Still, in a special way, this duty is incumbent on bishops, priests, and deacons. Jesus Christ came to proclaim the Good News of salvation to all. By virtue of their unique configuration to him through the sacrament of holy orders, bishops, priests, and deacons share the mission of Jesus Christ in a particular way. As *Fulfilled in Your Hearing* says, they are formed to be Christian witnesses in the world (43).

Of course, in calling "proclamation of the Gospel" the primary duty of priests and bishops, the Council was speaking of "proclamation" in the broad sense. They are not only called to proclaim the Gospel through the preaching of homilies but also through their celebration of the sacraments, through their administration of dioceses and parishes, and through their whole lives. Still, preaching homilies is one element of proclaiming the Gospel, and an important one, at that. The homily at Mass will be the focus of this chapter.

What does the preaching of homilies contribute to the proclamation of the Gospel? I want to focus on two things, following the lead of the Holy Father's Message for the forty-sixth World Communications Day. First: word and witness. Second: silence and communication.

Word and Witness

First, the preaching of the homily points toward the role of words in bearing witness to the Gospel. People are fond of quoting St. Francis of Assisi: "Preach the Gospel always; if necessary, use words." By this they usually mean that *deeds* are more important than *words* in proclaiming the Gospel. Fair enough. Words alone can be cheap; they need deeds to back them up.

At the same time, as the Second Vatican Council taught us in *Dei Verbum: The Dogmatic Constitution on Divine Revelation*: the "plan of revelation is realized by *deeds and words* [emphasis added] having an inner unity: the *deeds* wrought by God in the history of salvation manifest and confirm the teaching and realities signified by the *words*, while the *words* proclaim the *deeds* and clarify the mystery contained in them."[3] Words alone may not be enough. But deeds alone are not enough either. Words are necessary to make the meaning of the deeds clear.

If we look to the pages of the Old Testament, we can see that God always spoke through a combination of words and deeds. Jesus Christ himself proclaimed the Gospel in words and deeds. If we're looking for a pattern for the proclamation of the Gospel to all, we can't do better than God's own method! Through his words, Jesus gave people something to believe in; through our words, we can offer the world something to believe in. Through his deeds, Jesus gave people a reason to believe him; through our deeds, we must give people a reason to believe us.

In fact, as Benedict XVI points out in *Verbum Domini*, we need to reflect on the fact that God's word is performative: "There is no separation between what God *says* and what he *does*. His word appears as alive and active."[4] God's word in the Old Testament was *performative*—he spoke, and it came to be. Jesus' words in the Gospels were performative—he said to the leper, " 'I do will it. Be made clean.' The leprosy left him immediately, and he was made clean" (Mark 1:41-42, NABRE) Our words today are also performative. For example, every one of us knows the power of words to build up or break down a person's spirit. In many cases our words *are* deeds: they can make things happen, or prevent things from happening.

There may be a strong temptation in our day to use St. Francis' saying as an excuse *not* to proclaim the Gospel with words, to let our deeds speak for themselves. But we can't give in to that temptation because our deeds don't speak for themselves; we need words, too. This shouldn't surprise us. In the Old Testament, the Israelites couldn't figure out the meaning of God's deeds on their own. God used the words of the prophets to communicate with them so that they could know his will with clarity. In the Gospels, people couldn't figure out the meaning of Jesus' deeds on their own. Jesus spoke to us in human words so that we could know the Father's love with clarity. When the Holy Spirit came upon the apostles at Pentecost, Peter stood up and spoke so that people could understand what was happening and how to respond—and he had to speak because the actions of the apostles were obviously being misinterpreted by those who were saying, "They have had too much new wine" (Acts 2:13, NABRE).

The situation hasn't changed today. Our deeds are vitally important to the proclamation of the Gospel, but our deeds do not speak for themselves. The words of the preacher can be a witness and a reminder to everyone that words are an essential component of the proclamation of the Gospel. People of a certain generation are fond of saying that the longest distance in the world is the eighteen inches between the head and the heart. Of course, good preaching certainly has to help people make a connection between the head and the heart. But to stop there is to miss one of the major challenges of *today's* world. We aren't facing a rising generation that has been trained in head knowledge without heart knowledge. We're facing an entire generation (and more) of people who are comfortable being "spiritual but not religious." Their issue is not so much the interior gap between the mind and the heart as it is about the equally large gap between the heart and the lips, between faith as an interior reality, which many admit is essential, and the visible expression of faith as an exterior reality, which many think is optional. They are perfectly happy to wear the colors of their football team in the public square but hesitant to wear the colors of faith in the public square. Why the double standard? For many in today's culture the greatest distance in the world is not the eighteen inches between the head and the heart but the nine inches between the heart and the mouth, the distance between the comfort of our own spiritual interiority and the challenge of giving public witness to what we believe. The relationship between Jesus Christ and his heavenly Father was not only a matter of his own interior life; it was lived out publicly—thanks be to God! The homily can remind us that unambiguous exterior witness—including words—is required if the Gospel is to be proclaimed today. If we would preach Christ crucified, we must use words!

Silence and Communication

At the same time, one can also say that there is an overabundance of words in contemporary culture. Every one of us knows that e-mails are becoming incessant, sometimes more of a burden than a help. Everyone and their aunt has a Facebook account. Texting and tweeting have become the addiction of a new generation. In almost every other realm of life, besides the faith, the immediate public expression of every thought and feeling, often without reflection, has become the rule of life. The Delphic oracle's advice to ancient men and women was to "know thyself." The Facebook oracle's advice to contemporary men and women is "show thyself."[5]

In this context it's not enough to show that the word is essential to the proclamation of the faith. In this context the homilist must also exemplify and call forth another dimension of the word: its capacity to serve as an instrument of heart-to-heart communication, that is to say, communication that moves *from* the Heart of Christ *to* the hearts of the hearers *through* the words of the preacher. How can we do that?

Mark Twain is often credited with the statement that "lecturing is the process whereby the notes of the teacher become the notes of the student without passing through the mind of either." Much the same can be said for words and heart-to-heart communication: if our words are not rooted in silence, they will go in one ear and out the other without touching the hearts of anyone. As the Holy Father said in his message for World Communications Day 2012, "Silence is an integral element to communication; in its absence, words rich in content cannot exist."[6] Words have become abundant, but an abundance of words hasn't led to a richness of communication. If anything, people seem stuffed with words and starved for communication. Silence makes room in us to receive. This is why the rubrics of the Mass specifically call for periods of silence, especially after the homily and the Eucharist. These periods of silence allow us to absorb—or rather be absorbed into—Christ.

In his *Brief Reader on the Virtues of the Human Heart*, the philosopher Josef Pieper said that "All reasonable, sensible, sound, clear and heart-stirring talk stems from listening silence. Thus all discourse requires a foundation in the motherly depth of silence. Otherwise speech is source-less: it turns into chatter, noise and deception."[7] Chatter, noise, and deception—that sounds like an apt description of our blogging, texting, tweeting world! When we give homilies, we certainly want to avoid driving up the quotient of chatter, noise, and deception! But Pieper's words also suggest a remedy: if we aspire to reasonable, sensible, sound, clear, and yes, even heart-stirring talk in our homilies, then our words must come forth from the motherly depth of silence.

This is a point the Holy Father underscores for us in *Verbum Domini*. There he says, "Ours is not an age which fosters recollection [truer words were never spoken!]; at times one has the impression that people are afraid of detaching themselves, even for a moment, from the mass media [we've all seen this in our younger people!]. For this reason, it is neces-sary nowadays that the People of God be educated in the value of silence [there's the antidote—and, I dare say, people *want* it—the more their lives are filled with empty chatter, the more they hunger for pregnant silence!]. . . . Only in silence can the Word of God find a home in us, as it did in Mary, woman of the word and, inseparably, woman of silence."[8]

There it is—there *she* is—Mary, the Blessed Mother, Our Lady of the Lake. As you know, the word *silent* contains all the same letters as the word *listen*. So the Holy Father holds up for us the listening silence of Mary as our example and as the antidote to a world of chatter, noise, and deception. How fitting, here at Notre Dame, to propose that Mary is the model for the homilist because Mary is the model for a proper relationship to the Word.

Mary allowed the Word to come and dwell in her heart, in her soul, in her very body; the homilist must imitate her receptivity to the Word. Mary nurtured the Word in silence and, when the time came, she brought forth the Word for the salvation of the world; the homilist must imitate her silent nurturing and her giving birth. The last words of Mary in the New Testament are, in effect, her final words forever: "Do whatever he tells you" (John 2:5, NABRE). This must be the fundamental attitude of the preacher's every word.

I know a priest who, while the Alleluia is being sung, will quietly pray in the presider's chair and repeat "Lord Jesus, speak through me; Lord Jesus, breathe through me; Lord Jesus, live through me; your words, not mine." He gets it! He's striving toward what St. Paul was talking about when he said, "It is no longer I who live, but Christ who lives in me"

(Gal 2:19-20). It is no longer I who preach, but Christ who preaches in me! If the preacher follows the example of Mary, then his words and his life will bear the same fruit as hers. Through the preacher's words, nurtured in silence, people will be brought to an encounter with the living Word, Jesus Christ himself.

The Current Context

Before turning my attention to the new document on preaching, I'd like to mention several aspects of the current context that I think preachers need to address. First, many people today find the Good News hard to believe because they have been raised on a steady diet of relativism. It is crucial that we understand relativism as a christological heresy and treat it with the same seriousness that was given to the great christological heresies of history. When all is said and done, the truth is a person. To deny the existence of the truth is to deny the existence of Jesus Christ. We must prove as tireless, persuasive, and holy as the fathers of the church in facing the great christological heresy of our own day.

Sometimes people deny the existence of truth because they're afraid that truth claims enslave. As preachers, we must find a way to show them that truth and freedom are conjoined, not opposed. We must preach clearly that freedom is not perfected in *choosing* but in *choosing the good*. As Blessed John Paul II said—and you can't help but think of his experience with Nazi Germany and Communist Russia as you hear these words of warning to our own day: "Once truth is denied to human beings, it is pure illusion to try to set them free. Truth and freedom either go together hand in hand or together they perish in misery."[9] If we preach this message consistently, then people will understand that without the truth we can never be free. G. K. Chesterton speaks of the open mind as being like an open mouth. If the mouth doesn't close on food, it starves the body. If the mind doesn't close on truth, it starves the soul. Today there are many malnourished souls!

Sometimes people deny the existence of truth because they're afraid that truth claims incite violence. As preachers we must find a way to show them that truth and compassion are conjoined, not opposed. Too many people today are convinced that because we must love all people, we cannot draw moral lines. At the same time, too many people are convinced of the opposite; that because we must draw moral lines we cannot love all people. The Gospel story of the woman caught in adultery shows us that Jesus did both! Jesus loved people *and* drew moral lines. Jesus *protected* the woman caught in adultery—he did not let her suffer violence. Jesus *did not condemn* the woman caught in adultery. But he did not condone her sin either. In fact, he gave her the *dignity* of naming her sin as sin. In doing so, he treated her as someone who *could* rise above sin; he treated her as someone who *wanted* to rise above sin; he treated her as someone for whom he wanted something better than sin. Can we do less?

It's interesting to note that because Jesus dined with sinners he was accused of loving sin. Nothing could have been further from the truth! Jesus hated sin, but he loved the sinner. Today the opposite lie is dominant: because the church speaks out against sin, she is accused of hating the sinner. Again, nothing could be further from the truth! We must love the sinner. But, like a good parent, we must love enough to speak the truth in love. No one can say this is easy. But no parent worth their salt looks the other way and ignores, or even encourages, behavior that is harmful to their child. Like Jesus, we must love our flocks enough to speak the hard and unpopular truths that they desperately need to hear to be truly free.

Many people today find the Good News hard to believe because of the shortcomings of its messengers. In particular, the sex abuse scandal still looms large in many people's imagination, and we cannot fault them for that. As preachers, we must address this crisis of credibility, and the only way to address it is to be growing in holiness. As Alasdair MacIntyre famously said in *After Virtue: A Study in Moral Theology*, the world is waiting for a new St. Benedict.[10] Let it be you! People will say, with resignation, "Well, the church is a hospital for sinners, not a museum for saints." Let me say loud and clear: that's a false dichotomy! There is certainly *some* truth to it. It reminds us to be humble, which we all need. But to the extent that it makes us comfortable in our sins, to the extent that it makes us lazy and causes us to stop striving for great holiness, its falsehood is unveiled. The Catholic Church is not into "defining the deviancy down." The church *is* a hospital for sinners. The church is also a launching pad for saints, a place where people are trained for holiness and launched into the world as rockets of love, joy, peace, patience, kindness, generosity, faithfulness, gentleness, and self-control (cf. Gal. 5:22). Our homilies are meant to be part of that launching. And we can judge our homilies, as we can judge our daily lives, by those fruits. When your preaching brings out love, joy, peace, patience, and so on, then the

Spirit is showing you how to preach! When your preaching fails to bring out those fruits, in your life and the lives of others, it's time to go back to the drawing board and pray for inspiration.

For our homilies to be a launching pad for saints, for our homilies to bear good fruit and ever deeper fruit, we ourselves must be growing in holiness. One way to do this, and a major recommendation of the Holy Father in *Verbum Domini*, is by increasing our use of the ancient practice of *lectio divina*. The depth of our relationship with the Word has a direct impact on our ability to proclaim the Good News. An ever-deepening encounter with the Word in our own lives will lead to an ever more fruitful proclamation of the Word for others. There is a kind of "spiritual gravity" to our words and our lives; the deeper we go in our relationship with the Word, the greater will be the gravitational pull of our words. It must be Jesus speaking through us, and our words as preachers will have the depth or shallowness of our relationship with the living Word, Jesus Christ himself.

There is a lie that keeps us from being the preachers we are called to be. One of the "spirits of the day" that is a false spirit and must be unmasked is a false sense of privacy. It's a spirit that tells us that everyone should figure out the truth for themselves, that we shouldn't infringe on anyone's right to figure it out for themselves by "imposing" our truth on them. It's a spirit that whispers "this is none of your business," or "this is too personal to challenge people on."

Remember: we have Jesus as our model! Jesus did not bow to this false sense of privacy. Being a man and a celibate didn't prevent him from calling men and women, husbands and wives, and fathers and mothers from the challenges of discipleship. We priests are called "father" for a reason. Any biological father worth his name speaks up and fathers his family. We are called to no less in the spiritual realm. I think this false spirit of privacy has affected our preaching and prevents us from really letting Jesus live and preach through us. In the name of Jesus Christ, let the false spirit of privacy be banished and sent to the foot of the holy cross!

Remember that the Word does not always *convert* hearts and minds. Sometimes the Word *reveals* hearts and minds, and when it does so, sometimes it reveals their opposition to God. We need to be ready for that push-back. But if we rest in Mary's affection—for us and for those we preach to—we can withstand it.

Introducing the New Document

Finally, as you know, in *Verbum Domini* the Holy Father called for a new directory on homiletics.[11] As you probably know, the U.S. Conference of Catholic Bishops' committee on Clergy, Consecrated Life, and Vocations is overseeing the preparation of that document. Let me give you a few comments on that new document.

First, the centerpiece of the document is not so much a particular theory of preaching as it is Jesus Christ himself. It might best be described as a reflection on the Gospel portrayals of Jesus as the master preacher and teacher. The document looks at certain aspects of Jesus' preaching that call for our attention and imitation. Jesus Christ is the Word made flesh, and our preaching is meant to serve people's encounter with him. By the way, it's worth studying *Verbum Domini* on that point—just notice how many times the Holy Father speaks of an encounter with the Lord.

Second, one of the main themes of the document is how the homily can and should help people see a deep inner connection between God's word and the actual circumstances of their everyday life. In that respect, you will certainly find echoes of *Fulfilled in Your Hearing*. In one section the document speaks of how two thirsts meet in every sermon—God's thirst for us and our thirst for God—and how the preacher needs to articulate the divine longing for us and stir up our longing for God. In addition to finding echoes of *Fulfilled in Your Hearing*, you will also find echoes of Pope Benedict's focus on the human heart.

So many people are like the disciples on the road to Emmaus. The Lord himself is walking with them, speaking with them. Their eyes do not recognize him, but their hearts are aware of his presence. The preacher's task is to help open their eyes to the reality already present. As the Holy Father says in *Verbum Domini*, "The homily is a means of bringing the Scriptural message to life in a way that helps the faithful to realize that God's word is present and at work in their everyday lives."[12] That is also an important feature of the new document.

Finally, one particularly important feature of the new document is its explanation of the proper way for preachers to enunciate moral judgment. As mentioned earlier, Jesus himself was a master of loving people and drawing lines. Preachers must learn to imitate him while always bearing in mind that order: loving people and drawing lines.

Why does the document draw attention to the importance of imitating this aspect of Jesus' ministry in our preaching? Because what Pope Paul VI said in *Evangelii Nuntiandi*—about "the split between the Gospel and culture being, without a doubt, the drama of our time"[13]—is even more true today than it was when he said it in 1975. Let me give one simple example: Have you ever reflected on the fact that six out of nine U.S. Supreme Court justices identify themselves as Catholic . . . and no one seems to care? Why wouldn't the secular and liberal media object? I dare say it's because we have done a good job convincing people that we can "fit in" with contemporary culture, that being Catholic makes no difference to our judgments or actions. Well, the time has come for us to do an equally good job convincing people that being Catholic *does* make a difference in how we think and how we act.

Perhaps there was a time when the predominant culture supported the values of the Gospel. That time has passed. We live in a culture that is not particularly friendly to the Gospel of Jesus Christ and is sometimes actively hostile to it. The Gospel invites us to choose life; the culture tells us that death is an equally legitimate choice. The Gospel tells us that Jesus is the way, the truth, and the life; the culture tells us that there are many equally valid ways, truths, and lifestyles. To be sure, not everything in our culture is hostile to the values of the Gospel. There are points of light as well as points of darkness. But the bottom line is this: if we can't point to a number of issues on which our values differ from those of the contemporary culture, then we have to wonder about the depth of our commitment to Jesus Christ. And if the world isn't aware of a number of issues on which our values make us think and act differently, then we've got to ask ourselves: How effectively are we proclaiming the Gospel to all?

As the new document tells us, the way to preach to people in such a culture is not to start with words of condemnation but to start with words of grace. But, as the document also says, the way to preach to such a culture is not to stop with words of grace and ignore the reality of sin. Within the context of grace, the reality of sin must also be named and addressed. As the apostle John says, "Everyone who does not abide in the teaching of Christ, but goes beyond it, does not have God" (2 John 1:9, NRSV). And as G. K. Chesterton said, if you're "progressing" toward a cliff, it's best to stop and turn around.

So the new document certainly has some important elements of continuity with *Fulfilled in Your Hearing*. But you also see some special points of emphasis that are called for by the needs of our time, especially the need for catechetical preaching.

Conclusion

Thirty years ago, *Fulfilled in Your Hearing* noted that "for the vast majority of Catholics the Sunday homily is the normal and frequently the formal way in which they hear the Word of God proclaimed. For these Catholics the Sunday homily may well be the most decisive factor in determining the depth of their faith."[14] Today, we can confidently say that the majority of Catholics don't hear the Sunday homily because the majority of Catholics aren't at Mass. What does that mean for the challenge of preaching in the twenty-first century?

First, we need to take a deep breath and remind ourselves that inattentiveness and disobedience are hallmarks of God's people throughout history! Adam and Eve weren't attentive or obedient to the word of God, and that's what got us into this mess to begin with. The vast majority of Israelites weren't attentive or obedient to the word of God; they were truly sons of Adam and daughters of Eve in that sense. The majority of people at the time of Jesus weren't attentive or obedient to the word of God; they welcomed him in one breath and called for his crucifixion with the next. That's our spiritual family tree!

As I said earlier, and as the Holy Father notes in *Verbum Domini*, God's word is *performative*—it makes things happen.[15] In the beginning, God spoke and the world was made; in history, God spoke and made a people his own; in the fullness of time, God's word became flesh in Jesus Christ, and the salvation of the world was won. God's word is *performative*—it makes things happen. That same Word has echoed forth in the words of the great preachers of history, and it has not returned to the Lord barren (cf. Isa 55:10-11). That same Word can echo forth again today in the words of our preaching. When our own lives are deeply rooted in an ongoing encounter with the Lord, then, through our preaching, people can be invited to a heart-to-heart encounter with the Word made flesh, Jesus Christ himself. That encounter will transform them into disciples of the Son and evangelizers on his behalf. That is the glory and the challenge of the preacher today.

Endnotes

1. *Presbyterorum Ordinis,* 4.
2. "Indeed, the proclamation of the Word of God is the responsibility of the entire Christian community by virtue of the sacrament of baptism" (*Fulfilled in Your Hearing,* 2).

3. *Dei Verbum,* 2.

4. *Verbum Domini,* 53.

5. See Zenit article, April 2, 2009: "When 'Know Thyself' Becomes 'Show Thyself.' "

6. *Message for the 46th World Communications Day (May 20, 2012).*

7. *A Brief Reader on the Virtues of the Human Heart* (San Francisco: Ignatius Press, 1991), 13.

8. *Verbum Domini,* 66. See also 124: "Let us be silent in order to hear the Lord's word and meditate upon it, so that by the working of the Holy Spirit it may remain in our hearts and speak to us all the days of our lives. In this way the Church will always be renewed and rejuvenated, thanks to the word of the Lord which remains forever."

9. *Fides et Ratio,* 90. See also *Veritatis Splendor* 4, in which he speaks of "currents of thought which end up by detaching human freedom from its essential and constitutive relationship to truth."

10. Alasdair MacIntyre, *After Virtue,* 3rd ed. (Notre Dame, IN: University of Notre Dame Press, 2007), 263.

11. "The art of good preaching based on the Lectionary is an art that needs to be cultivated. Therefore . . . I ask the competent authorities . . . to prepare practical publications to assist ministers in carrying out their task as best they can: as for example a Directory on the homily, in which preachers can find useful assistance in preparing to exercise their ministry" (*Verbum Domini,* 60).

12. Ibid., 59.

13. *Evangelii Nuntiandi,* 20.

14. *Fulfilled in Your Hearing,* 2.

15. *Verbum Domini,* 53.

Afterword

A Living Word of Hope for the Whatever Generation

Michael E. Connors, CSC

As this volume was being prepared, the U.S. Catholic bishops released *Preaching the Mystery of Faith*, the first new ecclesiastical document on preaching in thirty years, and the first ever to bear the approval of the full conference. While the text had been under consideration for some time, its promulgation still came as something of a surprise to many of us, given the many other issues and needs that have clamored for episcopal attention. The strengths and limitations of the document will, no doubt, be explored thoroughly in the weeks and months to come. Yet *Preaching the Mystery of Faith*'s most enduring legacy may be symbolic, a gesture in the form of a statement reminding the entire Catholic community, but especially its official preachers, that the church lives by the word of God—and thus the quality and vitality of preaching matters. Many of us in the Catholic homiletics community join in the document's own hope that the importance of preaching will again be pushed nearer the top of the national agenda.

But that agenda is already crowded. The Catholic community in the United States continues to be wracked by wave after wave of the clergy sexual abuse scandal. Our membership is hemorrhaging. Finances are constrained. The Catholic identity of some of our institutions is cast into doubt. The Catholic community in the United States today is badly riven—right versus left, liberal versus conservative, "Vatican II Catholics" versus "John Paul II" Catholics, social justice versus core doctrine—and these rifts are becoming hard-wired into our thinking, as if they were separate worlds of discourse. I have remarked to some of my students that the task of the next generation of pastoral leaders will be to heal the church divisions that have grown up over the last thirty years.

Signs of fragmentation and disintegration abound in our society, too. Public discourse consists of round after round of partisan bickering. Red states and blue states chart radically diverging paths, with drastically differing priorities for public funds. "Culture wars" pit the forces of religion against the forces of secularism. As one commentator puts it, we are devolving into an "Argument Culture."[1]

Timothy Radcliffe, OP, notes that there has been a massive breakdown of the sense of promise in the future. Despite widespread affluence, he says, we in the West are suffering from a "collective depression" felt most keenly by young adults, whom he calls the "Now Generation."[2] There are no more master narratives, he says, no more shared stories that fire the imagination and move us to walk and work together toward a common destiny. There is nothing to do, nothing to hope for but to live for the present moment. I have come to think of the undergraduates I teach and live with as the "Whatever Generation"—every assertion, ideal, political program, philosophy or religious path is greeted with a politely dismissive, "OK, whatever. . . ." They are bright and well intentioned but unaware of just how distracted, anxious, indifferent, or fearful they are. Many have been religiously educated in the church and yet somehow missed what Robert Barron calls the "grab you by the lapels" quality of the Gospels.[3] They're not hostile atheists, nor ideological materialists; they are simply conditioned to keep everything at arm's length, and to greet every great claim with a shrug, as just one more lifestyle choice on the market. The world as they know it isn't on the road to anywhere. As one of them remarked to a colleague of mine, "Our generation has no hope."

Nonetheless, Radcliffe finds this "potentially, a wonderful moment for Christianity. If we are able to find ways to live and share our Christian hope, then we shall offer something for which the world is thirsting. . . . Now we have something extraordinary and rare to offer, which is hope stripped of its secular crutches, new and fresh and desirable."[4] He continues: "We should not be fearful of crises. The Church was born in a crisis of hope. Crises are our *specialité de la maison*. They rejuvenate us. The one that we are living through now is very small."[5] Radcliffe suggests that in a world where talk is cheap and everything is assumed to be relative and perspectival, we may want to reclaim the power of symbolic gestures. He bids us return to the Last Supper, with its implications for a different kind of power, a power that evokes hope and trust. He points to Francis of Assisi as an example of someone who understood the power of gestures. Casting off the garments of affluence, communing with Creation, welcoming even Death—it is not for no reason that Francis' memory remains vivid in our collective imagination. Such gestures, authentically delivered, and grounded in a visible community of faith, can have great power in a jaded world.

Homiletic gestures are sometimes under-appreciated, even though some of the most profound insights in the biblical tradition have been conveyed most memorably by deed rather than merely by verbal message. Think of Hosea, Ezekiel, or Jesus. As this book was being finalized for publication, a good friend of the poor has been elected to the See of Peter. His very first homily was not a homily at all, but a simple bow before us, the People of God. Presumably in the months and years to come, Pope Francis will preach many homilies and write many texts, but it will be hard to surpass the eloquence of that first moment when he stepped onto the veranda, stood humbly before us, and begged our silent prayers for him and his ministry. His gesture spoke both to his humility and humanity, and to our identity as the Body of Christ, the place where God chooses to dwell. *Servus servorum Dei.* Behold the servant of the servants of God.

Sixteen centuries ago Bishop Augustine of Hippo admonished his clergy that the purpose of preaching is to teach, to delight, and to persuade or move to action.[6] I offer this same advice to my young homiletic students: every homily should appeal to the mind, the heart, and the will. Every time we lay hands on the Bible in the ambo, and raise our voice in response to it, we must offer the Christian people that truth that illumines the mind, we must fire the heart with the love of God who so lavishly loved us first, and we must inspire naturally lethargic wills to engage feet and hands and voices in the Lord's own work in the world. Jorge Mario Bergoglio's simple gesture before the throng in St. Peter's Square carried a poignant lesson and filled us with a sense of our tangible oneness in Jesus Christ. How will we respond? If Christian preaching is anything, it opens a vista upon who we really are: sons and daughters of the Most High God, temples of the Holy Spirit. It sends us to fulfill the vision we are being made into.

Blessed Basile Moreau, founder of my own Holy Cross religious community, called his religious family to be "people with hope to bring." It has been said that hope is the most distinctively Judeo-Christian virtue. It may also be the timeliest of the virtues—the one in shortest supply in today's world. Our Church and society seem stuck in a gridlock of cynicism and polarization. Hope does not flourish in such stony ground, and where hope is lacking, creativity wanes. What is the hope we have to bring to a divided, dispirited church and world?

We have more going for us than we often realize. Let me point to three things distinctive to our form of Christianity that deserve further consideration as we ponder the challenges of preaching today.

A Dynamic Understanding of the Word of God

What is "the Word?" The understanding of divine revelation that Catholics share with some other traditions is complex, subtle, and rich. Along with other Christians, we customarily refer to the Bible as "the Word of God." Liturgical proclamation of the Scriptures is punctuated by "The Word of the Lord" or "The gospel of the Lord." These are conventions of long standing that underline the privileged place these texts hold in our tradition and community. Yet Pope Benedict XVI says in *Verbum Domini*: "While in the Church we greatly venerate the sacred Scriptures, the Christian faith is not a 'religion of the book': Christianity is the 'religion of the word of God,' not of 'a written and mute word, but of the incarnate and living Word.'"[7] The Second Vatican Council had pointed us in this direction with its insistence on the close interrelationship among Scripture, tradition, and the teaching office of the church.[8] Thus our understanding of the Word is always dialogical.[9] That Word emerges in a dynamism of faithful coherence and fresh creativity, addressed to the needs of time and context, under the inspiration of the Spirit.

Benedict XVI claims, "Being Christian is not the result of an ethical choice or a lofty idea, but the encounter with an event, a person, which gives life a new horizon and a definitive direction."[10] The key word here is *encounter*, understood in a double sense. First, the encountered Word is an *event*, a present, here-and-now communication from a God who is living and acting today as surely as in the age of Jesus, the prophets, or Moses. Thus the reading of the Scriptures and the preaching serve that

Word in the hope that through them God will speak to us today, in the concrete circumstances of life in the faith community to which we belong. Catholic Christians gather in the expectation and hope that the Word, never under our control or merely summoned at our bidding, might break out in our midst at any moment.

Second, and distinct but inseparable from the first, the encountered Word is a *person*, Jesus Christ. "Now the word is not simply audible; not only does it have a *voice*, now the word has a *face*, one which we can see: that of Jesus of Nazareth." [11] It is Christ who embodies the *Logos*, the divine, eternal Word. Moreover, this incarnation of the Word goes on from all eternity past to all eternity present and future. He is a living Person, the perfect communication of God's own being, a word-gesture and more, walking among us, continuing his ministry of preaching, healing, exorcising, saving.

So we can say that our understanding of the Word is an event-person who comes to us with the fresh immediacy and relational availability of this present moment in which we are gathered around the Book and the table. As Benedict goes on to say, that Word is "performative";[12] it "accomplishes what it says." In other words, the Word is sacramental[13]—it effects what it proclaims. Although much of what we do is *anamnesis*, or remembering, the Word to which we are receptive is more than a memory or a historical narrative. Although we talk about the Jesus of the Gospels, about St. Paul and the patriarchs, we do so in service of heightening our awareness of the Christ who lives in the Spirit in *this* moment, in *this* day and age, "for us and for our salvation." Although we read the scriptural texts handed down to us, and wrestle with their interpretation, we are not satisfied with exegeting their original meanings. The homiletic task— and the liturgical task to which all the faithful bend their efforts in full and active participation—is not complete until we have received a "scriptural interpretation of human existence" [14]—a word for today. Our thirst is for nothing less than meeting the living risen Lord in word and sacrament. To put this another way, we believe in the Holy Spirit, the God of the present, the "God of the gathering." As Benedict XVI said, "There can be no authentic understanding of Christian revelation apart from the activity of the Paraclete."[15]

At first blush this might seem to put us at a competitive disadvantage in the contemporary religious marketplace. For some other Christians "the Word" is quite simply the text of the Bible, interpreted as literally as possible. They would seem to have an enviable simplicity and clarity upon which to stand in their proclamation of the Gospel—no hermeneutics required. Yet the reigning literalism and fundamentalism also have their downside. Such approaches tend to foster a merely mechanical obedience, not the ongoing voyage of discovery of the disciple—the fealty of an employee or beneficiary, not the impassioned relationship of the friend or lover. As the Jesus of the Fourth Gospel tells us more than once, God wants sons and daughters, not slaves. So the dynamic Catholic sense of the Word as a present event-person offers the contemporary hearer something she or he craves: not mere virtual reality, nostalgia, or moral direction, but real relationship. To hear this word spoken in time and space, in the company of a communion of seeker-followers, is to have one's everyday world rearranged and filled with a kind of promise, presence, and possibility that go well beyond wallowing in memories or poring over ancient texts. "We preach a living Word."[16]

A Liturgical Word

On cable or satellite television today, at pretty much any hour of the day, one can find somebody preaching. While delivery styles and theologies vary widely among these telegenic figures, there are some common elements. For one, denominational affiliations and other ecclesial commitments are downplayed or invisible. Second, the preacher ordinarily speaks in an environment that looks more like an auditorium than a worship sanctuary—sparsely decorated, visually suggesting that the personality of the preacher and the Bible are all that are necessary, all that matter. Third, such preaching is almost never linked to the Eucharist nor any other sacrament, ritual, or gesture. Even the gathered community is anonymous, passive, unidentified. We know little about them, and nothing at all about their lives off-camera or about how they have been changed by the encounter with the Word or the worship of God.

Some Catholic imitators of this style have arisen of late. In our social milieu it is always tempting to cut one's institutional moorings or hide the wires that bind us to the past, to authority, and to the troubled world. But for us the living Word's native home is the liturgy. Thus, Catholic preaching is always in close proximity to the eucharistic feast, or baptism, or one of the other sacraments, in the context of a specific local church gathered for worship. Richly biblical in themes, style, and content, Catholic preaching never forgets that the Bible is the church's book. Even preaching in settings that are not immediately liturgical never strays far, symbolically, from the table. As Benedict XVI says, "A faith-filled understanding of sacred Scripture must always refer back to the liturgy, in which the word of God is celebrated as a timely and living word."[17]

What underlies this fact is more than the inertia of tradition; it is a *yin* and *yang* of our theological anthropology, what theologian David Tracy calls the way of "word" or the "dialectical imagination" in tandem with the way of "manifestation" or the "analogical imagination."[18] Word and gesture go together in Catholic cosmology and preaching, and both word and gesture only make sense in the context of a stable, concrete, visible community. If Radcliffe is right about the hungers of our postmodern world, in which talk is regarded as cheap but gestures have renewed power, then it could be that insistence on keeping word, gesture, and community together offers our contemporaries a genuine alternative to disconnected, disembodied, privatized religion. The liturgy demonstrates and enacts what the words describe and point to, forms community and sends us in service to others. Word, gesture, community, doctrine, mission—all are necessary, complementary, mutually illuminating. All celebrate and plunge us into the mystery of God's loving self-communication, a mystery in which we become not only recipients but actors.

A Rich Doctrinal Tradition

We are a doctrinal church. Our faith is a dynamic relationship that invites—indeed demands—continued reflection, a mystery whose depths each generation must plumb and give witness to. We give pride of place to the Bible, but we also treasure creeds, hymns, patristic sermons, medieval treatises, modern biblical reconstructions, magisterial teaching, conciliar texts, contemporary witness. At first glance, this, too, might seem to be more of a liability than an asset for effective preaching in a sound-bite, internet-dominated world. All of us have heard preaching that was doctrinally correct but dry and unmoving. Many Catholics today are conditioned to believe that a homily can be doctrinal and catechetical, or it can be passionate and relevant to real life, but not both. It is a sad comment on the ecclesiological divisions of our time that we have allowed this false dichotomy to grow up and largely go unchallenged. Not only can we have preaching that is richly infused with divine truth, and at the same time deeply engaged with the realities of contemporary context, we *must* have both—to pit these against one another is to settle for half a loaf.

Perhaps we have forgotten that the doctrinal formulations so dear to our tradition were composed precisely to guide preachers in the care of souls. Doctrines are shorthand guides to the interpretation of Scripture, and thus they are not meant to confine but to open up the full potential of the sacred texts as they take root in our hearts, minds, and wills. They guard us from error and give us a way of speaking about what we have heard and experienced, and sharing it with others. Doctrines are not meant to be merely repeated; like maps, they must be unfolded, studied, and used to guide us to our true destination. To say that preaching has to be doctrinal is really to say no more than that there must be to our preaching some substance or *telos*—it must plunge us into the mystery of relationship with God, and offer us something to which we are invited to respond.

So the question is not whether Catholic preaching should be doctrinally informed—of course it must be. The question, rather, is *how* our preaching is to be doctrinal. A merely formulaic deployment of doctrines is worse than useless; it can be self-defeating. The language of doctrinal formulation is not, by and large, the language best suited to preaching. To import doctrinal language into preaching, without much further explanation or without resort to other literary forms, is an error of genre to which people in our pews are still regularly subjected, with predictably negative results. Preconciliar catechesis too often settled for mere indoctrination, purely cognitive and requiring little more than rote memorization. Some today seem to want to resurrect this method as the panacea for the supposed failures of contemporary catechesis. "The young don't know the faith," one hears it said. "They are catechetically illiterate." Often true. Some postconciliar catechetical efforts have been long on innovation and process but short on content and tradition. But, by the same token, some who know the doctrines have only a primitive, notional kind of faith; they don't believe anything with the full-blooded trust that characterizes biblical faith. The task of the hour is reintegrating head and heart; doctrine and relationship; mind, heart, and will. The purpose of doctrine is not a purely intellectual instruction but *metanoia*, conversion of the whole person to Christ. This is what the great Christian preaching of every age seeks to do.

Our doctrinal tradition is not opposed to the dynamic understanding of the Word as the living Word of a living God—far from it. Rather, our doctrinal heritage stands as permanent witness to the breadth and depth of what God seeks to do with humanity, not only in the past but in the present and future. As Mary Catherine Hilkert remarks, "Doctrine functions precisely to protect the fullness of the kerygma (the proclamation). Doctrine exists so that the church does not preach or believe half-truths (heresy). . . . Doctrine informs, disciplines, protects, and enriches the preaching of the kerygma—but it never replaces it."[19] Furthermore, as John Cavadini argues in this volume, the understanding of Scripture and the understanding of doctrine are intrinsically, reciprocally related.[20] If we allow doctrine to play its appropriate role, mainly in the background, guiding the quality and structure of both homiletics and catechesis, it will give our preaching something that much of contemporary religiosity and culture sorely lacks: substance. That is to say, a homiletic substrate faithful to our doctrinal tradition opens up before the hearer a new world to live into, and new dimensions of the invitation to authentic relationship with God, through Jesus Christ, in the Holy Spirit.

Hope

Christian hope has been described as a "passion for the possible,"[21] or what has been made possible by Christ. I take this in at least these three ways: (1) what is possible in terms of intimate covenant relationship with God; (2) what is possible in terms of community among us, the disciples of the Risen One; and (3) what is possible for the world, and thus what we aim at in Christian mission to build a world of justice, peace, dignity, abundance for all, and so on. Our age and every age yearns for authentic contact with the divine, for belonging to a healthy community in which each person is valued and contributes his/her gifts, and for a role in making the world a better place. If Christian preachers today could speak from a dynamic sense of the living Word, introducing us into the living presence of God—a Word embedded in a concrete community of worship and of visible service to the world's most pressing needs, a Word robustly understood by the light of long tradition—it would go a long way toward making Christian hope credible, even for the Whatever Generation. The antidote for hopelessness and despair is authentic and life-giving encounter, witnessed in word, gesture, and community, and in a mission for which one could really lay down one's life. Our bishops have charged us with this task again in *Preaching the Mystery of Faith*:

> Homilies are inspirational when they touch the deepest levels of the human heart and address the real questions of human experience.

Pope Benedict XVI, in his encyclical *Spe Salvi*, spoke of people having "little hopes" and the "great hope." "Little hopes" are those ordinary experiences of joy and satisfaction we often experience: the love of family and friends, the anticipation of a vacation or a family celebration, the satisfaction of work well done, the blessing of good health, and so on. But underneath these smaller hopes must pulsate a deeper "great hope" that ultimately gives meaning to all of our experience: the hope for life beyond death, the thirst for ultimate truth, goodness, beauty, and peace, the hope for communion with God himself. As the pope expresses it, "Let us say once again: we need the greater and lesser hopes that keep us going day by day. But these are not enough without the great hope, which must surpass everything else. This great hope can only be God, who encompasses the whole of reality and who can bestow upon us what we, by ourselves, cannot attain."[22]

Our world yearns for the "great hope" that will give meaning to our experience, overcome our divisions, and show us what is possible for our future. We preach Christ—crucified, risen, glorified, living—a gift of hope incarnate.

Endnotes

1. See Richard Lischer, *The End of Words: The Language of Reconciliation in a Culture of Violence* (Grand Rapids, MI: Eerdmans, 2005), 142. Lischer is drawing upon the work of Deborah Tannen, *The Argument Culture: Moving from Debate to Dialogue* (New York: Random House, 1998).

2. Timothy Radcliffe, *What Is the Point of Being a Christian?* (London: Burns & Oates, 2005), 12.

3. See Barron's essay in this volume, "The New Evangelization and the New Media."

4. Radcliffe, *What Is the Point of Being a Christian?*, 13f.

5. Ibid., 16.

6. Saint Augustine, *De Doctrina Christiana: On Christian Teaching*, trans. R. P. H. Green (New York: Oxford University Press, 1997; original text ca. AD 427).

7. *Verbum Domini*, 7; the interior quote is from St. Bernard of Clairvaux.

8. See *Dei Verbum: The Dogmatic Constitution on Divine Revelation*, esp. 7–10.

9. See, e.g., VD 23 and 24, where the pope speaks of "the dialogical nature of all Christian revelation."

10. VD 11, quoting *Deus Caritas Est* 1.

11. VD 12.

12. VD 53. See also the essay in this volume by Jeremy Driscoll, "New Perspectives on Preaching from *Verbum Domini*."

13. VD 56. See also the essay in this volume by Mary Catherine Hilkert, "Feasting at the Table of the Word: From *Dei Verbum* to *Verbum Domini*."

14. *Fulfilled in Your Hearing*, 29.

15. VD 15.

16. The title of the essay by Archbishop Gustavo García-Siller in this volume.

17. VD 52. See also the essay in this volume by J. Michael Joncas, "Preaching from and for the Liturgy: A Practical Guide."

18. See David Tracy, *The Analogical Imagination* (New York: Crossroad, 1981).

19. *Naming Grace: Preaching and the Sacramental Imagination* (New York: Continuum, 1998), 134.

20. See Cavadini's essay in this volume, "Preaching and Catechesis: Mending the Rift between Scripture and Doctrine."

21. Jürgen Moltmann, *Theology of Hope* (New York: Harper & Row, 1967), 20.

22. *Preaching the Mystery of Faith: The Sunday Homily* (U.S. Conference of Catholic Bishops, 2013), 17f. The interior quotes are from Benedict XVI, *Spe Salvi* (*On Christian Hope*), nos. 30–31.

Contributors

Robert Barron is the rector and president of the University of St. Mary of the Lake/Mundelein Seminary and founder of Word on Fire Catholic Ministries.

Robert J. Carlson is archbishop of St. Louis, Missouri. As the former chair of the USCCB Committee on Clergy, Consecrated Life and Vocations, he oversaw the development of *Preaching the Mystery of Faith: The Sunday Homily*.

John C. Cavadini is professor of theology and the McGrath-Cavadini Director of the Institute for Church Life at the University of Notre Dame.

Michael E. Connors, CSC, is director of the John S. Marten Program in Homiletics and Liturgics in the Department of Theology at the University of Notre Dame.

Joseph Corpora, CSC, is director of University-School Partnerships in the Alliance for Catholic Education at the University of Notre Dame.

Kenneth G. Davis, OFM Conv, is a spiritual director at Saint Joseph Seminary College in Louisiana.

Guerric DeBona, OSB, is professor of homiletics at Saint Meinrad Seminary and School of Theology.

Jeremy Driscoll, OSB, is professor of theology at Mount Angel Seminary in Oregon and the Pontifical Athenaeum Sant' Anselmo in Rome.

Gustavo García-Siller, MSpS, is archbishop of San Antonio, Texas.

Ann M. Garrido is associate professor of homiletics at Aquinas Institute of Theology in St. Louis, Missouri, and a formation leader with the National Association of Catechesis of the Good Shepherd.

Mary Catherine Hilkert, OP, is professor of theology at the University of Notre Dame.

Jan Michael Joncas is artist-in-residence and research fellow in Catholic Studies at the University of St. Thomas in St. Paul, Minnesota.

Tom Margevičius is instructor in homiletics and liturgy at St. Paul Seminary in St. Paul, Minnesota, and pastor of Our Lady of Mt. Carmel parish in Minneapolis.

Susan McGurgan is assistant professor of pastoral theology and director of the Lay Pastoral Ministry Program at the Athenaeum of Ohio/Mount St. Mary's Seminary in Cincinnati, Ohio.

Maurice Nutt, CSsR, is a member of the Redemptorist Parish Mission Preaching Team based in Chicago, Illinois, and a member of the faculty of the Institute for Black Catholic Studies at Xavier University of Louisiana.

Ronald Patrick Raab, CSC, is pastor of the Tri-Community Catholic Parish of Colorado Springs, Colorado.

Barbara E. Reid, OP, is vice president and academic dean and professor of New Testament Studies at Catholic Theological Union in Chicago, Illinois.

Theresa Rickard, OP, is president and executive director of RENEW International, Plainfield, New Jersey.

Craig A. Satterlee, a liturgical scholar and teacher of preaching, is bishop of the North/West Lower Michigan Synod of the Evangelical Lutheran Church in America.

William Wack, CSC, is pastor of St. Ignatius Martyr Parish in Austin, Texas.